"Lee Thayer has followed his own leadership convictions and insights in writing a book that is itself the art of leadership. It is refreshing, authentic, and has a penetrating integrity. Don't take it lightly."

—Max DePree
Chairman Emeritus, Herman Miller, Inc.
Author of *Leadership Is an Art*

"It's a great book (or 'guidebook,' as the author calls it), reflecting years of hard-won experience doing what he reports on here. And he's done his homework as well! It's an original, very creative. If you can't learn how by applying the leadership lessons here, you probably can't learn how. It's superb."

— James O'Toole
Author of *Leading Change*

"When we first met Lee Thayer, our company was growing slowly at about 10% per year. Within a couple of years of following his ideas, our growth rate was 100% per year. Our customers became raving fans. We were receiving prestigious awards. Most importantly, our employees were more productive, full of life, and dedicated than they ever were before...Some of his concepts were initially hard to grasp. But I came to see that he was right...The concepts presented in this book (which we didn't have the advantage of—we had only the author!) work. Once you begin the journey to high performance, nothing else will suffice."

—John T. McBeth
President & CEO
Next Century Corporation

"Our company was in the past decidedly 'average.' But we were determined to be the 'best.' It wasn't until we discovered Lee Thayer and started taking advantage of his experience and his wisdom that we got on the right path. I had to learn how to make a high-performance organization. To do that, I had to learn how to be a leader and how to nurture other leaders. What it takes to get on and stay on the path of becoming the best in the business is in this book. It works."

—Wayne Renken
Founder & CEO
SensArray Corporation

"You have to think like a leader to *be* a leader, as the hundreds and hundreds of executives who have attended Lee's seminars know. As a Chairman of The Executive Committee (TEC), I've championed Lee Thayer's ideas since I met him 20 years ago. Learning how to perform at the levels he talks about is hard work. It's long term. Lee is uncompromising. He walks his talk. Follow the 'leader's journey' offered in this book, and you will be rightly instrumented for your quest to achieve high performance. And richly rewarded."

—Austin "Ozzie" Gontang, Ph.D.
TEC International

"If you truly want to reinvent yourself, are perpetually dissatisfied with yourself and your organization, and have a deep passion to change and improve, read Lee Thayer's book. You won't find any quick fixes here. I've been working at this both on the job and at home for a few years now, and both are immeasurably the better for it. I had to question everything I knew. If you can let Thayer do this to you, you will become a far better leader."

—Larry Bull
Executive Vice President
Bergstrom, Inc.

LEADERSHIP

Thinking, Being, Doing

Lee Thayer

To order additional copies of this book, contact:
Xlibris Corporation
1-888-795-4274
www.Xlibris.com
Orders@Xlibris.com
21148

For K.T., for all reasons.

As long as people exist, some will
always strive for the best.
And some will attain it.

—Historian Barbara Tuchman

EXECUTIVE ORIENTATION

EVEN THE TITLE may need a little explanation, you may be thinking.

You can't learn to be "a leader." History decides that. All you can do is to be prepared, if you are "called" to provide leadership, to do so. Leadership is a specific role in a specific ongoing story. That role is to change the course of that story. You *can* learn how to perform leadership, to prepare to fulfill that role, if ever called to it.

So, about the title: If you intend to equip yourself to provide leadership—when, where, and how it's needed—this is your comprehensive guidebook. How successful you can be depends upon how you think, because that determines who you are. And who you *are* determines how you will do what you do. Thus the title: *Leadership: Thinking, Being, Doing*. If those three don't hang together rightly within you, your leadership won't amount to much.

Beyond that: There is no point in learning about leadership unless you have a *cause* that demands extraordinary performance. All the words about leadership ever written are worthless unless a great and worthy cause is at stake. This book is about high performance and the kind of leadership required to fulfill a great and worthy cause.

You would be drawn to this book because there is nothing else that can provide you with all of the thinking, being, and doing tools you will need. You need to know not only what the territory looks like when you are traversing it, but the whys and the wherefores. The ideas and navigational tools provided in this guidebook were forged in the trenches, working directly with the executives who were, and are, trying to make it happen. And from knowing the best that has ever been said or written about the subject of leadership.

The only people who really understand what it takes are the people who have done it, and who can effectively equip others to do it. I'm here before you after more than four decades in the trenches being directly involved in making it happen. Some successes, some failures, which will always be the case. What you need are the hows and the whys. That's what you have here.

The value of ideas cannot be measured in the abstract. The only real measure of an idea is what has been accomplished with it. The best "theory" is the one that works best. That's my job as your guide in what follows—to provide you with what works and to forewarn you about what doesn't.

Is the journey difficult? More difficult than you can imagine. Is there a simple formula? Only the ones provided by the business press, which simply don't work—for most people most of the time. In this book, we won't shrink from the difficulties of what's required, no matter how counter-intuitive that may be, or how difficult to implement. You will meet up with the most tough-minded, realistic perspectives on leadership ever brought to life by those who had what it takes to reflect honestly on their successes and their failures.

You can't be who they were. But you can learn how to develop your own capacity for thinking, being, and doing when trying to forge *your* way.

Finally, is this a "how-to" book? Yes, in a way. But it is not a book about how others did it. It is a book about how it can be done . . . by you.

Leadership is an art. You have to have a compelling cause. That's your part of it. And you need to have an experienced guide. That's what you have here.

This is your guidebook for learning how to do it by doing it.

Who Should Read This Book?

Anyone who is seriously interested in optimizing his or her leadership capabilities. It is for practicing CEOs or high-level executives. It is for anyone who presides over any type of organization or institution—commercial, government, voluntary. It is for anyone who intends to be the "best" at their roles in life, from managers and coaches to athletes and musicians to lovers and parents. It is for anyone who intends to perform optimally in any role. While the specific circumstances may vary, the kind of thinking required to make it happen is universal.

It is for anyone who wants to improve their ability to lead themselves or others in any enterprise or venture in life. It is about life. It is about achievement. It is about living with purpose, which is the only reliable source of quality of life and of rewarding engagement with life there is.

One Caveat

You may be inclined initially to disagree with some of the perspectives offered in the pages that follow. This is understandable. Much of what undergirds leadership thinking is *counter-intuitive*. It simply runs contrary to much "common" knowledge. If you want something other than conventional results, then you have to learn to think in certain unconventional ways.

HOW TO USE THIS BOOK

TO YOUR OWN purposes, of course.

A couple of suggestions about how you might maximize your take from what's available here:

The first is that you want to be able to dip into this guidebook at any place it may seem intuitively advantageous to you. But to be able to determine this most effectively, I would suggest that you first read, carefully, "Openers" and "Part I: How to Think about What Needs Thinking about." This will give you a perspective on the rest of the book and provide a basis for where you might dip into it for your personal advantage from there on.

The second is that you can use the "Annotated Chapter List" as your guide. There may be enough description there to take you where you need to go at any time, given your personal needs and interests.

Since this is a "guidebook," you will want to have it around to refer to certain key sections to help you think about and implement the ideas that personally most appeal to you in your situation. You won't always get what you need with one reading, particularly a once-over-lightly. What's here is here to be studied and internalized, not merely "read." So make it bear fruit for you, in the form of your improved performance as a leader.

It's impossible to write a book that is personally for you. In your use of this book, it is necessary for you to seek out and incorporate what you need. It's here. You just have to find it, and put it into practice. Your real learning lies in how you apply what is here.

If your learning journey is not fun and exciting, it will not bear fruit.

Some chapters, and some parts of those chapters, will appeal to you more than others. That's as it should be. Let your appetite, your needs, and your present circumstances be your guide. Explore. Be pulled by your own needs.

However: It is very important that you invest in the early chapters (about how to think about what you need to think about). They inform everything else in this book. If you don't get the thinking part down, you may not gain the perspectives that will make all the rest of it work for you. It's obviously yours to do with as you wish. It's just a matter of gaining as much as you can of what you need—of all of this distilled experience and knowledge about how it's actually done—about how to journey to real achievement.

Reading this book is not a measure of much. But using it to achieve great and worthy goals . . . that will be the measure of what you did with what's here.

ANNOTATED CHAPTER LIST

OPENERS: SOME PRELIMINARY STRETCHING EXERCISES

Offers an issue-by-issue overview of the unconventional paradigm one has to be familiar with in order to pursue extraordinary achievement—in any human endeavor, individual or collective. Sets forth how this book aims to lay out that paradigm and its implications, for any person who is serious about learning what has to be understood in order to achieve high performance..........1

PART I: HOW TO THINK ABOUT WHAT NEEDS THINKING ABOUT 19

Takes the reader on an expedition that explores, in the most fundamental way, *how* to think about what needs thinking about. What is it the leader of any endeavor to excel needs to be able to think about, and how?

CHAPTER 1: GEARING UP: SOME PRELIMINARIES THAT NEED YOUR ATTENTION 21

Offers a very comfortable introduction to some of the main terms and concepts that structure the mind-set required.

A series (10) of "think pieces" that make clear how differently from the mainstream one must be thinking in order to lead oneself, and/or others, in the pursuit of optimum performance. For example, "Conventional ways of thinking and doing invariably lead to conventional results." If you seek unconventional results, and being "the best" at anything would certainly be an unconventional outcome, you have to learn how to think habitually in that paradigm.

A "lexicon" is like an inventory of a person's thinking tools—the concepts and "theories" with which he or she thinks. It is the "content" of a person's mental repertoire. The purpose here is to draw out and examine in detail some key concepts that are fundamental to any successful leader's ready, everyday lexicon. This will illustrate how leaders understand common terms in an uncommon way.

Continues the "inventory" started in Chapter 3, starting with the consequences of how the leader (of self and/or others) thinks about "people." Missing this one guarantees failure in any attempt to provide leadership. Others include "Problems," the inescapable issue of "ROA" (Return on Attention), and how people who have excelled have understood such matters as "Time."

Part II answers the questions: What makes it so hard? And why do most people underestimate the difficulty of high performance? The perils are all there for the person who would undertake leading a change in that direction, as Machiavelli warned back in the 16th century. And yet a few are successful in changing "the order of things." How do they get past those obstacles and barriers?

From the earliest recorded history, adventurers and heroes have always encountered "dragons" on their quests. However, it was understood then (less well today) that those "dragons" were mainly internal. What people imagine is going to happen to them on the path to any goal or destiny bears more upon whether or not they set out, and how easily they are discouraged, than do any actual obstacles they might encounter. How do leaders deal with their "dragons"?

Nothing is more important than the way a person conceives of himself or herself relative to his or her goal or cause. That's because this is what determines how that person will perceive their path given the obstacles encountered, and also determines how others will perceive that person. There are pratfalls in the way leaders think, such as the fact that much of what comes with being "the boss" is addictive; if those addictions cannot be overcome, the prognosis for success as a leader is very low. This is but one of several such "obstacles" dealt with in this chapter.

This chapter examines in detail what actually drives human behavior (not the conventional ideas about this subject). If you're thinking about this rightly, you will be successful. If you're stuck with the wrong ideas about them, you won't. If you have misconceptions about the "drivers," yours or others, those misconceptions will function as a barrier to your becoming the person who leads the way to high performance.

People are under-empowered if they are not fully competent to do what they do, or want to do. People are "empowered" by their own competence at what they do. This is not something you can "confer" on yourself or on others. It has to be earned through effort, discipline, and diligence. This is one of the "keys" to achieving extraordinary performance. This chapter sets forth the obstacle that "under-empowerment" presents, and what has to be done about it.

Another barrier to the pursuit of high performance or of excelling is that of trying to support the endeavor with systems that work against the cause they are supposed to be aiding. These are "dumb" systems. Success depends upon learning how to identify "dumb" systems and to replace them with "smart" systems. This chapter explains what systems are, and how to distinguish the "dumb" ones from the "smart" ones.

One of the most potent obstacles to great achievement is the "popular culture"—the "formulas" for living that people consume when they attend to popular music, popular television or radio, popular magazines and newspapers, and the popular folklore that emerges in all of the talk that gets generated by the universal consumption of this fare. This chapter focuses on the false ideas that people pick up there and bring to their lives or their workplace, and how those need to be displaced by the kinds of ideas that are required for any elevated level of achievement and performance. The popular culture will take people in some direction other than the direction they need to be going to achieve extraordinary results.

The world we live in is almost infinitely more "perverse" than people believe. It is a person's own perversity that keeps him or her from carrying out even the most mundane of their dreams or goals in life. Assuming one can overcome his own perversity, it is still the case that the world does not aid people in their endeavors, but usually throws more perversity in their way. For leaders, this is a paradox: they must overcome their own perversities in order to see clearly the perversities they will encounter daily in their pursuit of their cause. And leaders have to have the "weapons" to slay or defend against those perversities that will otherwise defeat them.

So we've come to what some readers would consider the "good parts"—the how-to-do-it parts. For some, what follows might be the main target. But this book does not pander to what readers think they "want." You get plenty of that in the sop being spoon-fed to you in the hundreds of "how-to" and "recipe" books being hyped week after week. This book is intended to provide readers with what they *need*: as much real-world from-the-trenches reality about this whole process they can stand. There is an even more compelling reason for why this part of it comes now. Most attempts fail. They fail in large part because those who tried to apply the recipes did not fully understand what was required on their part to make those tools work. The better you understand the tools and what can be done with them, the more effective you will be. Using a tool not fully understood, to accomplish something not fully understood, is the formula for failure. There's a good reason why first things are first in this book. Leaders steep themselves in what they need to know first. This makes them who they *are*. Then they act. Your performance will be no better than your preparation, which is why all of those preceding chapters came first.

This chapter is about what it takes to perform superbly: preparation, luck, being "had by" one's cause or mission (as contrasted with merely "having" one), inexhaustible enthusiasm for that cause and, for leaders of enterprises— surrounding oneself with the people who are going to make it happen by casting the right people in the right roles. Then, the four covenants between the leader and those people who are going to make it happen. This requires engaging people directly and *necessarily* in what has to happen. Sounds easy? It's not. Most people give up and start looking for an "easier" way, for some "fairy dust" or other panaceas. There are none. What's required to make it happen is what has always been required, as this chapter makes clear.

What else does it take? Dealt with in this chapter: a robust plan, telling the story of how we get from here to there compellingly, and the role each person plays in that story. Keeping up the impetus and sustaining the change. The "power" required to make it happen. Some right-headedness about "communication" and why "communication" can't do what you'd like it to do. And why leadership and "communication" are so intricately interrelated.

The preceding chapters described "what it takes" for the leader to *think about* how to put together the people, the organization, and the systems to make it happen. The next three chapters describe some of the specific and tacit tools leaders use to align others with their mission. It is the competency of the user that makes any great tool effective. These tools will not work for those who have not equipped themselves (along the lines of the preceding chapters) to be extremely competent users of these "tools."

The basic tools are those that contribute to making elevated performance **possible**, and those that contribute to making the required level of performance **necessary**. Making higher levels of performance possible requires (a) developing the competencies of people in their roles, (b) making the systems in which those people are embedded "smart" enough to both encourage and accommodate higher levels of performance, and (c) having a critical mass of leaders who exemplify the kind of culture that makes higher levels of performance simply the order of the day—day after day. The most basic tool is that of "Role Descriptions." This chapter describes in detail how this extraordinary tool is conceived, and how to use it.

The next most basic tools for raising performance are "Performance Goals" and "Learning Plans." Role Descriptions provide an idealized description of what a virtuoso in that role would accomplish over the long term. Performance Goals describe mutually-agreed-upon accomplishments, objectively measurable, on a time-line. These are integrated with the goals of the organization, top to bottom and side to side. Learning Plans address the competency shortfalls exhibited by any role-holder. Again—**demonstrated accomplishments**, on a time-line. Other tools dealt with in this chapter include measurement, how "problems" can be used for development of people and of systems, how organizations can be "composed" as a tool, and a thorough exploration of "smart systems," which could be considered as "meta-tools."

This chapter focuses on the best "power" tools the leader can ever have in his or her tool-box: communication (again), this time looking at the sheer capabilities the leader has for listening—and for being listened to. Then, how to design and implement communication *systems* that may facilitate productive communication, or might actually eliminate non-productive communication interactions—

like "meetings." If you want to get "lean," more effective communication and communication systems offer the greatest cost-savings to be found. A key leadership competency is pure word-power, which is the ultimate source of leadership power. Little-used power tools like "ambiguity," "seduction," "unreasonableness," and "luck" round out this chapter.

PART V: CODES, VALUES, AND STRATAGEMS

Codes of conduct, values and beliefs, and the core stratagems comprise the next three chapters.

CHAPTER 17: CODES OF CONDUCT

A "code of conduct" gets internalized by people in the process of acculturation. It is made up of the "rules" of comportment provided by the culture. A person may become a "member" of that culture if and when that person demonstrates that the "code" has been internalized. It functions tacitly, and makes up the operating rules for that person's conscience. If the pursuit of great performance by the organization is to be successful, the "code" by which the critical mass of key people operate in that organization must be what's needed to make that happen. This chapter explains why and how.

CHAPTER 18: VALUES & BELIEFS: THE TACIT MEDIATORS

People do not maneuver *by* their values and beliefs. They are the pawns *of* their values and beliefs. A person's values and beliefs, imported largely from the cultures and subcultures to which that person belongs, are the tacit mediators of the world the person "sees" and understands. All of a person's thinking, doing, and saying are mediated by those cultural values and beliefs. They determine not only a person's performance. They also determine over time that person's destiny. It is the collective and common values and beliefs of the people who comprise an organization that determine the organization's performance and *its* destiny. If you can't get those "right," you can't arrive at your chosen destiny. This is where "change" has to occur.

The "core stratagems," which also operate implicitly— or tacitly—distill most of the key issues from throughout the book into a handful of very broad strategically-oriented concepts. Get these right and you get most of the rest of it right. They are not a "summary" of all of the other ideas in the book. They are more like key foundation stones, which enhance the fit and function of all that precedes.

One meaning of "envoi": A message to send you on your way. That's what this is for.

Not exactly a "summary" of all that has come before. More like a capstone. This is short. The more it reminds you of what was here to be learned, the more useful it will be to you.

OPENERS: SOME PRELIMINARY STRETCHING EXERCISES

ALTHOUGH IT IS also about **real achievement** in any form, this guidebook (or handbook) is mainly about making high-performance organizations, and the kind of leadership required to do so.

The kind of achievement we're talking about is a little bit like winning at Wimbledon or the Masters. If you haven't done so, it may be because you don't know how. If you do know how but haven't actually done it, it amounts to the same thing.

So there's much to think about, much to learn. A mental "stretching exercise" occurs when you encounter something you haven't encountered before. There's much in this guidebook that you haven't encountered before. The other kind of "stretching" exercise occurs when you have to accommodate a way of understanding something that runs contrary to the way you've always understood it. Much of this book is devoted to challenging you to understand something you already understand—but to do so in a different way. Most people avoid both kinds of stretching exercises as ingeniously as they can.

The sheer fact that you have come this far—the sheer fact that you are even skeptically open to being stretched into the mental shape you may need to be in to accomplish what you want to accomplish . . . is evidence that you are a very unusual person.

Most people assume they could do "it" (especially this "it") if they "wanted" to badly enough. They would be wrong.

Most people's minds are already made up. Their position is: "Don't confuse me with the facts." But it is precisely the *facts* that call for the rethinking that has to be done. Here's an example of a "stretching exercise" to get started on:

• People can't figure out what they need to know. People can figure out only what they are personally capable of figuring out. So they seek "advice." And here a paradox rears its ugly face: *If you know the difference between good advice and bad advice, you don't need advice.*

In other words, the most useful advice is the kind that helps you to develop your capacity for distinguishing good advice from bad advice. So a lot of the advice you are likely to be exposed to is "bad" advice because it doesn't raise your own abilities for discerning the good from the bad.

The more you think about this, the more effective your mental muscles will be. In what follows in this guidebook you will encounter, page after page, the kinds of challenges to your thinking, based on the *facts*, that will put you in the mental shape you need to be in to accomplish what you want to accomplish.

Just for fun, here is another stretching exercise that can produce great benefits to your thinking, your being (who you are), and your doing (what you do and how you do it):

• *Conventional wisdoms always and inevitably produce conventional results.* This means that if you perceive some problem or some opportunity in a conventional way (just because that's the way your mind works), you will come up with a conventional solution. But high performance, real achievement, is far from being the norm, far from being "conventional." So the implication is that if you want to achieve extraordinary results, results that are not more or less "average," then you have to produce those results out of some fairly unconventional wisdoms. This guidebook is full of the kind of unconventional wisdom you may need in order to achieve high performance. Many of the facts and perspectives you will meet up with in the pages ahead are counter-intuitive. That is, they run contrary to what most people already believe. You have to stretch your mind to accommodate them. You have to be open to the kind of stretching required to get into the mental shape necessary to make it happen. And to practice, practice, practice, particularly a different way of looking at things.

Some Immediate Challenges

Here are some immediate challenges. Exercising your thinking on these will help you to get in good mental shape, ready to take full advantage of all that follows in the rest of this guidebook.

- One is that *many try, few succeed.* How ought you to understand this? Why are there so few successes when there are so many who long for real achievement, at work or at home? You're going against the odds. Two-thirds to three-fourths of business organizations in the U.S. have tried some formula for becoming "excellent." The "key," the blurbs blare, is TQM, or reengineering or "transcompetition" or "open book management" or simply "teaching the elephant to dance." There have been as many proprietary schemes for easy success sold as there have been people who thought they could make money off of them—off of you. But of all who have tried, in less than 10% of those attempts was there any noticeable improvement. In the case of "reengineering," there were many organizations that ended up worse off.

There is clearly a hunger for getting better, or of transforming into "excellence." Those who bought the panaceas of the month must have gotten a lot of empty calories.

There's no trick to beating the odds, here or at the game table. You just have to know what the odds are. And you need to be able to see through to the reasons why they are what they are. You can change *your* odds by avoiding the reasons why others have failed.

The main reason is probably this: that these consumers of the panacea of the month are led to believe that the logic required to get to high performance is the same logic that is required to become "average" or mediocre. It's not.

Another basic reason for these failures is that those who undertook some scheme for producing real achievement didn't understand that being great at something requires that you be *different*. And most of the people you know would like to be superior, but only if they can be like everybody else. In other words, trying to be different by being the same just doesn't work, no matter what the recipe says.

Another reason: Wimpy or inconsistent commitment. People get all fired up, and then lose their enthusiasm. Something to think about here: Enthusiasm without relentless commitment and devastating competencies never produces much of anything worthwhile.

Still another reason: It's nice to think that if you really wanted to achieve high performance, to make an organization that was hands-down the best, you'd get a lot of support from other people and from the rest of the world. You would be wrong. You will encounter daunting obstacles and barriers at every step of the way. And you can't look to the world to make it easier for you just because you've undertaken to "try." (As Yoda says in "The Empire Strikes Back," there is no "try." There is only "do or do not.")

Some Additional Stretching Exercises

Well, that's but one stretching exercise, and some examples for thinking how to go about it. Here are some additional stretching exercises. The better you can think through them and get yourself in the mental shape required, the better your odds.

- In spite of how seductive the "13 secrets" or the "49 steps" or the "8 habits" may be, there are no easy answers. Any real achievement requires great effort, sacrifice, pain, and utter, utter determination. You fail if you can't or won't pay the price.

- The difficulty of making a high-performance organization, of fulfilling any great and worthy cause, has never been *over-estimated*. It's mediocrity that is easy, not excellence.
- The media will lead you into confusing what's merely in fashion with what actually works. There have never been any fashions in what it actually takes to excel.
- The "answer" to something is never the same thing as accomplishment. There are words, and then there are real accomplishments. Dilettantes and celebrities deal in words. Those who are actually doing it are too busy to talk about it.
- If you think you can buy a process or a technique that is going to do it for you, you would be as wrong as you can get. The best tool works only if wielded by the best wielder.
- The number of recipes increases as the overall competencies of cooks decrease. The less able people are to do something, the more the predators will feed them about how to do it.
- If you don't know what real achievement *is*, if you don't know what it looks like and what it feels like, and how radically different it is from luck or talent or magic, you are not ready to launch *any* effort.
- It doesn't really make any difference whether or not you "understand" something. The only thing that makes a difference is what you accomplished with your understanding.
- What you think this book is about is not what you think it is about. It is about what it *is* about. To learn, sometimes you have to un-learn.
- There are many things we do in life that we can learn to do only by doing them. Walking would be an example. Making a high-performance organization, and developing the kind of leadership required to do so would be another.
- The "how-to" industry (books, magazines, seminars, talk shows) are not there to solve your problems. They exist to

solve *their* problems. Which include taking your money for ideas or "theories" that don't work because they need your money next month.

- Real achievement is not an idea. It is an accomplishment. They are measured very differently.
- The more people there are who believe in the latest panacea, the less likely it is that you can make it work for you.
- In the past twenty years, there have been more than 10,000 books published on how to manage and how to lead. Why does the failure rate remain more or less constant?
- How is it possible that a recipe for how to be "the best" can be a best seller? Is it even possible that the question of how to be "the best" could have 10,000 answers?
- How is it possible that your organization could be unique if you think like everyone else does?

And so on. You get the point. But unless you think through, and then think through again and again, these issues, you won't have done the mental exercises that you need to do to get in the mental shape you need to be in to go on. Have you?

Revisiting The Lobby

Entering this (or any) book is a little like entering a building. You arrive first in the lobby. There you have your first glimpse of what the building is like. And your question is always, How am I supposed to navigate this book (building)? What are my impressions thus far? How can I develop a mental model of this place so I can use it to my advantage? How do I assess what kind of advantage there is here for me?

Fair enough. Let's leave the exercises for a bit and go back to the "lobby." You'll encounter some of these mental exercises again later on.

This book is all about what you need to know—and do—in order to be successful at making a high-performance organization. Such a real achievement is something most heads-of-organizations who have tried, have failed at. So what is it you need to know, standing right here in the lobby, that will tell you whether or not this is for you? What's the problem?

After four-plus decades of being intimately engaged in this effort with scores of those who run our organizations, of every size and type, here and abroad, I'm convinced (in spite of how more or less adequate many are) that most American organizations are plagued by many of the same old problems. Some of those perennial problems are at least implied in the "stretching exercises" you have just considered. But to cut to the chase, there are at least three basic impediments. If you cannot honestly see yourself overcoming these, this book can't be of much help to you. Here they are:

1) People who sign up to make this happen fizzle or fail because they did not have or could not muster the level of commitment required. It turned out they didn't have the overriding passion for it or the level of perseverance required.

2) And those who didn't make it either (a) didn't have what it takes to make it happen, or (b) didn't have what it takes to develop in themselves those extraordinary ways of thinking, being, and doing that were simply necessary.

3) They never *really* understood what was required to make it happen.

The first of these impediments is totally your problem. You can't get the gumption required from reading a book about it. You can't get the needed passion, zeal, or stick-to-it-ness from reading a book. You either have those, or you have what it takes to perform them whether you actually have them or not. Real achievement cuts you no slack on these. If you don't have what it takes to see it through, then you're better off not commencing the journey.

By this time, you've already figured out that the second of these impediments also belongs to you. With some collaboration here. If you don't right now have what it takes to develop those extraordinary ways of thinking, being, and doing, you've come to the right place. With an experienced guide (distilled in this guidebook), you *can* develop in yourself what needs to be developed to make it happen.

The most valuable thing I can provide you with is how to really understand what is required to make it happen. That level of understanding is indispensable. If you don't really understand how to do something, it's unlikely you'll be able to do it. So if you do your part, you can depend upon this guidebook to help you with all the rest of it.

It *can* be done. Not by belief. Not by faith. Not by desire or ambition or effort alone. It requires understanding. Real understanding. And that requires some real collaboration between you and me, represented here by the tough and challenging perspectives and facts presented in this guidebook. If you can do your part of it, then you're in the right place.

Why Would An Otherwise Sane Person Take This Path In Life?

If you persist, you will find yourself wondering, when the going gets tough, Why am I doing this? It's the right question. Don't suppress it.

There are three basic reasons why a few people in history have committed themselves to real achievement:

One is, but this is fairly recent, for money or notoriety. A large proportion of those who fail come from this category. That's because you can't buy anything that is really worthwhile. You can't "buy" real achievement. And fame is fickle. Those who head up businesses are often like shooting stars. The belief is that if you pay them enough money, they can make real achievement happen. But for the person on whom so much depends, if the primary focus is on money, then it won't be on achievement. The media, more full of myth than substance, identify their celebrities of the month. Then they move on. Sustained achievement isn't newsworthy.

Two, some people are just naturally perverse enough to pursue greatness for their own reasons. They are internally driven to compete and to outperform their peers. These "lone ranger" types also disproportionately contribute to the ranks of the failures. That's because they often can't get along with other people—the very people they would need to make it happen, or to sustain it.

Three, there are those who see it as a *moral obligation,* if for any reason they end up in charge of an organization, to make of that organization all that could possibly be made of it. To make it great. These are the same people who deeply believe that they have a moral obligation to make of themselves all that could be made of that unique raw material they happen to have. It seems clear that most of the real successes come from this category. That may be in part as follows: Anyone who seems to be seriously engaged in the pursuit of outstanding performance these days (either individual or organizationally) is looked upon by other people as marginally insane. So you are always going to get the question, "Why in the world are you doing this?" Presumably it is unthinkable that a person would choose that difficult, less materially-rewarding path rather than the easy path of self-indulgence, greed, or of "balance." To be able to answer, "Because I have to" may limit the conversation so each can get back to the different paths they have chosen.

"Because, for me, it's the only right thing to do." "Because I wouldn't be able to live with myself if I didn't strive mightily for being the best." "Because there's a high road and a low road, and I personally have to take the high road." "Because I can't take my toys with me but I can leave behind a legacy that will affect other people for years to come."

These are some of the kinds of answers you might get from a person who is rightly cast and fully dedicated to his or her role in making it happen. For most other people, it is usually a matter of doing much the same thing, over and over again, while hoping for a different outcome. You may recognize that as an old Chinese description of insanity. So there may be a real question about which one is "insane"—the person who does what is necessary in order to achieve what is possible. Or the person who does the same thing over and over again but merely "hopes" for a better result.

The Immediate And Inevitable Challenge

If this is the path you choose—of doing whatever is necessary to achieve some great and worthy purpose—you will be quickly challenged by other people who might have to be involved. Those other people are going to ask you: "Why should I be doing this? Why should I buy in? What's in it for me?"

If you don't have a convincing answer, if they can't read you as *being* the answer, your attempt to achieve a high-performance organization will essentially be dead in the water. You have to understand right from launch that a high-performance organization, while it can be measured in many other ways, is fundamentally an organization that is *good* for people. Most people work in organizations that are unhealthy, and for bosses who are not good for them. Most people go to work in the morning and come out at the end of the day no better off as human beings than they were at the beginning of the day. Many are worse. If the people who work at your place are not measurably better off in terms of the quality of their lives at the end of the day, or when they get their 10-year "pin," then you do not have a high-performance organization.

It is not just money, although they will have more of that. It is not just the fact that they will have far more control over the conditions of their lives at work, although they will have much more of that. It is something very counter-intuitive in the American culture. It is that the one condition that predicts to happiness and to relevance in life—to the very meaningfulness of life—is *competence*. The more competent people are in their roles in life, the more stimulated and satisfied they will be in their lives. And a high-performance organization is based in the competence of the people in every role in the organization. To have a competent organization, you have to have competent people in every role.

Seeking "happiness" directly, as we all know now, is the surest possible way of not getting it. That's why the more you try to provide for people's "happiness" or satisfaction at work, the less likely it is to happen. It doesn't come from what people are given.

It comes from how competent people are to live their lives at work (the bulk of the day). So what is needed for an organization to be extraordinarily competent at what it does is the competence of every person in that organization. It's win-win.

Here are some stretches:

- Most people don't know what you have just read. It is part of the power of every compelling leader who has ever lived.
- The less competent people are at work, the more they lose interest in their work and in everything around them. No wonder the day seems so long to less-than-fully-competent people!
- Competence is the only thing people have that is portable. They certainly cannot take their "politicking" gains with them to some other organization, which many failed CEOs have learned to their dismay.
- "Work" is not a way for a person to sell her time or soul for a paycheck. It is an integral part of one's life. The better a person is at it, the better a person's life will be for it.
- As someone's "boss," if you are not good for yourself in this sense, you won't be good for other people—the kiss of death for any would-be leader. If you can't effectively and advantageously lead yourself, then there's little hope that you can lead others.

Will those people be clamoring for you to make it necessary for them to be more competent at what they do? Not bloody likely. They will resist you every step of the way. After all, you resisted *you* in much the same way. If you didn't win with you, you aren't going to be good for them.

The more broadly and deeply you can understand how to answer their questions and their objections, the more likely you are to succeed in your venture. This guidebook can supply you with the way of thinking you will need to be able to do this. You just have to make it a part of who you *are*.

"Wanting" Vs. Doing

In the top executive seminars I conduct around the world and where I sometimes talk about such things, I'm frequently asked, "How many top executives can actually do this, based on your experience?"

My answer, "All of them *could*. Are you asking how many will actually carry it off?"

"Yeah, that. And what's the difference? What do you mean, all of them *could*?"

"By 'all of them *could*,' I'm acknowledging the fact that whether they can or not depends ultimately on whether they did or not. And we've all been surprised from time to time by our judgments of people and what they actually do. In all cases, it's possible. It might take one person a few years and considerable effort. It might take someone else a lifetime and incredible effort. But perseverance counts for more than potential. So how many will actually produce great outcomes? Out of every ten or so who really, really *want* to be responsible for great achievements, maybe three or four will actually make some progress. But it's likely that no more than one out of ten will see it through."

"So it's not potential? It's not motivation?"

I have to answer as follows: "It's not potential. More potential goes to waste than anything else. But by itself, what we're calling potential won't do it. Motivation? I don't even know what that means. It's a weasel word. People use it to excuse themselves and put others' achievements into the hands of psychological fate. It's nonsense. A person either accomplished what she set out to accomplish or not. Nothing is added by saying 'She was motivated to do so.' But the key point to focus on here [a stretching exercise for readers] is that 'wanting' to do something and 'doing' that thing aren't even in the same universe. People who aren't going to do it will waste everyone's time by talking about how much they 'want to' do it. They are delaying in hope that someone or something will do it for them. The person who is going to do it just does it. Nothing is added by saying 'I want to' do this or that.

It's more like a way of bonding with other people who would rather talk about what they 'want' than to make the effort needed to bring it about."

There is nothing easy about being the best at something. And there is nothing easy about learning how to be the best at something. "Wanting" is the easy way out. "Doing" is what it's all about.

Then comes another often-asked question: "So how do you decide who you're going to work with? If you're picking one out of ten, how do you do that?"

"I don't always do a good job of picking the winner. By the time an executive has made it to the top, he or she is really good at deceiving other people. So I've been had—mainly by enthusiasm, as we all are. It is very intuitive, like Michael Jordan's decision to shoot this one is ultimately intuitive. Based on experience. Asking a lot of questions But it probably comes down to how much experience the candidate has had at strategizing and putting whatever effort is required into accomplishing impossible things. It may not seem so at the outset, but it won't be long before the task will appear to be impossible. That's what will separate those who do from those who don't."

The key, certainly, is preparedness. If you read carefully and apply the distilled lessons available in this guidebook, you can be optimally prepared. Beyond that, there are factors over which no one has any control.

Competence And Control

People often talk about competence as if it would permit you to control things over which you do not and cannot have control. Competence alone will not ensure your success.

Competence is what optimizes your preparedness. The real world will function as it functions, whether you will it to do so or not. It is oblivious to your wants and needs, even to your competencies. What extravagant competencies are for is to take advantage of good luck, and to take advantage of bad luck. "Luck," which is how we might describe the workings of the larger world in which we have to seek real achievements—a way of naming what we cannot control—is blind. Luck favors only the prepared. As one golfer put it, "The more I increase my abilities, the luckier I get."

We try to control what we cannot. And we fail to control what we can. What we can positively control are our own capabilities, our own competencies. To perform any role, from concert pianist to multinational CEO, a person's competencies can be enhanced every day . . . forever. What this means is that the person who is daily enhancing his or her competencies is optimizing—even maximizing—his or her chances of real achievement. They don't give that person any more control over the uncontrollable than others have. It just means they are more prepared for whatever happens.

So when we talk about making high-performance organizations, and about the leadership required to make and sustain being "the best," we are not making the stupid mistake of imagining that we can create superhuman people or organizations who can bend the world to their will. We are talking about the relentless pursuit of greater and greater levels of competence at everything we do, and everything that is done in and by an organization.

You will never be invulnerable or omniscient. But you can outpace others if you never cease developing your competencies. That's as good as it gets. And this guidebook cannot provide you with immortality or certain success. But it can, uniquely, help you equip yourself to be prepared. No "magic bullets." No "secrets" of sure success. No easy "steps" or panaceas. Just the stuff you *can* control: your unremitting passion for the journey. And the mental tools and provisions offered here that you will need to make that journey.

So Who Is This Book *For?*

Good question. It may be for you if you've got what it takes.

Or, if they've got what it takes, it may also be an invaluable guidebook for anyone who is put in charge of any kind of human endeavor. For anyone who has to achieve something great through themselves or other people. Thus, by definition, it is for parents, for coaches, for military leaders, for private sector leaders, indeed for the would-be leaders of any human endeavor that has some great and worthy aim, or purpose, or mission. It is for teachers, for mentors, and for any kind of "role model."

It is for anyone who has to carry out real achievement, whether by choice or by happenstance. There are, after all, no "leaders," at least not until historians dub them thus. There is only "leadership." That's what's required when one can take on that role for purposes of changing history.

That could be you. That's because it could be any one of us. But only if we are competent and prepared to fulfill that role. You could be. You could make this a better world—for yourself, but as well for all the rest of us.

Here's your guidebook for how to do that. Bring your passion, your zeal, and your determination. The pursuit of real achievement is the pursuit of real life.

Thinking Tools

- *As you think, so will you **be**. And as you are, so will you **do**.*

I've met many top executives who simply did not have the mental horsepower to avoid getting into a problem in the first place. Or the mental wherewithal to extract themselves from it once they had gotten themselves into it.

In that sense, most of the problems such "leaders" face are self-inflicted. If they had the thinking tools needed, they could have avoided, or at least anticipated, most of the problems that predict to their future. If they had the kinds of thinking tools they needed, they might have been able to get around the problems they face, and move on.

This book is a book of thinking tools. You need to think in a certain way to provide the kind of leadership required for the pursuit of real achievement. If you intend to be the primary cause of making a high-performance organization, you have to think in a high-performance way. The logic that enables the achievement of high performance is not the logic that leads to being adequate or mediocre.

Reading an advertisement about a new tool does not thereby equip you to use it effectively. You have to learn, thoroughly, what the tool does and how. And you have to learn what you and the tool can do collaboratively.

Many of the thinking tools you will encounter in this guidebook may often be expressed as axioms. Like the one above. The most generally-applicable axiom I know of, and the one which best explains what most needs explaining for leadership, is this:

- *Most people prefer a problem they can't solve to a solution they don't like.*

To put this in the immediate context, what this means is that most people will go on being pretty much like they were today. If their problem was how to create a great organization, or even a reliably effective one, they will be likely to have that same problem next week and even ten years from now. The reason: The effort required to eliminate that problem and to get involved in real achievement just looks like more effort than they feel like putting out. It just looks more difficult than they want to deal with. So they deal with the problems of mediocrity—and all of the insoluble problems that go with the nurturing of, or tolerance for, mediocrity.

This is a difficult book, because the process is a difficult one. You could buy a book that promises success in a couple of minutes or by simply owning the "panacea."

Well, there are none. And I would be insulting your intelligence and further tarnishing your credulousness by making it look easy. It never was. It is not now. It never will be. Can you "buy" an answer that does not, ultimately, depend upon *you*? You can, but it won't work.

So let's get on with what will work. If you can incorporate the thinking tools you need, then you will be the person you need to be. Only then can you do what needs doing.

N.B. You will meet up with some of those tools more than once in the pages that follow. This is not careless repetition. It just means that internalizing a tool and how to use it usually requires more than one encounter. When you've really got it down, you can skip it. Otherwise, you may want to stretch your thinking with it again, whenever the opportunity to do so arises. But, then, most people prefer a problem . . . .

PART I

THIS FIRST PART takes you on a trip. A mental expedition to explore, in the most fundamental way, how to think about what needs thinking about—and why. It will turn out to be indispensable. Besides, you'll like it.

But only if you have a keen interest in great performance. Or in leading your organization on the long and difficult journey to great achievement.

And then only if you have what it takes to undertake such a rigorous and challenging journey. Only if you have what it takes to learn what needs learning, and to persevere.

Chapter 1 offers you some essential provocations to help you get into the needed frame of mind for what's to come.

Chapter 2 provides a series of "think pieces"—brief engagements with what needs thinking about—and how.

Chapters 3 and 4 put before you a few key terms and how you may have to understand them if you are to provide the leadership required. Real achievement requires understanding basic terms, but sometimes in an uncommon way. How you define things (your "lexicon") will determine who you are, and how you do what you do.

CHAPTER 1

Gearing-Up: Some Preliminaries That Deserve Your Attention

IF YOU WERE to read every book ever written about real achievement, about organizational excellence, and about the leadership required even to undertake such an audacious cause—even if you were to memorize them all, that still would not enable you to do what has to be done. You have to learn how *by doing it*. Even then, it would still depend upon who you *are*. And upon how doggedly determined you are to fulfill your mission in life. And upon how well you can surround yourself with the people who are going to make it happen. And upon having a strategy for getting there. And, always, upon a certain amount of the right kind of "luck."

No scheme for making you "successful"—even your own—comes with an iron-clad guarantee. The reason is simple. The only person who can make you successful in such a venture as becoming extraordinary is you. Your personal mental and emotional resources may be superior or not. Your timing may be fortuitous or not. Your people may be better equipped—or not. If your business or personal strategies are wrong—forget it. If you do not pursue your mission in life ruthlessly enough, you're likely to get whatever is dealt to you. About "luck," that's easy. Good fortune favors the best prepared. And that's accomplishable for those who are incorrigibly determined—and willing to pay the price.

A large part of that "price" is how you think about the things that make a difference. That's what this book is for.

This *book* will not transform you into a high-performance person or your organization into a high-performance organization. Nor will this *book* make you into the leader you would need to be. No book, no seminar, no "program" can do that.

But if you internalize the way of thinking this book offers, and if you implement these ideas by putting them into daily practice until they are habits, then you will have the necessary wherewithal for undertaking the journey of becoming "the best"—personally or organizationally.

This *book* won't do it. But if you take to heart and mind what it offers, *you* can. The ideas are like the launching pad and the vehicle. *You* have to be the engine. *You* have to power these ideas. *You* have to make it happen. That "launching pad" cannot be made of words. It has to be dug down to bedrock—to belief, to habit, to a commitment from which you cannot escape or abandon, to a way of thinking and doing that becomes who you *are*.

It's not these words—these or any other. It's the passion and the competence behind the words. It's not the understanding—yours or anyone else's. It's the passion and the competence that focuses the understanding, like an overwhelmingly powerful magnet that is unfailingly energized by how you think about the things that make a difference. And about what you do with that thinking—with how you put it into everyday practice. So if you're ready, willing, and able, let's collaborate in the building of this "launching pad."

1.　Behind and under and before every perception, every feeling, every decision and every action, there are habits. Habits of mind, habits of perception, habits of feeling, habits of reaction and action. "The world" about which we speak so loosely does not "inform" us. We are "informed" by our own thinking and feelings about what that world is like and what is going on in it.

In short, the first and last leadership lesson is this:

We are led by our *habits* of feeling, of thinking, of perceiving, and of understanding.

Get those right, and everything beyond becomes possible. Get those wrong, and the outcomes will always be something you didn't choose.

A leader's perceptions, thinking, and feelings about the world inside or outside are informed by that leader's cause in life. Most people believe that the world around them is a given, that when they look at it they are seeing what's there. And that what people say about it tells them about "it." The leader knows that a perception or an interpretation of something is never more than just that. Reality is not obligated by what we say or fail to say about it.

The leader also knows that people do not choose their trajectories through life.

How we live and maneuver through life is not something we can have simply by "choosing" it. It is our habits that drive the way we think, and feel, and have, and do, and see, and say. We cannot choose our ways of being and doing. But we can choose, within our capabilities for doing so, the habits that inform our perceptions, our thinking, and our feelings. What makes the leader different is that he or she depends upon the habits *chosen* and developed to drive the direction and the outcomes of life. Not upon "hope." Or "intention." Or "desire."

What characterizes the leader is the mental models or the heuristics used to assess the world and the strategies for undertaking his or her cause in that world. It is the habits of thought, feeling, and action that underwrite the leader's success in his or her endeavor.

- You do not get those by reading about successful leaders.
- Or what celebrities imagine was *their* recipe for success.
- You get those by working backward from your cause and laboriously building into your thinking and feeling and doing those habits that are going to propel you in the direction of your cause.
- Thinking. First things first.

2. You have to be dissatisfied. You have to be sufficiently dissatisfied with yourself and your performance in your roles in life to do something about it. To be satisfied with the habits that will determine your life is to endorse them and to acquiesce to wherever they take you. Most people seem to prefer whining about their lives, or their work, or their friends, or the world, than to doing something about the only thing we have the prerogative to do something about—ourselves. Leaders understand that they cannot get to a place they have chosen to get to by being victimized . . . by *themselves*, which opens the door to being victimized by all the rest of the world.

- The leader changes the world by who he or she *is*. That *might* occur as the result of some one-in-a-billion genetic or historical accident.
- But the only leadership worth pursuing is not got by accident. It's got by the habits of thought, feeling, and action required by the circumstances.

3. Even so, the leader understands that pursuing any significant cause in the "real" world requires doing so in a complex web of interdependencies. The stand-alone hero who single-handedly achieves what appear to be impossible goals exists only in myth, in the movies, in the imaginations of lazy journalists, or in our dreams.

We all need someone who will make us do what we ought to

do. If you have a powerful conscience, that will function as the "other." Or, if you have the kinds of habits that make it necessary for you to do what you *ought* to do (your "duty"?), those will also function to make it necessary. For the rest of us, what's required is surrounding ourselves with the kind of people who will not let us default ourselves, who will make it necessary for us to do what we have to do in order to pursue our cause in life. Without an inner or outer context that absolutely makes it necessary, we will, more likely than not, fail by defaulting.

The leader is **first** of all interdependent with the historical moment. If the timing is right, he or she may become "the leader." If the timing is not right, if there is not a compelling need sensed by the potential followers for that person's leadership, that person will be unknown to history.

Second, "the leader" (of course we're talking about the would-be leader) is totally interdependent with those people on whom the success or failure of the leader's cause depends. You've all heard the sing-song-y thing about "For want of a nail, the shoe was lost/ For want of a shoe the horse was lost . . ." and so on, until it is revealed that the battle was lost. That's the kind of interdependence we're talking about here. Patton understood that "his" success as a field general depended upon the competencies of the lowliest recruits. That's why he paid so much diligent attention to the development of the competencies they would need under adversity.

Third, "the leader" and the success of his or her cause will always be interdependent—inseparable—from the strategies and tactics put in play to make it happen. If they're "right" for the historical moment, there will be success. But it will never be known whether or not those strategies were the "right" ones until the results are in. No guarantees. Just intricate and inescapable interdependence.

Fourth, any leader will remain over the course of the endeavor interdependent with whatever happens along the way. These may be happenstances. These may be a competitor's counter-moves or strategies. These may result from the fact an alarm clock didn't go off. Stuff happens. And the test of the leader is how nimble he or she is with respect to improvising and moving on, whether it is only oneself involved, or thousands of other people.

- The fancy term for all this is "systems."
- What this concept enables us to understand is that everything that happens—certainly everything that happens in the human world—has to happen in the context of other things that are constantly happening.
- Linear thinking won't work for leadership. What's required is thinking "systemically"—that is, understanding that everything is related to everything else. In *some* way.
- The leader understands that everything is what it is because everything else in the system is what *it* is.
- That may sound like gobbledygook to you. If you can't make it fundamental to your way of thinking, you'll never have the leader's edge.
- Not cause-and-effect. But interdependence, interrelatedness. You will never be more than those on whom you depend will permit you to be. And you will never accomplish more than the circumstances with which you are interdependent make possible.
- You can't change that. But you can equip yourself to pursue your cause in *that* world—for the leader, the "real" world.

4. Leaders seem to have more LIFE brimming behind their eyes and ears, within them and around them, in the evidences of their "spirit," than the rest of us have. That's a major part of what makes successful leaders so seductive.

They have so much LIFE in them that they can give it away. They seem to infuse those around them with more of this . . . LIFE. What is it? Exuberance? Zeal, passion? Clarity of purpose? Single-mindedness? Openness? Whatever it is, it seems to be infectious. We see it in their eyes. In their movements. In the way they listen and ask questions. In the way they speak and engage others. In the way *they* grab hold of LIFE and won't let it go.

- Does LIFE grab them more? Or do they grab more LIFE?
- Or, given that they are a part of a system that has everything in it that is there for the rest of us, maybe it has something to do with how they *think about things*, or with their habits.
- They inhabit the same "world" we do. So it must have something to do with *them*.
- Maybe the difference is that they had no interest in the difference.
- Maybe the difference emerged from their total immersion in the pursuit of their cause?

5. There is the perennial issue of "change." It has become so popular it functions like a "mantra"—people frequently mouth or pen the term but it has ceased to mean much more than suggesting that the speaker or writer is "with it."

What leaders know:

- Things are changing all the time.
- Most of the changes that swirl around us are not within our control.
- Who people *are*—*because* that is a function of a whole bundle of habits exercised every moment of every day—is a primary source of resistance to change. We want to be tomorrow what we were today. For that to happen, the world tomorrow has to be reasonably like it was today.
- To attempt to change the world, which would require people to change is, as Machiavelli wrote, the most dangerous and uncertain undertaking there is.
- But this is what leaders do. It is the appeal of the alternatives they describe that makes any significant change *possible*.
- But it won't occur unless it is *necessary*.
- Change cannot be generated or sustained by rational means.
- The systems in which people are embedded are fiercely resistant to change because they are tacit, accessible only by habits of belief.

- Leaders understand that they are wholly interdependent with the forces that resist change, **and** with the forces that enable change.
- Leaders don't "make" change. They midwife it.

6. Leaders don't just measure. They measure what counts.

7. About *anything* they imagine might bear upon the journey undertaken to fulfill their mission or cause in life, leaders have a minimal threshold. Being intensely curious about anything that might bear, one way or another, on the path they are on, leaders are in the business of asking questions. Asking questions of themselves, of others, of all of the world's wisdoms and its histories and current complexifications, leaders aim not to "know" everything. But only to gather the intelligence they need, from any source that bears upon their cause, beginning with themselves, that they can use to accomplish what has to be accomplished.

- There is no leadership "trivia."
- Leaders either know what they need to know in order to carry out their mission, or they fail.
- Their communication is that critical.

8. What matters? Holding people accountable for the results? Or holding people "accountable" for how well prepared they are, at all times, for pursuing those results? "Managers" seem to prefer the former, leaders the latter. Something to think about.

9. Leaders often seem to be "ruthless." On themselves? About what? Was there ever a leader who wasn't ruthless—about what might contribute significantly to the success or the failure of their endeavor?

How often have leaders failed by being reasonable? How often have they succeeded by being unreasonable (again, about what really matters)?

Given that most people have no particular aims in life, beyond having a comfortable "job," a comfortable spouse/lover/family, a comfortable house in a comfortable neighborhood with comfortable friends, a surfeit of comfortable leisure, and a comfortable retirement (the operant term being "comfort"), can you achieve your aims in life by soliciting and indulging those people? Especially if one of them is *you*?

> 10.   It does hinge profoundly on how the would-be leader *thinks about things*, doesn't it? The leader understands this: *As we think, so we will* **be.**

The leader knows that leadership is not a characteristic of a person. It is a *role* that needs playing in a *story* that needs writing. If it isn't the *leader's* story that gets written, the leader knows that it will be someone else's story, and that he or she would then be no more than a bit player in those other stories.

It is only when this kind of outcome is intolerable that the irresistible desire to lead gets born. The leader knows that leadership, being a role that needs to be played, is, metaphorically, a performing art. How the would-be leader plays that role will determine whether or not there are followers, and thus whether or not that leader's aims make a difference . . . or not.

It may be that "All the world's a stage," but the only one that matters is the one on which you appear. And upon how well prepared you are.

- Prepared with a way of thinking that makes a difference in *your* performance.
- Unconventional.
- A way of thinking that powers your performance.

The leader understands people better than most. The leader understands, for example, that if you want to know how a person *really* wants to live, you look at the way that person lives. If you want to know what people mean by what they say, observe what they *do*.

ch more ahead on this.

11.   How to have a **mediocre** organization:

- Be a conventionally-minded manager or executive. Think like your peers do.
- Put your own immediate interests and feelings first.
- Make sure you have a conventionally-designed organization, with conventional systems, processes, and procedures that take precedence over performance.
- Hire only mediocre people, especially those who put their own immediate concerns and interests first. They will be more comfortable to have around if they have no particular aims in life.
- Navigate solely by the "bottom line." The shorter the time frame, the better.
- Don't expose yourself to excellence, except to critique it.
- Do what you can to force your customers, suppliers, and other stakeholders to "understand" *you.*
- Make sure all of the people and other sources whose opinion you value are no better than you are.
- Get excited only about what has *happened* to you in the past.
- Defer learning to your leisure time.
- Appear always to know everything.
- Use your thoughtways until they become comfortable "ruts."
- Depend on habits that you didn't choose.

That's all worth thinking about. How? Shall we move on?

CHAPTER 2

Getting Underway . . .

Think On These Things

THIS CHAPTER OFFERS you an opportunity to exercise even more your thinking muscles. What follows is a (minimal) set of "think pieces" to use as examples for how you might think through short quotations or epigrams that (for any reason) intrigue you. They are not intended as recipes for how to think. They are intended as *exercises* for how to think about what needs thinking about.

Let's start here:

1. **If you want to know what kind of organization you deserve, look at the one you've got.**

Maybe you've never heard chief executives whine about the performance of their organizations—or the people in them. I have. Many times. They seem to be suggesting that they somehow "deserve" better. A little bit like parents trying to get others to agree that they did "the best they could" raising their children, so why those children didn't turn out wonderfully is certainly no fault of theirs.

Here's an example:

I arrive at the office of a client. This client—we'll call him

Frank—is livid, enraged. I wait. You would never ask why a person is angry; it encourages them. After a while he says, "I'm absolutely beside myself. Why so-and-so would do such-and-such is beyond me. He's done it before. What makes him so stupid?"

My reply (not kind): "Do you mean what makes him so stupid or what makes you so stupid for choosing him and casting him in that role?"

"What do you mean?" Frank replies, some of his anger now targeted at me. "He's supposed to know better than that."

"How?" I ask. "By behaving like you do? If everyone behaved as they are supposed to behave, from whose point of view would that be, yours or theirs?"

"Well," Frank said, finally pointing the finger back at himself and, being unable to muster the same level of anger at himself, "it just seems like I deserve better—you know, smarter performance."

"You probably do," I replied. "Does that begin with you?" You get the point. Them who can, do. Them who can't, whine about the reality they have surrounded themselves with. They use words like "supposed to" and "ought." If something they consider "smart" happens, they are quick to take credit for it. If, however, if something wrong or "stupid" happens, they start pointing fingers at anyone or anything but themselves.

So, what do such people as we are, deserve? Better than we are?

- The people in your organization are there because you directly selected them. Or because you selected the people who selected them. How people perform throughout the organization is your mandate—directly or indirectly. If you can't get that part of it right, you're going to have trouble getting any of the rest of it right.
- The person who performs in a way that pushes your frustration or anger button is likely not as fully competent to perform his or her role as may be necessary. Who is ultimately responsible for *that*?
- The attitudes and the performance of every person is directly or indirectly (through *your* choice of *their* boss) influenced

by who you *are*, because who you *are* determines how you do what you do.

- If you overlook performance shortfalls or the failure to grow in role until you finally "blow up," that makes those shortfalls and failures as much your fault as it is the other person's. From day one, *if there are no consequences forthcoming for sub-par performance, then you are responsible for your own frustrations or anger.*

- Were those expectations clear and mutually understood? As Sun Tzu said, if people do not perform as expected because the expectations were not clear (to them), then the fault lies with the boss—with the leader—with you.

With rare exceptions, the organization you deserve is the one you have. Shall we press on?

Over time, the organization isn't going to be much better—or perhaps much worse—than its leader. If you want an organization, or an athletic or musical performance, that ranks you among the "best," you have to be the kind of leader who *deserves* that outcome. And what needs to be changed at the outset is not the organization. It is the leader.

If you can't become the kind of person with all of the capabilities required to lead a great or high-performance organization, then it is just not going to happen. If you can't put your organization on and keep it on the path to becoming "the best," then you are not—yet—the kind of leader who deserves such an organization. *Fix that first.* The rest will follow.

- If you want to know what kind of organization, or performance, you "deserve," look at what you've got.
- That deserves thinking about. If you're not sure what you "deserve," ask your followers.

2. Like it or not, believe it or not—it will all depend first and last on who you *are* and thus on your leadership. It will

depend on how you think about what needs thinking about, which is the *source* of your leadership. Let's revisit this one:

Conventional thinking always and inevitably leads to conventional ways of doing things. And conventional ways of doing things always produce conventional results.

Short version: Conventional thinking leads to conventional results. It's always easier to think like everyone else does. That way you never have to justify your ways of thinking or of doing. And you'll end up in the middle of the pack, like most everyone else. How to have the most ordinary life? Think like everyone else does.

And it's always easier to think like you have always thought. Thoughtways—ways of thinking—are like the paths sheep make on the hillsides, as they follow in one another's footsteps. Your thoughts follow each other like they always have. The more they are used, the more ingrained they become and the harder they are to change. We get deeply into our mental "grooves" and resist any happening or any person who challenges them. We twist present "reality" so that it fits past "experience." We'll think like we've always thought.

One of my clients was a very smart fellow, a good engineer, a person who wanted to be an adequate—or better—CEO. I arrived in the middle of an almost plant-wide involvement in figuring out what a certain machine wouldn't "register"—it just wouldn't perform the sophisticated operation it was "supposed" to perform. The CEO, his staff, and several other "experts" were engaged in trying to figure out why the machine wasn't doing what it was "supposed" to do. They had even called in the machine manufacturer's people, a consultant or two, etc.

I asked," Why are you doing this?" In fact, I asked two or three times, looking right at him. Finally, he said, "Okay, you keep asking me that question. I'm trying to fix a problem. So, what the hell do you mean, 'Why am I doing this?'"

At least I had his attention. "You're a good engineer," I said. "So if you figure out why the machine isn't 'registering,' will that tell you how to make it do so?"

"Well . . . no," he said, thoughtfully.

"Let me ask another question, then. If you wanted to make this product, could you set up a plant across the street and just do it?"

"Yes, I reckon we could."

"In that case," I said, "why don't you do it that way? Why don't you take a blank sheet of paper and figure out what has to be done to fabricate that product? Why are you wasting your time looking for a 'cause' of something that went wrong when knowing that won't in itself tell you how to do it right?"

I waited. He was deep in thought. Then he took a blank sheet of paper, called a couple of his key people in, and they "solved" the problem. Not by going head-on at it, but by going around it. Sometimes people just do the same thing over and over again, but "hope" for a better outcome. As retired Army General Gordon Sullivan and many before him have observed, "Hope is not a method." Thinking and doing in the same ways over and over again, while trying harder and hoping even more for a better outcome is, as ancient wisdom has it, a form of insanity. But you can see how common this is.

There are two traps here: One is that conventional ways of thinking are simply easier. They are likely to go unchallenged by others who think the same way. Or by others who have come to expect us to think or act in those familiar ways.

The other is that a way of thinking that may have resulted in some modest successes is likely to take root and defend itself against any alternative. We come up with a success "paradigm" and then use it to fit all circumstances until we fail by applying it where it does not fit.

Here's the corollary: If you want something other than conventional results, then you have to start with some uncommon ways of thinking.

Conventional thinking is a byproduct or a symptom of the inability to think afresh about a common problem. What this requires:

- Being totally accomplishment minded, not being shackled by routines.

- Having great mental resources that come from honing them against great thinkers, and
- Having the sort of disciplined mind that enables you to be creative, to *invent* or improvise ideas and stratagems that enable you to leapfrog current thought and beliefs. The more commonplace the "stuff" you feed your mind, the more commonplace will be your thinking, and thus the results of your thinking. If you want uncommon wisdom, you have to go after it ruthlessly. And you have to figure out how to generate a way of accomplishing what needs accomplishing. Leader's lessons?
- An accomplishment is always in the future. Exactly what is it? And what is the most expedient path from here to there? Leaders often have to **create** the outcomes they seek. If those could be had from experience, or by prescription, we'd all have been successful long ago.
- Leaders have to calculate what needs to be done in always-unique and ever-changing circumstances, *given their own aims*. If you're looking at circumstances *in terms of* your own aims, it's obvious "conventional" won't work.
- Leaders are the makers of the world and its consequences for their purposes. They are not the victims of it. Change the world? Change your thinking.

Here's another corollary: There is no competitive advantage in doing *anything* conventionally. That simply places the outcome directly in the clutches of chance or "luck."

- When everyone thinks like everyone else, the winner is determined by the roll of the dice.
- Maybe what drives leadership is a loathing for living that way.

3. Here's an easy one: **There is no quick fix.** We all know that's true. Yet why do so many executives, so many "wannabe" leaders, continue to lust after the latest and

greatest of the "quick fixes" being hyped by the business press—or by one another? Not only is there no quick fix. There certainly isn't a one-size-fits-all prescription for greatness, for unparalleled success. Why? Because no two leaders are ever that much alike. And the circumstances in which it all has to be worked out are *never* the same. Few leaders have ever been able to replicate their success at another time and in different circumstances. So the imagined prescription which made them successful won't even work for them in changed circumstances. They are themselves different from who they were.

There are no shortcuts. There is no fairy dust. There are no "secrets" to be revealed if you just buy this or that magazine or book or seminar. You are offered every day all kinds of "magic wands" to wave over your place and make it wonderful. As someone once said, "Hope springs eternal." We seem to be seduced by every panacea that gets hawked by the panacea-hawkers. Why?

There is only one way to achieve something intended that is really worthwhile. And that is the hard way. To achieve great things, you have to pay the price. That's just the way it is. The "price" is not what you pay for some fairy dust. The price is the long-term investment, it is great effort and dedication, discipline, smarts, and an unwavering passion to achieve.

Here's the reality. Becoming "great" is not a goal to be reached. It is a way of life, gained and maintained by superlative discipline of mind, body, and spirit. It is character. It is pursuing a purpose or a cause even if it requires more than your own lifetime.

It might take a hundred years. So what? There is no better way to live than by what is required to be solidly on the path of becoming—forever *becoming*—the best at some truly human, and humanizing, endeavor. This way of life makes "getting there" a non-issue. Whether or not you are securely and irreversibly on the path is the only thing that matters at the end of the day.

A quarterly financial statement is certainly important. It has frequently been observed that you can't have a future unless you are healthy in the present. But making any short-term measure the only one that counts will guarantee that you are not on the path of becoming anything other than short-term. You will be pushed here and there like a reed in the economic winds. You will always be a victim.

A short fable: There was this CEO who said that things were not going well because "the economy is weak." There was this same CEO who, when "the economy" was robust, said, "Look at what I did!" Which of these CEOs are you going to believe?

- You have to be up to something great in order to have any possibility of making progress in that direction.
- If you are not interpreting the world in terms of your own designs on it, then it will interpret you in its terms.
- If you don't know (or care) where you are going, you're likely to end up someplace else—but with tons of advice about how to get there.
- To compete on any criterion other than becoming "the best" leaves you vulnerable to even the poorest competitors.

There is no "quick fix." You *can* buy one, and then the next one, and then the next . . . . You can be known as the person who pursues "the flavor of the month."

Or . . . you can get on the path of real achievement, which means practicing today in order to perform "perfectly" tomorrow. And then tomorrow you practice again. So you are forever practicing to do it better. That's the path.

- If most of your focus is on the short-term, in pursuit of quick-fixes or just ways of accommodating the posture of firefighting, then thinking about what needs thinking about to get somewhere you have chosen will never become a priority.
- You will put it off until your own aims and intentions have atrophied.
- A "quick fix" is the one you need before you need the next one.

4. Getting from here to there requires getting into a different "paradigm."

The "here" refers to the present you. And to the present circumstances of your organization. The "there" refers to the point at which you are irrevocably on the path of determined achievement. A "paradigm" refers to your standard ways of looking at and thinking about yourself and your organization—and the world in which both function. Different? Well, if you use the same "paradigm," you will stay in the same place. Or, at best, you will be on the path of becoming whatever is inevitable in your present paradigm. Your destiny will either be given. Or it will be chosen. To choose requires getting into a way of thinking and doing which is different from the one that presently holds you hostage.

What this means is that there has to be a "leap of faith" for the first person to transition from the "here" lily pad to the "there" lily pad, from the one way of thinking to the other way of thinking. This would be the leader. Once there, and thinking and doing in this different paradigm, he or she can reach out a helping hand—provide a bridge—from the one to the other. It is only the leader who must believe in his or her vision of that future way of life. It helps if the others—particularly your other leaders—also believe. But, *ultimately, they have no choice.* They can choose *not* to make the journey. But they cannot choose to participate, yet not go where the leader is going.

- Leaders are roused to commitment and action through *dissatisfaction.*
- Dissatisfaction with the status quo, with being merely adequate, with being victimized by whatever happens, with the deadly suffocation of mediocrity, with the mundane same-old, same-old.
- Leaders *lust* to live in the rarefied atmosphere of being exceptional.
- The faith required, the effort required, the perseverance required—all fade to irrelevance in the face of the raging

dissatisfaction of being no more than a pawn in the clutches
of yesterday forever recycled.
- To make a story of your own, you have to be powerfully
  dissatisfied with the one you're in.
- That's part of what it takes to lead the struggle from "here"
  to "there."

A reminder: You can't live in the conventional world, wallowing
in a conventional lifestyle, with its conventional orientations and
attitudes, and still expect to be a real achiever. A would-be leader
who does not have the courage to follow that proverbial "path less
taken" will not make much of a difference in his or her own life, or
the lives of others.

In spite of a persistent myth to the contrary, history is not
made by the masses of people who do not have to think because
their thinking is done for them. It is the leader who derails
inevitability by refusing to let the past determine the future.

You need followers. Radical followers—people who will make
your vision into reality in spite of your own shortcomings and
weaknesses and regressions. Without leadership, they have no aim,
no direction, nothing toward which to channel their energies and
their pursuit of something greater than their present lives. Without
those radical and unreasonable followers, the leader's cause will be
stillborn.

The journey from "here" to "there" is a matter of *realizing*—of
making the mere vision into an absolute reality. How incorrigibly
committed the leaders are will determine the life—or the death—
of a cause, a vision, a dream. If it is "life or death" for the leader,
that leader will have the followers needed to realize the "there."

We humans have to understand the world by looking at the
past. But we have to live it going forward. The future is not subject
to past analyses. It gets created by what people say and do every
day. We can neither predict nor control that. But we can align
people to a cause. It will never be perfect. But it's all we have. The
leader makes allegiance to the present "paradigm" difficult or even
impossible. And the leader makes saying and doing consistent with

the alternative "paradigm" *necessary*. You can't align people by exhortation. You have to make the thinking and doing that will get you from "here" to "there" **necessary**. For people to go their own way cannot be an option. If it is, the organization will not go the leader's way.

What's required of our thinking and doing is not more of the same. It is not a comfortable extension of present thinking and doing. What's required is a profound shift in orientation and attitude to what's going on, made necessary by where we're going— from "here" to "there." This is, at the outset, what the leader "leads." For example, here are some faulty assumptions:

- Working "harder" at being a manager will turn you into a leader. Hasn't happened yet.
- Whatever makes us "successful" could make us "the best" if we just worked "harder" at it. Won't happen.
- Knowing-*about* is almost the same as knowing-*how*. Never.
- An adequate organization will evolve into a great organization. No. That won't happen.
- The future we desire will be produced by our desire. Does anyone *really* believe that?
- Most people are willing to leave their comfort zones of their own volition. Does it work that way for anyone you know?
- The future is determined by the past. Only when you don't intervene.

You have to be overwhelmed, totally seduced by your zeal to get from "here" to "there." Those who cling to their present paradigms like shipwreck victims to anything that floats are not neutral. They will thwart you if they can. Ever try to save a drowning person? They will welcome you with open arms only to take you down with them.

You have to think and do in a way that will make your cause be realized whether they welcome you or not. Great achievements are always *in spite of*, never "because of." Change is brought about by an unreasonable person.

- It's tough. The road signs are all on the well-traveled road being taken by most others.
- You have to make your own. You have to *make* the road, not take it.

5. Most people, and thus most organizations, are *event-driven*. Leaders, and their organizations, are *purpose-driven*.

What this means: In an event-driven organization (or life), the day begins with the first event that hits, followed by the second, and then by the third, each more or less random event being superceded by the next more or less random event until, at the end of the day, people are exhausted. "Fighting fires" is not very inspiring or energizing work. People finish one day of being event-driven, only to look forward to another day of the same. It is like a squirrel-cage—a squirrel-cage being cranked by anyone and everyone else who has a problem that you look like a target for.

One thing leads to another. You sort them out according to which one seems the most threatening, *or* has the least risk, *or* whatever one's random feelings are for dealing with these random events at the moment.

Well . . . you've been there, done that. You know how it feels and how it leads to nothing other than more of the same. If you like that, forget the rest of this. If you are really, really dissatisfied, read on.

What's different about being *purpose-driven*? After all, the same events can occur whether you are event-driven or purpose-driven. The primary difference is that you look at those events in terms of their relevance to your purpose, your aim, your cause in life. You interpret events in terms of their bearing on outcomes you have chosen, not in terms of those events themselves. A "fact" is a fact only because it relates to some purpose or cause. To deal with it as a thing in itself is exhausting because it is meaningless, a mere exercise in getting through the day. For the purpose-driven, one's purpose is the measure of an event, not the other way around. In a purpose-driven organization, the agenda precedes events. Events get put into a more meaningful context—in terms of their relevance, not to people, but to the larger purpose—the reasons for the organization's existence and its destiny. Leaders help us to put the horse before the cart, the context before the event.

- To be event-driven is to measure things by *their* demands.
- To be purpose-driven is to measure life through *accomplishments* that move you toward your purpose.
- Preparing yourself, and then others, to get on the path of real achievement is being purpose-driven. Mere *activities* diminish everyone to a life of being event-driven.
- If it gets on your agenda without your permission, or is not a means to **your** ends, it is because you prefer being event-driven.
- A person who is event-driven will never become a leader.

6. **The pursuit of a cause is not a goal.**

   It is, however, the best way of life.

The pursuit of a great and worthy purpose in life is an endless *journey*. The world will not stop just because you got a little better. There are those who are struggling to overtake you, always. You will not be exempt just because you tried. Real achievement is not a place. It's an attitude, a set of habits, a way of life.

- Those who seriously pursue a purpose in life cannot afford to tarry at any level of "success."

- Getting better, making progress, is about preparing today for tomorrow's trials.

- If this striving ends before you do, you have failed.

- It is the striving that enhances our lives, not the arriving.

- The question, "Are we there yet?" is the kiss of death for your mission in life.

The quality of the life you have while pursuing your goals is more important than achieving them. You can be successful by accident, by sheer "luck." And you can fail through no direct fault of your own. But you cannot pursue a purpose in life except by choosing to do so. And it is the character that comes as a byproduct of being committed to that path that measures the quality of one's life—or an organization's life.

The critical difference: the pursuit of a great and worthy purpose in life requires you to develop and maintain an increasing capacity for learning. Learning produces growth. And life is always enhanced to its current limits by growth, which in turn increases its limits. By putting people on this path, the leader incites and inspires their lives. Having something larger than themselves to live for generates and raises the sheer quality of life. The leader is a life-maker, first his own and then the lives of followers. Arriving is a form of death. It is the end of something. *Striving* requires forever *beginning*. There is more life in beginnings than in endings. There is more life in striving to achieve something great than in being forever buffeted by "events."

A client once said to me, "We're not getting there."

There's only one answer to that: "You're not getting there *today*? What are you doing *today* about that?"

- To live in the thrall of the habits required to pursue a great and worthy purpose in life generates endless adventure.
- Achieving one's goals too soon or too easily is the end of the adventure that life could be.
- To compete with the best in order to surpass the best puts you in the "best," the most exciting, company.
- The schoolyard game "King of the Hill" teaches us that being the one on top is temporary, at best. It was those who were trying to knock you off your perch who were having the most fun.
- But, the critics say, suppose we "fail." "Fail" at what? At having richer and more rewarding experiences of life?
- Where's the downside? If you don't do it, how much life will go un-had, unrealized?

7. You like "practical"? Here's an extremely practical one:
Take your eye off the bottom line.

That must look like some whack-o advice. It's ancient advice. It's advice not much heeded in our world. We're "bottom line" people. But you'd be surprised by how valuable this simple bit of advice can be.

Some managers believe that "the numbers" tell them what they need to know. How wrong they could be. The conventional bottom-line numbers may tell you a little bit about the current and most recent financial history of the company. They may tell you where you are relative to where your forecasts were. But those numbers won't tell you where you ought to be. They won't tell you what's wrong. They won't tell you what to do about what's wrong. They won't tell you what the situation might be if you had prepared differently. They won't tell you, won't even give you a clue, about what your purpose in life ought to be. They won't tell you how to get from "here" to "there," or even where "there" is.

Those numbers will tell you something about your current state of purely financial health (and you have to read that into them). But managers who don't have a fairly accurate intuitive grasp of that without the numbers are not going to learn much by any literal interpretation of the numbers. But those numbers won't tell you whether or not you got to the present situation out of incompetence, stupidity, or (good or bad) luck. They won't tell you how good your competitors are, or where the next real threat is coming from. They won't tell you if you have the right business strategy. They won't tell you whether or not you have the right people in the right roles (including the CEO), or the right organization architecture for what you want to accomplish.

"The numbers" are a conventional talisman produced by a conventional accounting practice. Here's something accountants won't tell you about "the numbers": that they do not, can not, partial out the contribution of the environment from the contribution of the organization to "profit." Thus some organizations do all the "right" things, but fail. Other organizations do all the "wrong" things, but succeed. The numbers may tell you *something*. But they won't tell you what you did right, or wrong. They won't tell you what you need to do next, beyond doing whatever it takes to make the numbers measure up to some preconceived pattern.

Enough? The point is that taking your eye off the bottom line (except as you might use a thermometer) sets you free to put your eye on what *drives* the bottom line. Things like towering competence. Like intensity and zeal. Like preparedness for whatever happens (or doesn't). Like reserve energy and acumen. Like the kind of intelligence that matters. Like being committed to a level of performance that forever pulls the bottom line along in its irresistible wake. Like focus, or the right strategy, or the right organizational design. Like "smart" systems that underwrite exceptional performance. Like practice.

- Bottom lines do not improve by analysis or interpretation.
- They are produced. What produces them is measurable.
- Put your eye on what *drives* the bottom line, develop those capabilities, and the numbers will always meet or exceed your expectations.
- What's most easily counted is rarely what counts most.

The financials are the result of many forces—some of which are controllable, some of which are not. Leader's lessons:

- Those who pursue real achievement will focus on what *is* controllable, what *is* developable.
- Leaders focus on being the *best prepared* there is in the game. Better than this you cannot do.

8. **Don't let what you can't do define what you can do.**

People who have abandoned themselves to mediocrity or merely being average do this all the time. What most people get good at is explaining why something can't be done. They use their arguments about why they think something can't be done to define what they think can be done. Unacceptable. (You've probably never been in a meeting where this has occurred.) How leaders have thought about this is as follows:

- There is probably *always* some way of figuring out what has to be accomplished if the obvious tack doesn't work.
- You just have to be determined and smart enough to figure out what that alternative tack is.
- If ingenuity or determination are lacking, then you are doomed to succeed—or fail, in no more than an ordinary way—merely by chance.
- You have to measure *capabilities* by figuring out how to do something that others have considered "impossible."
- Give us the difficult. What's easy brings no honor, no joy, no glory.
- Never confuse an activity with an accomplishment.
- Never let what someone imagines we can't do define the future.

9. **What drives extraordinary performance is *necessity*.**

NOT threats. A boss's threats are a symptom of a bankrupt manager. NOT blackmail. Not "rewards" or "punishments." NOT exhortation. None of these engenders any real *necessity*. These are games that require no more than the complicity of the other players. They are testimony to a bankrupt imagination.

What, then?

The kinds of necessity that make a difference in thought, feeling, or behavior take many forms and have several sources. Here are some of those:

- The most pervasive and powerful of all the forms of necessity is **habits**. It is our habits that behave us. We are merely the visible evidence of their pushes and pulls. Our habits function as the necessity that produces what we do (or don't do), what we think, what we feel, and what we say. There is rarely any possibility of compromise. We don't choose. *They* do.

- A person's **competencies** are also a source of considerable necessity for that person—for you, for others. The more competent people are to do something, the more likely they are to do it. Conversely, a person who is not competent to do something is not likely to do it. An incompetency works like this: The more incompetent a person is to do something, the more necessary it is *not* to do it. What a person is capable of doing, that person will do. What a person is not capable of doing, that person will not do. Our incompetencies provide one kind of (negative) necessity. You will never observe people doing what they cannot do, or thinking in a way they cannot think, or feeling in a way they cannot feel, or seeing in a way they cannot see. It is *necessary* for them *not* to do so. Or, looking at the positive side of it: it is simply *necessary* for people to do what they are competent to do, and in the way they are competent to do it. Practical implication: If you are not (or any other person is not) performing at the required level, it's most likely that you or they are simply not competent enough to do so. Fix that first.

You can't know for sure if there is another explanation—"laziness," for example—until you fix this infrastructure shortfall. In other words, fix first what's fixable.

- Some people are more conscientious than others, and about different things. Some people would never cheat a friend, but might be stealing time from you. A person's **conscience** is a formidable source of necessity for that person. The more conscientious a person is, the more necessary is his or her way of doing things. Conscientiousness requires self-control. People who have developed significant levels of self-control live by a greater sense of personal necessity than do those who feel far less responsible for themselves.

- There is a destiny in every way of thinking. There is a destiny in every person's history and present circumstances. There is a destiny in every organization's history and structure and mode of operation. Everyone belongs to a culture and to one or more subcultures. These are evolving in some direction. And the people who "belong" to them will be greatly influenced in their future destinies by virtue of their membership in them. Who you hang out with, who you talk to, what you read, will affect your destiny. Your mind works the way it does because it is interdependent with the other minds it associates with.

If you seek a certain destiny, you have to have aligned the conditions that will produce that destiny. Necessity is in the way circumstances work themselves out. You have to put in place **all of the factors** that will produce a **necessary outcome**. Necessity is far more powerful than theories, or mere desire or effort.

- **Consequences.** Of all of the sources of necessity, none is more potent than the imagined or foretold consequences. We like to think that children become more "angelic" when they are told at Christmastime that good children get the goods, and bad behavior takes stuff off their list. We like to think that the "sticks" and "carrots" we use makes people perform better in the long term. Wrong.

But if there are no consequences, if people don't imagine consequences that are worse than what needs be done to avoid them, then there is no real necessity. My own father bought basketball shoes for me (6th grade, proper shoes required) with the proviso that I would be "first team." Guess what? (Yes, he would have taken the shoes back if I had failed to keep up my end of the deal.)

When there are no consequences for poor performance by the CEO, there is little he or she can say about consequences that will carry any necessity. You see the point. It is that the level of performance will reflect the level of necessity operating—internal and external combined.

For these and like reasons, the leader knows—

- That the best path for gaining predictable and enhanced performance forever is to surround oneself with people for whom that level of performance is simply *necessary*.
- Or to inculcate that level of internal necessity, which requires more leadership capabilities than most people can muster.
- Or to be the kind of seductive leader who so enchants followers that they *assume* the necessity for always pleasing that leader with their performance, and never displeasing that leader.
- The leader knows . . . that it must be one of these ways. And that extraordinary performance will always be a function of *necessity*.

10. It isn't the recipe. It's the cook.

Like necessity, this will be a recurring theme throughout this guidebook, so we don't need to spend much time on it here. Even so . . . .

You'll recall this basic caveat:

Many have tried. Few have succeeded.

There are three reasons.

The **first** is that the person who undertook to make it happen was not the leader he or she needed to be. It may have been a shortfall of passion, of dedication, of necessity, of competence. Whatever it was, something was missing in the person who had the role of leading the charge.

The **second** reason for the fact that most attempts fail is that the leader did not persevere. Thinking of real achievement as a destination rather than a way of life may have contributed.

Third, that person didn't have what it takes to implement the process—to "make it happen"—which is about 95% of the process. What has to be done to make it happen has to be done by the leader(s) in place, in the context of the condition of the organization and the circumstances of the real world at that time.

You can't put that in a bottle, a can, or a nutshell. It cannot be reduced to a recipe. One size does not fit all. We suffer especially in our civilization from the delusion that knowing-*how* to do something—like having a recipe or a set of "steps" got from a celebrity—is all that's required. Wrong. It takes much more than following a recipe. Ask any chef. Or champion golfer. Or great lover.

People are not interchangeable with respect to a set of instructions. We want to "buy" something that will compensate for our incompetencies. That might work with unimportant things. But the greater the aim, the greater the capabilities required.

Where they are required, there is no recipe that can overcome individual ignorance or incompetence. You've probably seen it tried.

Let's cut through this. The best recipe in the world in the hands of an incompetent person will produce a poor product or service. Are we to believe, after 30 years or so, that "computers" have made us all a lot smarter? Or our organizations significantly more capable? Isn't the failure rate of businesses about the same as it always was? If our "productivity" has actually *decreased* over the "hi-tech" era, why do we cling to the myth? Do we get better "customer service" (that's the claim) because our calls are handled electronically? Why are we *less* literate than the pioneers? Do we really make better marriages, better families? Have these new recipes that we are bombarded with every day by the business press enabled us to make *better*—more competitive, more resilient, more prepared, more secure—business organizations in this "global" economy? Have all of our problems gone away yet?

The ancient wisdom is simple enough: "Talk does not cook rice."

Here is how leaders understand this:

- There is no recipe that is better than the cook.
- Great cooks, like great leaders, are well beyond recipes. Recipes are for amateurs.
- There is no recipe that will turn out the same regardless of the cook. Poor cooks can ruin the best recipes; great cooks can make great food out of the most mediocre of recipes.
- No "recipe" or scheme or "theory" the leader can buy will be any better, in its implementation, than is the leader.
- Great leadership cannot be taught. But it can be learned.
- The key variable will not be a recipe. It will be *you*.
- In the hands of a great leader, *any* recipe will work. And has.

* * *

These are but examples of how to use "think pieces" to your advantage. They can come from anywhere. Whenever you come across a quotation or an epigram or even an offhand comment that runs contrary to what you believe, do what we've just done here. Think through what you could advantageously make it mean to you on your journey on-behalf-of your cause in life. Here are a few more to whet your appetite:

- Exceptional performance is not "because of" but "in spite of." Turning the lights on does not make people smarter. Put your money on the person who is going to accomplish what needs to be accomplished . . . regardless. The *bricoleur*.
- People don't learn from "experience." They learn from their *interpretations* of their experiences. What they learn will be no better than their interpretations.
- Most people prefer a problem they can't solve to a solution they don't like. Observe carefully a person who does not make his or her problems go away and you'll see why this is so.

- "Good enough" is the *enemy* of great performance. It's not a step in that direction.
- The most important things you have to learn by doing them. That's the great chasm between "knowing-that" and "knowing-how."
- People love doing what they do in direct proportion to how good they are at it. Pop psychology will have you exactly backwards on this.
- Security "kills."

Or, as Thoreau said:

**"What can the person who is dissatisfied
with himself not do?"**

CHAPTER 3

The Leader's Lexicon: I

BE PATIENT. WE'RE all eager to get to the "good parts"—like the how-to-do-it stuff. That includes me.

But we need to put depth of understanding first. Think about it this way: Many more people fail than succeed. And the main reason for this? It is that *a technique that is not supported by a superior understanding of why things work the way they do is a technique that will likely fail.* We're all eager to do things. People are urged to read the instruction book first. But most don't. Most people launch into things with the shallowest understanding. They consult the instruction book only when all else fails.

Where people and the dynamics of doing life and business are concerned, no technique can be any better than the depth of understanding of the person who exercises it. No matter how prestigious the source. Imagining that a great idea offered by a guru will solve all your problems is a (widespread) delusion. People imagine that, because they read somebody's words, they now know all they need to know to do it. But no mere reading of John Wooden's thoughts on coaching will make a better basketball coach of anyone. He was the one who gained the potent understanding. It is *his understanding of the game* that you need, not his words. It is *this* understanding of the game you need, not just the words.

If doing is not profoundly supported by understanding, it will, in any critical test, fail. That's why we have to dig down into the *understanding* part of it.

We cannot visit this guidepost too often: The more difficult and challenging the journey, the more critical the preparations and the provisioning. Any great achievement requires that kind of intense preparation and provisioning.

Most of those preparations and that provisioning have to do with *your* thinking, *your* attitudes, and *your* overall readiness for the journey. That's what all this upfront stuff is for. The more thoroughly you understand and internalize these provisions for your thinking, the better able you will be to **implement** your leadership aims. "Measure twice, cut once," is the carpenter's wisdom. This means that the most important part of your journey is *your* preparation for it.

So it is not simply a matter of being patient. It is a matter of being thoroughly equipped—mentally and emotionally—before you are put to the test.

So what we want to delve into and understand here are some critical terms for your thinking. We think with the terms we have available to think with. If we get those right, we get our thinking right. Most of these are common enough terms. But, as you will recall from the last chapter, conventional thinking always leads to conventional results. You want *unconventional* results. So you have to start with more powerful ways of understanding certain terms that you will use every day.

An example would be "thinking" itself. Most people think they can think. But most people can't. They've lost it—through misuse, or disuse, or by being "dumbed-down" by the millions of words, ads, images, and other information they are exposed to every day. Many people believe that being able to tell others what they heard on the news, or from other people, constitutes "thinking." Not even close.

So when someone begins a sentence directed your way with "I think . . . this or that," you can be fairly certain that what they are saying is something like "The way my head works, I couldn't help coming up with what I am about to say to you." In other words, don't be led to believe that there is any significant thinking behind the use that other people make of "I think . . . ."

As Henry Ford put it: "Thinking is the hardest work there is, which is probably why so few engage in it." Thinking requires great depth and breadth of real intelligence, and the tools for combining and recombining pertinent facts productively. Thinking is perhaps a little like improvising in music. All of the fundamentals have to be at your command without thinking about them. Years of practice may enable you to "think out of the box": to use your unique tools on your unique stockpile of knowledge and your unique capacity for pitting your imagination against a difficult or "impossible" outcome. What does imagination have to do with it? Einstein reminded us that "Imagination is more important than knowledge." And knowledge is far more important than facts.

Here's another angle: Picasso insisted that computers are not good for anything. All they can give you, he said, is the answers. So what's wanted in "thinking" is not the answers but the questions that lead you to insights, ideas, solution paths that would otherwise not be available to you. That's what thinking is for: to take you where you have never gone before. "Thinking" is not opinion. It is not someone's interpretation of something. It is not bringing to bear what one already knows on a situation never before encountered. It is the capacity to take yourself mentally to a more advantageous point of view, a more powerful perspective on things.

So it is dangerous to imagine that others are offering you their "thinking." In all likelihood, they are offering you something they just happen to know, hoping it might fit. They haven't learned how to "think." As Ford said, it's hard work. As for your own "thinking": don't give credit where it is not due. If you pay careful attention to this and the following pages, you'll be thinking better than you ever have in your life. It'll be a start for the great journey of learning how to think—a prerequisite for the journey to any great achievement—including compelling leadership.

1. Let's start with the obvious. **We are led by words.** A better
    way of putting this, perhaps: *You* are led by how you
    understand the words that are used—whether your words
    or others' words.

What this means is that the way you understand things
determines what you are going to do about them. So your
understandings of things go far toward determining how things
are going to turn out for you. Given the outcomes, there are better
ways and worse ways of understanding the terms by which you
describe present and future circumstances.

Let's look at some of these (common) terms, and consider some
better ways of understanding how they reveal the world to us.
Before we do, are you wondering whether or not people can change
or improve their thinking abilities? If so, that's a good question.
The answer is . . . yes. But how much people can change, how
good they can really get at this business of thinking, depends upon
how determined and how ruthlessly they are committed to some
future great achievement—as, in this case, becoming a compelling
leader. Lukewarm desires and intentions will produce little, if
anything. Many people "want" the outcomes. They would probably
even "like" to be able to think. But getting there requires hard
work, *change*, passionate dedication to the outcome. And discipline.
What's provided here are ways of disciplining your mind. Learn to
lead yourself with these ways of understanding.

If you don't have these characteristics in sufficient measure,
you have two choices. Develop them. You can use what follows to
do that.

Or forget it.

"Reality" And "Communication"

You can't talk about the one—sensibly—without talking about
the other one. But here, just for ease of understanding, we look at
each and then put them back together where they belong.

"Reality." We talk as if we are dealing with "reality." But this never happens. We are stuck with dealing with what we say about "reality." With what we think about reality. What's in our heads is not "reality." It has already been transformed into what things *mean*.

This is not a "philosophical" issue. There is nothing "academic" about it. It's as practical as we can get. It may be hard to "get it." But if you don't, you will be forever disadvantaged. And if you don't "get it," you can forget about any illusions you might have about leadership.

The world is, in and of itself, no matter the object or the event, meaningless. It is we people who render it meaningful. We have to. Our minds—the only tools we have ever had for dealing with the world—work only with the meanings of things. Think about anything which is meaningless to you, and you will get the point. You can't do it.

So our grasp on "reality," so *your* grasp of "reality," is necessarily limited to the way your own mind works. Maybe we both wish it wasn't that way. And maybe we have been able to become comfortable with the fact that "reality" is what we think it is. But there is a "reality" out there, and it keeps on spinning out things and events. Different takes on what people agree is "reality" may permit us to exercise more—or less—control over some aspects of it. We can nullify the limits of our "natural" capabilities by inventing airplanes. Or by contacting each other via satellite. But the "realities" of the world in which we have to perform, with all of its social/economic/technological/political ramifications, are things we can understand only by thinking about them in the way we think about them. And no one of us controls the twists and turns of the economy or of the society. We can't even control each other. We can only control ourselves, and that only within limits.

So what's the point? They are these:

- All human conflicts can be reduced to the struggle over whose "realities" will prevail. Who has the power—or the good fortune—to determine whose "realities" we will have to live by.

- All misunderstandings come down to the fact that one person's view of "reality" was not the same as some other person's view of "reality."
- More people (and thus organizations) get messed up by their misassumptions about "reality" than any other single thing.
- Our takes on "reality" consist of hypotheses, hunches, and assumptions about "it." We can never know whether those are right or wrong. We can only know and assess where they took us.
- "Truth" is always a red herring. "Truth" is whatever we agree it is. There is no test beyond a test that we might devise, which will be as fallible as we are.
- What's in your head (your way of seeing and thinking about things) isn't "reality." It just happens to be the way you think about things. Inescapably, it's just the best you can do.
- You either have to trust your view of "reality," or someone else's. You are no more infallible than they are.
- How you happen to see things doesn't obligate them to be that way.
- Your sense of certainty you're right doesn't make you right.
- People try to "understand" the existing world. Leaders try to make an alternative world. Along the lines of Einstein's observation that "Imagination is more important than facts."

Any argument over whether something is "true" or not is, for the leader, a silly waste of time. The issue is simply this: Where is this way of understanding things, of looking at things, going to get us? All of our thinking, all of our talking, all of our claims on "reality" come down to the consequences for doing so one way or another.

Got it? Whether you're right or wrong is given in how things turn out. Every other argument is an academic one. No conflict ever determined whose opinion about "reality" was "right." It merely determined whose view was going to prevail.

Got it?

If so, let's cast the same lens on "communication."

When people think (talk to themselves) or talk to one another, they are always and inevitably talking from their perspectives on "reality." People can only tell you what they know. They can't tell you what "is." What something means is what it means to that person. When people talk a lot with each other, they come to have similar meanings for things. They come to see the world in similar ways. Their "realities" have the same furniture and similar understandings, assumptions. When people want to collaborate for some mutual purpose—becoming lovers or partners, for example—they try to make sure they are "on the same page." They want their views of "reality" to coincide. So they talk to determine how "compatible" their views of "reality" are.

We acquire from other people and other sources the intelligence we imagine we need to pursue our interests. We have maps and signs and reports to "tell us" where we are. We read books, and ask others, to figure out who we ought to be, and how we ought to go about it. We tell other people what we think might bring us closer together or otherwise enable us to manipulate them in some way to our advantage. That's what advertisers do. That's what buyers and sellers do. That's what politicians do. That's what artists do. That's what we people do.

The "real" world is the one people construct when they talk to themselves or to one another. That may not be very satisfactory. But that's as good as it gets. It's the one they have in their "heads." It's the one they work from when they observe, or assess, or debate. Like all the rest of us, you are stuck with the way your mind works. Until or unless, of course, you change it. As may be possible here.

The point: People may be presuming to "refer" to some "reality" when they talk to you. But if they can think about it or talk about it, it has already been adapted to their way of thinking or of talking. When they talk to you, they are not referring to some "reality" that is independent of them. They can only refer to the way they understand it, the way they see. They can't tell you what's in the world. They can only tell you what's on *their* minds.

So we're back again to the all-important criterion. What something means lies in the **consequences** for having or applying that meaning. What you infer from your perception of the world, or of what others say to you, ultimately lies in what the consequences are for those interpretations.

- When you observe something first hand, it is your interpretation that you come away with. When you listen to others, it will be your interpretation of their interpretations. (I know that is awkward. But how otherwise to put it?)
- Your ability to provide yourself with the interpretations you need to get where you are going—whether these interpretations are yours or others'—will determine whether or not you can get there.
- Yes, indeed. You have to know what the present circumstances are, as best you and/or others can assess them. But they will still be interpretations. It's just that some are better (or more efficacious) than others. But not even a perfect assessment of present circumstances will be of any help if you don't know where you are going.
- The value of any "communication" lies in its **consequences**. For you. For your cause.
- Some people believe that "communication" is a way of solving problems. They forget: that's how we got into the problem in the first place. So you can see how "reality" and "communication" fit together. They are two aspects of the same thing—the ways in which we "see" and comprehend the world. And ourselves. If you can't get the "ourselves" part of it right, you won't be able to get the "understanding" what is going on part of it to your advantage. The more flaws there are in your interpretations of yourself, the more flaws there will be in your interpretations of other people and of the world you function in . . . with them.

"Knowing" And "Believing"

Another bugbear. A "bugbear" is a problem that won't go away because we're not seeing it for what it is. By not knowing how or not wanting to go to the source.

Consider this: You say something to someone. That person nods in agreement, adding, "I know." Dilemma: Just because two or more people agree doesn't mean that you can't be wrong, or that all of you can't be wrong. Agreement validates what you know. But it doesn't guarantee that what you know is what you need to know.

In a leadership coaching session where we were talking about this, a favorite client said, "Okay. What's your point?" What's the point? Not a very satisfactory one, I'm afraid. It is that there is no necessary correlation between what you know and what the actual situation may be. The correlation lies in the fact that others agree with you. This guarantees nothing. Entire civilizations have disappeared from history, agreeing with one another to the end that what they knew was what they needed to know. The point is you can't "fix" this dilemma. It's just part of being human. People in power always imagine that their view is the right one. Their organizations have failed. Whole nations have failed. There is no happy ending here. The best you can do is to be aware of the following:

- You know what you know basically because people told you so, directly or indirectly. You may have improvised on what you started with. But you had to improvise from what you already knew. So what you had as sources is crucial. As one writer put it, "It makes a lot of difference who you choose as parents." Or teachers. Or friends. Or "experts." Or conversational partners.

- We can live with that. We do so every day. Pretending, probably, that what we know is what we need to know. But that's even more irresolvable. The point is that you don't know whether what you know is what you need to know. Because that evidence is not available until after the fact. Did what you knew get you where you wanted to go? Were you able to achieve your goals? Did what you knew keep you from trouble and harm? The answers to all of these are revealed solely in the **consequences**. Figure out what the consequences are that matter to you. Then figure out what you would have to know to achieve those consequences. Part of that is knowing what to do and what not to do. No one has ever been able to do better than that. Small consolation.

Not much in the way of consolation, for sure. But it's far better to start with the facts, no matter how difficult they are.

"Knowing" is a sucker's game. How do we get suckered into it?

- By believing you know something you don't know. It's old wisdom, but still not very common: the first step is *being clear about what you do not know.*
- By believing that what you just happen to know is an accurate picture of some "reality" independent of your thinking about it.
- By failing to understand what you know is far more determined by what you already know than by any "reality" external to you.
- By assuming that what you don't happen to know is probably irrelevant.
- By ignoring the fact that other people's perceptions are only that.
- By not realizing that any argument about who is "right" and who is "wrong" may change the future. But it doesn't change present reality one whit.
- By pretending that other people, events, and things in the world are somehow obligated to be as you "know" them.

[An aside: you're supposed to be thinking about this stuff. Are you?]

- What you know is what you made of the past. What you need to know is what to make of the present and of how that bears on the future you aim to get to.

- By concluding that others are "right" to the extent they are certain and outspoken about their opinions, and that you just might therefore be "wrong."
- By making the opposite mistake. Just because you believe you know better doesn't mean that you don't. Is there any tougher issue in leadership than when to take others' advice and when to take your own?

Here are the constraints or limits on your "knowing." It pays to know what they are.

The **first** of these is that you can know only what you are capable of knowing. The less capable you are, the more likely you are to be drawing on faulty assumptions. "Knowledge" is a hoodwink. You can know only what you are capable of knowing.

Second, what you know is limited by the words and ideas you regularly consume. You know the saying, "We are what we eat." It applies here.

Third, you can't know everything. You will never know more than a tiny fraction of what might be knowable—by someone. What you don't know in this world of ours will always outpace what you do know.

Fourth, what you know becomes a part of who you *are*. And who you are is immensely resistant to change. Habits will trump the facts every time. Add to that: what you know at any point in time precludes what you could know. Especially if knowing that would call into question what you already know.

Fascinating, these facts. Most people avoid ever confronting them in any serious way. The leaders who have made a difference don't have bigger brains or even better luck than you do. But they have confronted those facts about their own knowing—and others' knowing—in a deliberate way. If your aim is to raise your own performance, or the performance of your organization, you will be advantaged by the kind of thinking that accommodates these facts.

Lessons? Well, you've heard the expression, "Know thyself." And you've heard it said that the leader must first demonstrate self-leadership. That's what those expressions mean. That, where "knowing" is critical, it's far better to ask a provocative question than to offer any statement that represents what you "know."

Now . . . what does "belief" have to do with all this? This one's easy. What you "know" is already a belief. Otherwise, you would have long ago traded it in on something better.

One last suggestion from all of the leaders who have preceded you. They knew, as you must know, that people who don't know *how* they know—or *why*—are dangerous people. To themselves. And to you, if you play follow the leader with them. This is the source of "the blind leading the blind" proverb. It's risky to fail to make that central to one's thinking.

Some thought-prodders to have some fun with:

- What you "know," or what you "believe," is indifferent to whether it is good for you, or bad for you.
- You cannot *know* what the present would be like if something different had been done in the past. You can only fantasize.
- Similarly, you cannot *know* what the future will be if you do "X." You can only speculate.
- What you don't "know" could be to your advantage. Choose carefully what you do not want to "know."
- When you're talking to someone else, it is their thinking that constitutes their reality. Not yours.
- What leaders do is create a reality out of a vision of it.

If you need a reminder—the value of what you "know" (or what you "believe") is given in what you accomplished with it.

"Explaining" Things

Of all the creatures on earth, we humans can be best characterized as the species that has an inexhaustible need to "explain things." This has gotten us to places where we wanted to go. "Space," maybe. A drug for everything, maybe. But it has also gotten us to places where we perhaps didn't intend to go. War after war and every other kind of human tragedy, for example. When spouses start explaining *the other person*, they cease to be lovers. We seem to be unable just to live life. We have to "explain" it.

We "explain" ourselves and then define everything else in the world to fit that. Or, we "explain" everything in the world and then define ourselves to fit those explanations. It amounts to the same thing. We describe (explain) our organizations and that defines us in them. Or, we explain ourselves and then define our organizations to suit. It's a bit both ways, isn't it?

Not just that we *have to* "explain" things, but how we do so . . . has consequences, consequences, consequences. But let's get practical here. How you "explain" performance bears upon the kind of performance you get, whether individual performance or the performance of organizations.

It's easy to get waylaid by popular explanations. For example: It seems that most problems you face will be traceable to some painful discrepancy between what people said was going to happen, and what actually happened. And we (you?) seem to prefer the problems we get that way to even the obvious solutions. Dilbert gets a lot of laughs out of the fact that people are quick to take credit for any success that occurs. But when there is a failure, it's "explanation time"! People don't get good at performing. They get good at explaining why their shortfalls were never their fault.

If there is to be reliable collaboration that produces the intended outcome (as is always the case for organizations), two conditions have to be met. One is that the people involved have to be supremely competent in their roles. This means avoiding problems, but having the capacity to improvise through or around them if they can't prevent them. The second condition is that the "ensemble"—the set of people who are supposed to be collaborating—is a supremely competent ensemble. They are prepared not only to perform, but in any imaginable contingency. And this means that they will have to have a communicative and logistics infrastructure that is adequate to the task.

The point here is a key one. It is that the only measure of performance is performance. Either people (including you) did what they said they were going to do. Or they didn't. (Did they—

or you—lie?) If you accept an "explanation" in lieu of the promised accomplishment, that's what you will get more of. Treat an "excuse" as if it were the same thing as the accomplishment, and that's what you will get more of. In our world, excuses are often equated with accomplishment. But an intention is not an accomplishment. Did you ever treat it that way, especially when you were "explaining" your own performance? If so, you are going to get far more intentions and then excuses than you will performance. The *only* measure of performance is performance.

Some thought-prodders:

- Performance is either *necessary* or it isn't.
- If outstanding performance is not necessary, it won't happen.
- Achievers blame themselves first. That's fixable.
- Winning at the "excuse" or explanation game makes losers.
- The way you "explain" things will be your destiny.
- Competence at explaining shortfalls makes those shortfalls inevitable.

Cause Vs. Choice

It all depends on which end you look at it from. Things may be seen to be "caused" by certain events that preceded the outcome. OR, events may be made to conspire to produce a desired outcome . . . by choice. Examples: You want a "zero defects" organization. You choose that. Then you decide what has to happen to get there. You choose the people and the practices out of which that outcome will be produced. All great athletes do it this way. All great actors and musicians and artists and thinkers do it this way. All great leaders have done it this way.

When you get hung-up about cause-and-effect relationships in your organization, and go on witch-hunts to find the "cause," you've got people with their heads buried in the past and not directed at the future.

"Cause" carries with it a sense of being determined by what happened in the past. Things are "caused." So you look for "the cause." You feel compelled to "explain" why what happened, happened. If you had chosen the outcome, and put in place the conditions necessary to produce that outcome and it didn't happen, you wouldn't be looking for the cause out there somewhere. It would be reflected in your mirror.

The illusion that what happens in the real world is independent of the people in it and how they think about it may make people feel they are being rational and objective. But if you did this, you would be missing the core causes of things. Those would be: Incompetence, inattention, indifference, and the capacity (in your organization?) to get away with an explanation that puts the blame somewhere else.

Here's what you do: If you take the position that whatever happens is by **choice**, you'll get far more "knowing-how" and far less "knowing-that." It's the "how" that gets you where you want to go. "Explaining" what-caused-what is the biggest waste there is in most conventional organizations. That's not the issue. The issue is how to get from here to there. The "there" has to be chosen. Then the "how" is chosen." If the "hows" turn out not to be quite right, you can change them.

If you are a "cause-and-effect" person, you are a person trying to figure out how you got victimized by what happened to you. Before long, you will be a *victim* of whatever happens. It's a way of looking at things. But it's not the way of looking at things that you need.

Key question: Do people learn from their mistakes? Rarely. That's because there are two preconditions.

First, you don't learn from your mistakes. You *might* learn from your *interpretations* of your mistakes. This would require you to be able to see what part of the problem you were. Most people can't look at it that way. So they can't learn from their mistakes. Most people aren't smart enough to do so.

Second, learning from your mistakes requires that you have a great and worthy cause in life. Or at least that you have a very specific destination in mind. People who live from day-to-day, without a long-range destination to which they feel obligated, don't learn from their mistakes. What's to learn? So they get good—really good—at being "victims" and expecting the boss to make them happy. Or the pols to take care of them.

Here, for your amusement and edification, some thought-prodders:

- If you want to be a part of the solution, make certain you are not a part of the problem (which could be yours).
- The first obligation of competence, therefore, is not to be a part of the problem.
- An explanation tells you more about the explainer than it does about the happenings being "explained."
- Practice what needs to be accomplished, not what can be "explained."
- The conditions of our organizations, like the conditions of our lives, were *chosen*.
- If you don't believe you chose them, they will choose you.

We could, of course, "predict" future outcomes. This would be like "explaining" things forward. And, like all explanations, these will be a mix of hope, fear, ignorance, and guesswork. As has often been observed, if you want to predict the future, create it.

That's what leaders do. Perfectly? Never. Determinedly? Totally. They know the outcomes are not controllable. They know their preparation for accomplishing what needs to be accomplished is within their control. So they concentrate on that.

As the prize-winning biologist famously said about the study of "cause" in biology: Things are the way they are because they got to be that way. Indeed. And things will turn out the way they do because they turned out that way. But you could intervene. You could redirect. You could set another direction.

Here's a brief version of a typical exchange about an organizational "problem":

CEO: "Why is this happening?"

ME: "Do you mean you didn't choose this to happen? Are you sure you know what your role is here?"

CEO (huffy, of course): "What do you mean by that?"
ME: "I would have thought your job was to *make* happenings, not to be made *by them*. Anyone could do that."
CEO: "Come on. I don't control what happens."
ME: "Agreed. But did you choose the outcomes and then choose how those outcomes were to be achieved?"

A little more discussion and he got the point. And, by the way, his organization is doing far better than it did when everyone assumed they were just victims, when the best they thought they could do was to figure out why things went wrong.

It's also useful to remember that nothing has a single cause. There's always "The straw that broke the camel's back." It wasn't the one straw that broke the camel's back. It was the accumulation of weight. Same thing in organizations. Things happen because the conditions are ripe for that to happen. People make mistakes because they are incompetent. Because they weren't paying attention. Because they weren't thinking. Because someone else didn't perform. Fix the conditions first. There is always "luck." But being fully prepared makes you luckier.

Well, here are some interim thought-prodders, if needed:

- The smartest leaders partner with serendipity.
- Nothing that involves people has a single cause.
- Things do not turn out as we *want* them to. Things turn out the way they *have to*. Make that work for you. "Luck" can't. "Hope" won't.
- A leader is not the sole "cause" of anything—except himself or herself.
- Leaders who make a difference are those who have successfully limited the difference randomness makes.
- Surround yourself with people who are not part of the problem. Then they could be a part of the solution.
- Out of what "causes" does a person emerge as a "leader"?

Here's a partial list of questions that help to absorb people's spare time at work, along with a potentially useful alternative formulation:

1. Why *were* those customer deliveries late? Try, what would we have to do to ensure that no scheduled delivery is ever late?

2. Why didn't we know what our competitors were planning to do? How about: What would we have to do, and how, to be competitor-driven?

3. Why did the stock market (or the "economy") go up or down? What would you do with any "explanation" of that? Try this: "How can we optimize our immunity to things over which we have no control?

4. What caused this problem we're faced with? Why not be faced with the problems you think are going to get you where you want to go?

5. How did that accident happen? Try this: Who ought to own the problem of not causing an accident, or of being a victim of one?

6. How can we explain the slump in sales? Depends on who you ask, doesn't it? Maybe a better question is: How can we prepare for the ups and downs of our revenues?

7. Why did the people who said they would buy an Edsel not do so? What would you be able to *do* with an explanation of that? There was only one Edsel. How about: What constitutes a *valid* prophesy?

8. Why is it that what you tell people to do sometimes doesn't get done? Well, what part of that problem are *you*?

Did we forget something? Maybe it was this: Outstanding performance is not *because of* (because of the resources provided), but *in spite of* (in spite of any and all impediments). If people don't think that way, they won't be that way. If the *leader* does not think that way, no one else will take on that way of thinking.

You have to make the future out of the present, not out of the past. If you can figure out what causes the right outcomes, use those causes to drive the future, to *cause* your aims. It's not likely that knowing what caused the wrong outcomes will enable you to do this, beyond simply avoiding *those* causes. The leader's challenge: How do you *cause* something that didn't exist in the past, doesn't exist in the present?

> *It isn't that impersonal "cause" is not a perfectly useful way of explaining things in the nonhuman world (although it doesn't always work there). It is that this way of thinking has steadily eclipsed the role of human choice in life and social life, and especially life in organizations.*

The "Founding Fathers" of the U.S. were not "caused." The republic they envisioned was not "caused." It was chosen. We live in the nation we do not by "cause" but by choice. A person *could* choose not to smoke or not to overeat. Abe Lincoln thought a person *could* choose not to be illiterate. But times are a-changing in this freedom-loving, permissive world of ours. We're raising young people to believe that they have a "right" to do whatever they want to do whenever they want to do it. And it's somebody else's problem to take care of any untoward consequences—parents, social agencies, pols, the "society."

You will have more and more of these people in your organization. Where everything is your fault because people are "innocent" victims of what *happens* to them.

Corporate "Welfare"

There could hardly be a better term for it. As our government and private and commercial organizations become more like day-care centers, we will arrive . . . where? It may even be an okay idea in the abstract. But there will never be the heart for the pursuit of great achievements to emerge from that environment—neither individual nor collective.

Is it a world you would choose?

I heard a college graduate report by public radio that the "American Dream" was dead because no one came to him and offered him the kind of "job" he thought he deserved. Who could have imagined that? I understood that the "American Dream" was that everyone had an equal *opportunity* to make something of themselves and of their organizations. What they might *choose* to make of themselves. I must have been wrong. We train our young people—at home, at school, in health and illness, and in that welfare state we call our colleges and universities—how to expect and even demand whatever they can imagine they "deserve." Not what their responsibilities are but what their "rights" are. All because we've elevated "cause" above "choice," rights (as victims of anything and everything) above responsibilities (to self and others). It is now only barely imaginable that a person could *choose* not to smoke or overeat. Or to choose a future rather than be determined by past or present. Or to choose not to be incompetent. Or to choose not to be an eager victim, *before* becoming addicted to that way of life. Welcome to the 21st century.

But you can see how important our understanding of things— our thinking—can be. As you think about things, so you will be. There's the source of the power of *your* choice.

This concept is crucial to leadership thinking. So we will meet up with it again later on.

Moving On

Here are a couple of thoughts to chew on as you move on:

- If you believe in "cause," then the most important thing in the world for you to know is what causes *you*. If you are "caused," put in place what will cause you to be who you intend to be, or who you *ought* to be.
- Trick, right? You can do that only if you *have* a cause. Only if some future achievement has you "by the skin and the hair," as a prior VW CEO put it. Otherwise, you will be a

random event. The "welfare" required to support that outcome is limitless. Cradle to grave—no matter what befalls every man, woman, and child on the list of "victims" with a claim for which there is, or could be, a service. What can be made of those who can't, or won't?

Passion causes. Does it cause you? Is your passion a cause of others, of a real achievement in the world as given, with the hand you were dealt?

The leader does not so much seek to know the causes of things as to *be* the cause of something. Is there a "key" here to what needs unlocking?

In this topsy-turvy world of ours, you will either make your own path as best you can. Or your path will be made for you by whatever randomly comes your way.

Most people get around this by refusing to choose either way, and thus by pretending to be blameless. Are you prepared to support that habit in yourselves or in others? If so, you need to remind yourself that leadership lies in the opposite direction. Leadership requires competence, responsibility, and performance. The more necessary these can be made to be, the more possible great achievement will be. It's worth thinking about.

Chapter 4

The Leader's Lexicon: II

WE'VE DEVOTED A good bit of time to examining the idea of "cause." For good reason. This is not a "philosophical" issue. There are two fundamentally *practical* reasons why leaders need to grapple with the idea of "cause":

The **first** is that leaders have to know what causes them. There is no more direct route to knowing who you are. Leadership is not primarily about what you do. It is primarily about who you **are**.

The **second** reason is that leaders have to be able to figure out, once they have an accurate perspective on who *they* are, what they can and cannot "cause."

There may be remote "causes." But the immediate causes of who you are and what you do (or how you do it) will always be in the way you **think about** things.

So while it may still try your patience to devote more time to this matter of the leader's lexicon, it's much like practice and preparation for the game: the better you get this stuff, the more effectively you are going to "get" all the rest of it. To "do" what leaders "do," you have to think like leaders think. And that's why you have to think deeply—and make a part of who you are—what has preceded in the previous chapter, and what follows in this chapter.

"People"

Small word. For the way you think about people—HUGE consequences.

People: the source of all of our problems. And yet, we have no other source for solutions. So the way you think about "people" will either preclude or contribute to the problems you face, and will either contribute expediently to the solutions to those problems, or to persistent inabilities to resolve them. In other words, the way you think about "people" will determine what kinds of problems you will have *and* how solvable those problems will be.

Let's start at the beginning. If you don't truly "like" people, it is unlikely you will ever be able to provide leadership, for yourself or for them. If you do not truly **care** about people, it is unlikely you will ever have followers. And it is unlikely that you would ever be able to lead them to extraordinary levels of performance/achievement.

Why is that? Because if you do not like people, they don't have much reason for liking you back. If you do not truly (in their perspective) care about people, they have no compelling reason for caring about you, or about your purposes in life.

This is not a pop psychology issue. There is some logic here that you might as well accept, because you are not going to get around it.

Yet there is a twist here that leaders have to learn how to understand, but which seems to be lost to those whose minds have been colonized by the popular culture. It is that "liking" people is given in how genuinely interested you are in them, in their lives, in *their* problems and concerns. Trying to get them interested in you, in your life, in *your* problems and concerns, will not be interpreted by them as your caring about them. They have to know you care about *them* before they will join you in your cause.

About "caring." Most people have this all wrong. To "care" about another person doesn't mean that you accept that person as she is. If you want to learn how to think like a leader, *caring about others means refusing to let them default themselves.* It means caring about the person they should *become*. It means caring about who they *ought* to be—potential realized—not where they are presently stalemated. This is the way the leader has to look at himself. Caring about people means looking at them in the same way. "We should love people," the German poet Goethe said, "not for who they are, but for who they ought to be." That's real caring because it is win-win. Every other form of "caring" has at least one loser in it.

A common complaint: "I just don't understand people." It's actually not that difficult. Modern "psychology" has made it seem so. The lesson (for leaders) is this: If you want to know how people think, watch what they do and how they do it. If you want to know what people's beliefs are, or what they are really going to do or to be in the future, don't listen to what they *say*. Watch what they *do* and how they do it.

There is no necessary correlation between what people say and what people do. Leader's lesson: Never mistake what people say for what they can or will actually do. You've had the experience. When people want to work at your place, they'll promise anything. Could be the answer to your prayer. But after a few days or a few weeks, that same person may turn out to be as marginally mediocre as the one being replaced. People are far more likely to talk a good story than they are to provide one. Many—if not most—married people may have observations on this.

It's the everyday version of "walking the talk." Most people don't. Or can't. That's largely because they have never had to, which is key to "understanding" people. We'll return to that enthusiastically below. The lesson here is that you don't have to be a psychologist to "understand" people. In fact, the less "psychological" you are about all of this, the better off you will be. The lesson is that you will have a far more reliable "understanding" of people if you base your understanding on what people actually do than if you step into the psychological swamp of their "intentions," their "motivations," their test profiles, or their enthusiasms (sucking up). If you are a mind-reader, go for it. But leaders don't try to get into people's heads. For leaders, *the reality of who people are and what they are capable of lies entirely in what they actually do.*

This is not a book about "people." It is about how you may need to think differently about people in order to move in the direction of real achievement—personally or as a leader. So our concerns are operational, pragmatic, practical.

One of the most useful questions you can ask is this one:

Why DO people do what they do?

You could ask a roomful of psychologists this question and you'd get a roomful of answers. Those answers would be interesting—if you wanted to be a psychologist. But if you want to be a leader, those "theories" would be largely irrelevant.

Books and articles abound about how to "motivate" people to do something you want them to do. Or to be the someone you want them to be. Some of this is entertaining (it is meant to be). But none of it would explain very accurately what "motivated" those writers to write those books or deliver those seminars. Why is that?

Most of what you will get in those books and articles is "pop" psychology. Consume this stuff and it will help you to think like and be like most everybody else. But it won't help you in your quest to achieve. That requires you to be different. And *that* requires you to *think* differently. You can't think differently if you feed on the same mental junk food as everyone else.

Consider "motivation." This is about "causing" others to do, or be, in ways consistent with your intentions. But most people can't even cause *themselves* to be different. So why would you believe you can cause in them what you can't cause in yourself? What makes you think you can "motivate" others to do or to be in ways they are not even capable?

"Motivation" is largely a myth. A very popular and deeply ingrained cultural myth. It is a mystical term—intended perhaps to give us the illusion of power we don't have. It is a term invented to account for why laboratory mice (literally) did what they did, and was then generalized to account for why *people* do what they do.

These lab mice were deprived of things like food or sex, and were then carefully observed under controlled conditions to measure how "motivated" they were to get to the one or the other. On the face of it, only a psychologist would believe that some great and profound truth had been discovered when a starving animal seemed determined to get at some food. But then it would also take a psychologist to prefer playing with mice rather than with people—under conditions that would never occur in the mouse's real world. So what was the psychologist's "motives" for pursuing the study of the obvious?

"Motivation" and "incentives" don't work in the long run. And they seem to work reliably only with the kind of people who have already bought into the "rat race." They seem to work best with people who intend to do only as they are told.

Even if they did work with extremely competent people, how many of you out there would sign up to live in a world where people would perform solely for "rewards"? If psychologists are themselves performing solely for "rewards" (if their theories about people included them), what exactly are those rewards? And in that world where everyone is being manipulated, what rewards "motivate" the motivator? Who is pulling *your* strings or pushing your buttons, without which *you* wouldn't be "motivated" to do what *you* do?

So if we're not going to be "psychological" about it, why DO people do what they do? The best—and the most potent—answers you will ever find to this question have little to do with either "motivation" or with things like desire or intention. As a practical matter, people do what they do, first, **because they CAN**.

Simple. But powerful. You will never see a person doing something that person cannot do. If people *can* do something, they will. If they are totally incapable of doing something, then you won't see them doing it.

So leaders attend to that shortfall—that condition—first. They make it necessary for people to be competent at what they are going to be required to do. Only then can they conclude that if they don't see the performance required, the under-performance is by *choice*. If you don't cover this base, you can never be certain where the shortfall lies. It will never be in "the circumstances." It will be in the failure to prepare for those circumstances.

There are two useful implications here: One is that the best way of accounting for performance is not to grasp for something like "motivation" or desire, or even "talent." It is simply recognizing that the level of performance is a reflection of the level of competence for performing in that way. The other is that being a mediocre or even a poor performer also requires competence. Poor performers are not "incompetent." They are simply competent to perform in that way. Ultimately, it takes just as much practice to do something poorly as it does to do something well. It's a matter of practicing only what you want to get good at.

It may be challenging to think this way. Here are some thought-prodders:

- People do not become virtuosos even at being lazy except by practice.
- People do not become adept at *not* being engaged in what they are doing except through practice. Everyone is born with his or her "lights" on. You have to work at turning them off.
- Leaders' rule of thumb: Don't practice what you don't want to get good at. Don't let others practice what you do not want them to get good at.

To be *competent* means that a person is fully prepared for what will occur, or for what might occur, between where they are now and successful achievement of the goal. So another word for competence is **preparedness**. A person is not "competent" unless he or she is fully prepared to accomplish what needs accomplishing.

To develop what it is people are capable of doing therefore requires first equipping yourself, and then those others, to be fully *prepared* to accomplish the mission from start to finish.

Why do people behave as they do? Because they are competent to do so. Why *don't* people do what they are supposed to do, or even what they say they are going to do? Because they are competent at *not* doing what they are supposed to do. Conscientiousness works both ways. Every achievement (+ or -) requires competence.

There is a second very practical understanding for why people do what they do. It is not that they "want" to. It is not that they "intend" to. It is not that they have a "desire," or even the talent or the background, to do so. These all count for something. But we are looking for a more powerful, more universal explanation. And that would lead us to this realization: People do what they do, second, **because they *have* to.**

This doesn't mean that they were somehow "forced" to perform, because you cannot force a person to do something that person is incapable of doing. Some external "necessity" may help the process, of course. Tiger Woods' father could attest to that.

But by "necessity" or "have to" here, we are referring to such things as *habits*, as *competencies* (which provide their own necessity—if you're competent to do something in a certain way, it's altogether likely that you will do it in that way), as *duty*, as *interdependence* with respect to mutual survival, or even DNA. The culture you grew up in will make certain things "necessary" and other things irrelevant. Spouses may even provide you with certain "have-to's" in your life. The joke is that if you're not a good boy or girl (in the other's eyes), you may have to sleep on the sofa. That may provide a certain level of "necessity" for some people.

Necessity comes in many forms, as we will examine more carefully later on. It is enough here to think through the fact that "necessity" will turn out to be a far better explanation of why people do what they do than all of the "psychological" reasons you could muster. The idea is to be a powerful thinker, not a conventional one.

From all of the preceding, you might conclude that leaders are inclined to think as follows:

1) There are only two kinds of people in the world, "Them who do, and them who don't."
2) And the *only* difference between "them who do and them who don't" is that "them who do, do," and "them who don't, don't."

This is old wisdom, of course. What it is intended to suggest for the way we think about things is that the only measure of whether or not someone accomplished something has to be found in the accomplishment and not in the desire or the intentions of the person involved. And certainly not in his or her words. Those are merely "promises."

It is probably also intended to suggest simply that the main difference between the person who accomplished something and the person who didn't is that the one did and the other didn't. You can, as unthinking people often do, get involved in "explaining" the differences in some other—usually "psychological"—way. But this will suck you right into the psychological "swamp" which is full of psychological "alligators" and other dangers. You might say, for example, that one person is "smarter" than the other person.

But what have you said here? "Smart" is as "smart" does. And a person's "potential" is observable only in what that person does with it. It's the same with any form of "intention" to accomplish something. Leader's lesson? Actual intention can be measured *only* by actual accomplishment. See the difference?

So we can add a third condition:

3) If you think you know some underlying difference between them who do and them who don't, then you are a part of the problem because you have opened the door on every "psychological" explanation that has been or could be created. And those will be used as "excuses." It is sufficient to use objective measures. It makes the problem more complex and increasingly resistant to any solution to get

into this stuff we can only talk about. It is far better and more humanizing to use objective measures.

Some thought prodders?

- You needn't ask people why they did something they weren't supposed to do or didn't do something they were supposed to do. Unless it was consciously intentional, they don't know either.
- Most words that follow "I" are promises, not facts. "I will" do so-and-so, for example, is no more than a casual statement of intention. Whether or not a person "means" what she says can be determined only by the accomplishment.
- The people who make a difference in the world—or to you— are the people who make good on their promises.
- If you want to know why people do what they do, ask a person who has done something. Don't ask a "psychologist."
- If you want to know what people are *for*, ask a person who knows what real commitment requires of them.

"Problems"

For us people, a problem is some sort of sensed *discrepancy* between the way things are and the way they believe things *ought* to be. So every "problem" depends upon how a person or a set of people "see" the way things are, and the way they think, imagine, or project the way things "ought" to be. What constitutes a problem for one person may not even be "seen" by another. What some people fret about others may be blissfully unaware of.

So the first thing that leaders learn—and learn to the bone— is that "a problem" is **something that is had only by people**. Whether or not that is a problem worth having, or a reasonably true picture of any actual reality—depends entirely on who those people are, how competent they are in their roles, and how committed they are to the mission they are engaged in or the goal(s) they are trying to achieve. Got it?

Human enterprises—like your organization or your love life—rise or fall on the basis of random events, and then on how you and every other person involved "see" the "problems" that arise in the context of those uncontrollable happenings. More than that. There is not just the matter of being aware of the obstacles and opportunities on your path. Problems also have to be identified. They have to have a name.

Leaders recognize that the names people have for problems will largely determine the problems they "see." What people don't have a name for they are unlikely to be aware of.

- So the problems a person "has" are going to be primarily a function of the problems for which he or she has a "name." They are going to be related to that particular person's perception of the world, whether they are related to any actuality or not.
- And, thus, the problem you try to "solve" is the one you have named.
- How well you do all of this problem stuff will depend on the names you have handy, and the repertoires you have for dealing with them.

Interesting? What we're spotlighting here is that there is certain mental machinery that determines all three steps in the process: (1) what people "see" as constituting a "problem," (2) how *those people* "name" that problem (for how they do that will) (3) determine what they're going to do about it. The perception of the problem, the name given to it, and the solutions applied are primarily functions of the minds involved, not of any actual "reality."

So *the problem we try to solve is the one we name.* And the one we name comes with a "solution." This means that the chief cause of problems in an organization is solutions. How we put together an organization, and the competencies of the people we staff it with, will essentially determine the kinds of problems we are going to have—at least the kinds of problems we are going to pay attention to. Think about it.

You also have to consider this: every solution to every problem causes more problems. You do not eliminate forever problems in any organization. You merely replace the ones someone believed you had with other problems that grew out of the solution(s) employed. So leaders need to think not just, how do I solve our problems, but what kinds of problems do I want to generate out of the solutions we employ? Might as well. Problems will arise out of those solutions in any case.

The right solution to the wrong problem will make the problem worse while adding some new ones. The wrong solution to the right problem will do the same. There must be a better way than merely learning some technique for "problem-solving." Such techniques assume that the problem is independent of people. That is never going to happen. Such techniques also assume that anyone can see accurately what the problem "is" by using the correct procedure (e.g., the process for getting to "root" causes). Note that the procedure for determining what the problem is—was itself devised by people who were solving *their* problem. A procedure for arriving at the best name for a problem may help, of course. But the reason why the "root cause" rarely turns out to be stupidity is that the problem sleuths have no solution for that. Incompetence has to be the most common "cause" of problems. But identifying the cause as something else seems to most people more readily fixable.

Here are some more thought-prodders for this provocative subject:

- Most people prefer a problem they can't solve to a solution they don't like—or which is not in their tool box.
- Many people mistake a solution method for a problem definition. That is, they define the problem by a known method of solution.
- The acceptability of a solution to a "tough" problem is likely to be inversely related to the time it takes to provide it.
- If you can't imagine how your understanding of the problem might be wrong, you don't understand the problem.
- Believing that a problem named by people has only one

right solution is the same mistake as believing that a problem has but one "cause."

Is there a better way? Is there a way to escape the contributions people make to misnaming problems because those people imagine they have the "solution"? If we look carefully at the centuries of leadership wisdom and practice, yes, there seems to be a better way.

And that is to create a way forward that obviates the problem. Problems arise out of the ways things are done. Change a procedure, change a habit, change an attitude or change a goal, and the problems you have will change. If you change the circumstances or the conditions that made a problem possible, or that nurtured it once it emerged, then you may indeed make the problem evaporate.

What would you do, and how would you do it, to make a particular problem impossible? That's what leaders do. The crux of the matter is not to explain the past or the present. It is to create the future out of whatever you've got or can get. That requires a far different logic, a far different mentality.

"Solutions" to problems, no matter how expert, always create problems in their wake. We (people) are problem-creators, not problem eliminators. Leaders focus on the outcomes. Problem-solving procedures, no matter how elegant or popular, will reproduce the status quo.

There is always our complicity in the problems we encounter. The lesson to be learned is that the determination of what the problem "is" and what to do about it will always be more a function of the people involved—including yourself—than of any actual circumstances.

So what does the leader do? The leader, knowing that problems are inevitable, attempts to create the circumstances out of which will emerge the problems he or she *prefers* to have. Creating the future means picking the problems that you intend to have there, or along the way. The leader refuses to be "victimized" by problems. Leaders make victims of problems and obstacles, not the other way around. The tougher or loftier the goal, the tougher the obstacles are going to be. That goes with the territory. Most people "solve" this one by not having any particular goal or aim in life. Even this doesn't work. The problems a person encounters in attempting to live a conventional life will be . . . conventional problems. They are often more onerous and more difficult to deal with, simply because they are universal and are therefore assumed to be unavoidable. This is one reason why the most common problems in conventional organizations recur and recur. Sloppy work, for example.

Another view of great value to would-be leaders comes from some ancient wisdom. It is that we are given the problems we encounter not to eliminate them, but to learn from them. We have the problems we have for a purpose. Your task: to figure out what that purpose is, because such problems do not come with an instruction book.

People who are never challenged to grow by figuring out a way around the problems they encounter on their quests in life are people who are not on a quest. Outstanding leaders welcome the problems that come their way, knowing that the tougher and more challenging they are, the more there is to learn, to grow on. If you have the same problems everyone else has, that means you are not different enough, or on a different enough path, to have your own. The "self-help" industry (even in "management") preys on those whose problems are the most common.

We've only opened the door on this subject. But here are some thought-prodders to help you take your thinking further:

- Don't ask, "What is 'the' problem?" Ask, rather, "What is **whose** problem?" (Problems always arrive at your door on two feet.)
- Don't solve problems that rightfully belong to others. Help them to "own" and to solve their own problems.
- "Ownership" means the ownership of problems. And that means owning the consequences of what is done or not done.
- "Responsibility," "accountability," etc. are a function of ownership—owning the consequences.

- In the valley of problem-solvers, the problem creator is king.
- Your first obligation—to yourself, to others, to the organization—is not to be a part of the problem, because the more you are a part of the problem, the less you can be a part of the solution.
- Finally, think on this one: Can any set of people "solve" a problem with the same mentality which they employed to be victimized by it in the first place (as Einstein once asked)?

Performance

As fundamental as this concept is to all the rest of your thinking, we can come to grips with it in short order.

Think of a continuum labeled LIFE. At one extreme are those people who are lived *by* life, and at the other extreme are those people who *make* the lives they live. In our culture, there seems to be a far greater tendency to being determined by what happens than determining those happenings.

Those are people who play the role of being "victimized" by life. Whatever "happened" to them made them what they are. They have the problems or the difficulties they have because that's what life dealt them.

We need to be clear about this. Bad stuff happens to everybody. And it seems to be randomly distributed—that is, no one is exempt just by presuming to be intellectually superior, or because they have more money or more power. No one on an airplane that is crashing has enough prestige, or political or spiritual power, to keep it from happening. Those who exercise regularly are not immune to heart attacks.

Whether life grabs a person by the throat, or a person grabs life by the throat is a matter of attitude. One can look at the world as a victim of it. Or one can look at the world as a given, simply the only place there is to work out one's destiny, one's life. Neither way changes the world. They merely change the way one goes at life.

There is a powerful way of thinking about this—the leader's way. It is that life is a performing art. It is certainly the case that *leadership* is a performing art. What this means is that we are either given a role to play in life or we forge a role for ourselves. In either case, our lives are given in how good we are in the performance of that role—not how elevated that role is, but how well it is performed. There are some plumbers who perform their role better than some surgeons perform theirs.

So, to develop the capacity to be a leader, you have to look at everything that people do or don't do in terms of **performance**. The leader intends to be the "author" of some aspect of the future—to interfere with the undirected unfolding of history, of the story that would have been if that leader had not intervened. Leaders are measured by their performance. If they intend to be successful, they have to measure others by *their* performance.

It is how well an organization performs that counts. It is thus how well the people who comprise it perform in their roles that counts. A healthy organization is one whose members have assumed full responsibility for shepherding their own lives in the context of the life of the organization.

The right measure of any organization is its performance. And that depends primarily on the performance of those who comprise it. You can get "lucky." But that too is a form of victimization, isn't it?

Performance is not about play-acting. It is the serious business of becoming fully and increasingly competent in one's role—individual or organizational. The real qualities of the good life come from being competent at life, at work or at play.

Necessity

So please, put on your thinking caps. This is not going to be what you may expect. There are two gates to this thinking "field":

What drives performance is necessity.

What drives extraordinary performance is extraordinary *necessity*. Not desire, not intention, not "motivation" or "inspiration," but . . . **necessity**. Not goals, not incentives, not rewards, but **necessity**.

"Necessity" has many sources. The most effective necessity is unseen, intangible. In general, the most potent source of necessity is internal—habits of thought and action.

What drives a person's performance is a function of the way that person is built. You can threaten and cajole, you can holler and scream, you can be gentle or you can be forceful, you can attempt to politic or to blackmail or seduce or entice. You can offer rewards or you can threaten punishments. You can offer heaven, or hell. You can do so articulately or by getting red in the face and huffing and puffing. You can be angry or sweet. You can try all of the tricks there are. But nothing you can do will work in every case. And nothing you can do will hold a candle to the drivers that are an intrinsic condition of a person.

The lesson here? Surround yourself only with people who are internally driven to perform—don't ever ask why or how. But it takes one to know one. Or to cope with one. If you don't have the internal drivers, you won't be able to surround yourself with the people who have those drivers. Simple enough.

- Competencies are bundles of habits. Whatever we are capable of doing depends upon bundles of habits over which we have no immediate control. If we are competent to do something in some way, that's what we will do and that is how we will do it. For a person to do something differently, or "better," requires fundamental changes in fundamental habits, no one of which can be dealt with tangibly. The path of practice by which these habits got ingrained is something we will never know—too complex, too subtle, too out of conscious intention or control. They have to be changed in the same way we got them in the first place—by practice, practice, practice. The habits that underpin our competencies can rarely be eliminated. But they can be displaced by other habits. There is nothing we do—including our thinking and our feelings—which does not hinge upon bundles of habits that got nurtured and took root long ago and out of memory.

- So why **do** people do what they do? Because they "have to." And the core have-to's are the habits that underlie and inform our competencies. So the main necessity driving people's performance, for good or for ill, from the highest levels to the lowest, is their competencies.

- The second aspect of internal necessity worth thinking about is that of **conscience**. Some people are conscientious, some are not. Quality at any locus in an organization is a function of "conscientiousness," not, ultimately, of some program or technique. People who are conscientious preclude the errors that lead to poor quality, whether in a product or a service. It's a big word. But it's a powerful driver. Look up this word in the dictionary. It is a concept that suggests certain people may have a strong sense of guilt if they do not do what is right. As conscience fades, so does what we call the "work ethic."

- A third concept that will help you understand what accounts for level of performance is that of **duty**. A very useful concept which, unfortunately, is much out of vogue these days. It is useful to any person who wants to lead a worthy life. It is indispensable to the leader, both personally and for the purpose of developing an organization capable of real achievement. The idea of **duty** was central to the leadership philosophy of General Robert E. Lee. "Duty," he said, "is the sublimest word in our language. Do your duty in all things. You cannot do more; you should never wish to do less." Yet you cannot do your "duty" unless you are *competent* to do so.

- If I see myself as a person who can be depended upon, no matter what, to do my duty, to perform my role, to achieve the goals or objectives set before me, it's far more likely than not that this orientation will be a driver. If I don't have such a sense of myself, then how I perform may depend upon the circumstances, or on whether I "feel" like it or not. Both self-images are drivers. They just drive the person in a different direction.

Another is what we sometimes refer to as "peer pressure." I may perform as required because others expect me to, and if I have a sense that they may punish me in some way if I don't perform as they expect me to. Great organizations of all types depend heavily on this kind of "driver." The Mafia, elite military units, team sports, marriage and friendship all control performance in this way. Given competence, of course. Nothing can "drive" performance if the competence required to perform at that level is not a precondition of the person or the team. That's why you start there. That's why you go there first to assess and to develop performance.

- Or, there may be something very personal. I may refuse to "let down" another person who means much to me. A coach, perhaps. Or a parent. Or a lover. Or even a leader. I may equip myself to perform at a superb level just to have the feeling, at the end of all the pain and effort, that I did not let that person down. Over time, everyone you associate with in any way has an image of you. Out of all of these images that are implicit in the way others treat you, you will create one for yourself that enables you at least to accommodate those that are important to you, or critical to your path. Some may see this as a negative, as a constraint on your "freedom." But it works both ways. The more "conscientious" people you have in your organization, the more "conscientious" people you *will* have. You don't make this happen. They do.

It is the way of the manager to try to get people to perform by rules, by rewards, by threat, or by trying to micro-manage performance. It is the way of the manager to exhibit and exercise power or authority. It is the way of the leader to build necessity into personal and organizational performance where the internal drivers are. This is what makes performance reliable and sustainable. This is what accounts for performance when the leader is nowhere in sight. People who have to perform because of who they are, because that's who they **are**, do not need a policeman or a mother at work, or at play. They do the right thing, they perform at the level required, because they **have to.** That is an aspect of them, not something that the leader does *to* them.

Given a *conscientious person* who is *competent* to perform at the level required, that person will do his or her *duty*. What leaders do is take all possible ambiguity out of what that duty is.

The leader puts into place first the bedrock preconditions for performance. The leader does not imagine that he or she can provide that necessity during or after the fact.

In a traditional society or organization, it is "tradition" that provides the necessity for performance. In a "modern" society or organization—such as we have today—it is **fashion** that guides, constrains, and drives us. Those who run organizations often do what they do out of the need to keep up with others, to be like those others are, to be up-to-date. In short, to be in step with what's fashionable.

It is the same for individuals. The less tradition-bound people are, the more fashion-bound they are likely to be. People say what is said, do what is done, and try to "be" as the fashion demands. If it is fashionable to think of work as drudgery and leisure time as freedom from that drudgery, people will drudge and trudge through the hours at work just to get the paycheck to buy the (fashionable) leisure time activities and stuff they think they deserve.

People may claim to be thinking for themselves. People may claim to be "individuals" in their tastes, their personalities, their attitudes. But in a world like ours, it's much more likely that they are just being fashionable. They are much more concerned with what's "in" and what's "out" than in any wisdom. So when people begin a sentence with the word "I," what the leader hears is a report on current fashions amongst that age group or economic group. To be "where it's at" is more important to most people than to carry out what would actually serve one's own best self-interests. Leaders become astute at looking for the unseen but operative sources of necessity behind people's thinking, attitudes, and actions.

Advice

Therefore the "advice" you get these days is more likely to be fashionable than it is to be useful.

Consider the fashionable idea of "empowerment." A person who has not made himself or herself totally responsible for his or her own destiny cannot be "empowered." People can "empower" themselves to be the instrument of their own destiny, but you cannot "empower" them to be the instruments of *your* destiny. Hollow words. Leaders do not mouth fashionable words. They say what they *mean* and they *mean* what they say. Repeating fashionable mantras is not a method that works.

Let's cut to the chase on this one:

- If you know the difference between good advice and bad advice you don't need advice, as the saying goes. But the only way *you* can know the difference is by having a purpose or cause which measures that.
- Whether it's free or you pay dearly for it, people cannot tell you what you need to know. They can only tell you what *they* know. The other problem is always yours.
- The worst advice and the best advice you will ever get comes from how you advise yourself. Fix that first.
- Power attracts advice like light attracts moths. Be certain your light is powered by your own thinking.
- No advice ever offered has had any more value than the receiver made of it. In other words: No advice exceeds a person's ability to implement it, including yours.
- If you don't want to know the answer, don't ask. If you need an answer, ask just the right question of just the right source.

Commitment

If there is something that is common to all of those who are the engines of great achievements, it is the fierceness, even the fanaticism, of their commitment.

There is a HUGE difference between "having" a cause and **being had by** a cause. A person who merely "has" a cause will usually be willing to compromise. A person who is "had by" a cause will be unreasonable, relentless, especially with himself or herself.

You'll remember this: "A passion to build automobiles has me by the skin and the hair." If you intend to be a leader, you must be "had" by your purpose or cause in life. You are a servant of your aim, and not the other way around. It is your cause that is your destiny. And you will let nothing stop you, nothing get in your way. The leader is the person who holds himself or herself to this standard with respect to what **has to** be realized, made into reality. "No excuses."

If you don't see the difference, you're probably not a good candidate for the role. If you **are** the difference, then you've come to the right place.

"But suppose," a CEO once said to me, "I don't have that level of commitment." ME: "No one will know but you. If you perform your role as if you were had by your cause, and people give you that role because you are utterly convincing, two things will result:

"One is that you **will** be had as a result of sheer and effective practice at performing that way. People judge you on your performance. They have no direct access to your mind or your heart. What counts in the real world is performance."

"Second, the more you are 'had' by your cause, the more likely it is that you will have 'followers'—those required to make you successful."

Change?

"Things" change. What leaders do is to *create* a world that would not have existed without them. "Change" is unavoidable. Changing some part of the world from the way it is to the way it ought to be is the work of leadership. Michelangelo said he "saw" the finished sculpture in the raw slab of marble. His task was to release it. To bring about something that never existed before. That's what leaders do.

Much of all this talk about "change" seems to suggest simply rearranging things. Leaders do not simply rearrange things. Leaders create a future out of their vision of it. In retrospect, they may have altered the course of history, if only of themselves or of their organization. But that was a byproduct of composing something that never existed before.

- Managers "change" things. Leaders "compose" the future.
- What people want is to be relevant. Changing them does not make them relevant. Being a part of the making of the future does.
- The leader's relevance and influence lie there.

ROA

Everyone knows about ROI—"Return on Investment." But not everyone appreciates the fact that the investment we all make which has the most far-reaching returns, plus or minus, is how we invest our attention. What we pay attention to, why, for how long, to what ends: these create the wake in which everything that follows will be thought, or done.

So the key investment for any individual or for any organization is that of *attention*. We can make ROA refer to Return on *Attention*. If you get this one right, most of the other hoped-for "returns" will occur without focusing on them.

Example: If you invest in what *drives* performance, you will get the desired performance without endlessly fussing with yourself or your people about it.

Randomness, "Luck," Etc.

There are ALWAYS factors over which you have no control that will bear on how things turn out. We could refer to these inevitable events as "luck" or as "randomness" or as one or more of "Murphy's Laws." It makes little difference what you call them. As we all know, "Whatever can happen will happen, and usually at the worst possible time."

So be it. The leader doesn't imagine that he or she has the omniscience to see what is going to happen. But leaders have learned that much of what determines the outcomes of any endeavor can't be foreseen. And that they could not control them if they were. What leaders have learned is how to collaborate with "luck" or chance happenings, how to roll with the realities—often the perversities—of their world. They develop a sixth sense about when to raise and when to fold in the face of unbeatable forces, as Sun Tzu suggested, and as every good poker player knows.

Leaders do not imagine that they have more power than the world has. They do not imagine that they could comprehend what is going on there in all of its dynamic complexity. They learn to play their hand within the context of whatever happens that is beyond their ken, beyond anyone's control.

A thought prodder?

- Leaders *partner* with "luck," with randomness.

Time

People who are clear about their purpose or cause in life have all the time they need to plan and pursue those ends. Those who are not clear about why they are here, or what their aims in life are, will have problems "managing" their time.

That's because people who always have their eye on "the ball" (their purpose in life) can sort out what is relevant to their path and what is not in nanoseconds. Others, sadly, will have to carry an "organizer."

- If you can't figure out what is relevant, on the spot, it's likely because you have no clear purpose in your life, or at that moment.
- This cannot be fixed by buying something.

There are many more that we will meet as we go along. A word is a handle on a concept. The lesson for leaders is that the concepts you carry around with you as tools to navigate the world are the critical part of your resources. Get those right, and your endeavors will be optimum. Not perfect, not always successful, just optimally so.

We all have to use the same words. But the way we conceive of those aspects of the world which those words trigger can be quite different. When we say that leaders **think** differently, that is what we mean: they are using the same words, but they understand those words differently. It's the difference that makes the difference.

We could take almost any important word in the dictionary and revise it for purposes of a "Leader's Lexicon." If these examples take, and if you study the rest of this book carefully, you will be able to build your own "lexicon," which will determine not only how successful you will be, but how much you enrich your own and others' lives in the process.

Some "thought-prodders"

- What's **necessary** is not what you think is necessary. It's what the person who has to do it thinks is necessary.
- The pressure a person can't bring on herself to perform is pressure you can't place on her to perform.
- People may do tricks for you, for money or recognition, but those will be no better than mediocre tricks.
- If it boosts your ego to imagine that you can manipulate someone, think about this: that is how they manipulate you.
- If it were necessary for you to *make* someone perform, that would measure that person's power over you, wouldn't it?
- What leads you to believe you could make people perform beyond their inclinations, when you can't make yourself perform beyond *your* inclinations?
- Why is it that you think you have to get the credit for another's performance if it is superior, but attribute the blame to that person if it is not?
- What is it, exactly, *you* want from others' performance?

A thinking test, just for fun:

- About *what* does the leader need to be a competent thinker?
- What or who makes the *leader's* exceptional performance necessary?
- Is it "wrong" to be content with being mediocre or just "average"?
- Even so, incompetence in the service of good will produce the wrong results. Incompetence is *always* misleading.

PART II

OBSTACLES AND BARRIERS

WHAT MAKES IT so hard?

No one has ever over-estimated the difficulty of great achievement. No one has ever over-estimated the difficulty of making a great—a high-performance—organization. No one has ever over-estimated the difficulty of leading people (the Moses story), or of changing the order of things (the Lincoln story). Here is what Machiavelli had to say in 1532 about the perils and difficulties of becoming an exceptional leader:

> There is nothing more difficult to take in hand, more perilous to conduct, or more uncertain in its success, than to take the lead in the introduction of a new order of things.

Consider every phrase carefully. He does not say that improving things for the benefit of the people will be warmly welcomed and aided. Just the opposite. It is, in fact, easier to do harm to people than it is to do good for them. Think about that.

If anything has changed since those words appeared, it is that they are truer today than ever. Machiavelli was trying to coach his prince (his "leader") about how to protect and preserve the state, about how to be a successful—a great—leader.

This book is about how to be the leader you need to be to make a healthy, long-lived organization. One that is full of quality and growth and real human life for all of the people involved. It is about how to make an organization that is actually good for people and for the society. An organization that enhances and enriches the humanity of all who are a part of it, or are touched by it.

Moses was told what to do (free my people from their slavery and deliver them to the life they should have). But not how to do it. Those people did not want to be led somewhere else. Nor were they all that pleased to have a guy with a speech impediment and not a clue about where the "Promised Land" was as their leader. There were no incentives or bonuses involved. So Moses's only problems were:

> How am I supposed to organize 6000 people,
> Get them on an unknown path to some unspecified future,
> Feed them and clothe them and take care of their needs
>   along the way,
> When they don't want to go anyway?

A challenge is always a challenge to your thinking. In the following chapters, you can continue to provision yourself with more powerful ways of thinking about what you need to think about. We'll start by examining in depth some of the universal obstacles and barriers you will face if you undertake to "introduce a new order of things." The better you anticipate these, the better you can prepare yourself to deal with them.

Such obstacles on the road to great achievements may be there for no reason other than that of testing how committed you are. Reason enough.

If it were easy, this undertaking, you'd be surrounded by the same people who hover around you today. Any easy path will lead you to exactly where you are today.

CHAPTER 5

Dragons

IF YOU GREW up with picture books, television, and cinema, you will imagine that "dragons" are those loathsome fire-breathing monsters that have been the standard depiction for decades. So it may be that what I have to tell you will seem, simply . . . wrong.

But for centuries before there were "illustrated" books, and for millennia before there were photo- and life-like moving pictures of these fantastic creatures, humans did not have a mental "picture" of them. Quite the contrary, in fact. For those who lived in oral cultures (most of the humans who have ever lived), a "dragon" was not a creature that came to scare us into some heroic defense of our lives or our lovers. "Dragons" had no corporeal existence.

They were indeed believed to function as obstacles to any journey or quest undertaken. But they were not real things on the path in front of us. They were metaphors for those attitudes, fears, and anxieties that existed *within* people that kept them from doing what they ought to do, that kept them from undertaking the quests they perhaps should have undertaken to make their lives what they ought to be. They were the mental ghosts and goblins that kept people from venturing forth, that people used to convince themselves that they should not undertake anything dangerous or risky. They were indeed seen as obstacles to any venturesome human undertaking. But they were not obstacles in our path. They were obstacles in our thinking, in our imaginations, about how treacherous any change (or any attempt to undertake something that might have a questionable outcome in the future) would be.

Nothing much has changed. We still have a love-hate relationship with the future. It is the unknown because we have not experienced it yet and can not look at it as we look for the answers to life in the rear-view mirror. The future is not in the rear-view mirror. We may want change, or even **to** change. But we are comfortable only with hind-sight. We like "hope." But we don't always want to deal with the realities we find there in the future.

The dilemma? We have to understand life backward, but we have to live it forward. We would "like" to be adventurers in life. But we would prefer to deal with the risks or uncertainties involved by doing it vicariously. Enter, thus, the "stories" that allow us to remain in our comfort zones while pretending to undertake dangerous missions. Most of these become the favorites of, today, large audiences of couch potatoes: "Mission Impossible," "OO7," "Star Wars," "Dinosaur," the "Super Bowl," "WWC," and on and on. We love "consuming" the adventure. We would prefer it in the comfort of our familiar surroundings and security.

So we entertain ourselves with the notion that there are "dragons" out there that are bigger than we are, fiercer than we are, and cleverer than we are. We like to look at them, and to be scared or thrilled by them. But we wouldn't really want to come face-to-face with one. So we've organized the world in such a way that we don't have to.

But this misses the point. The point is that any obstacles or barriers to achieving something in the future ALL belong to the person who imagines them. You can't escape the logic. What might keep you from doing something in the future can't be known in fact until you pass through that future. If there is an obstacle there, you can't *know* that until it is present or past.

It pays to be realistic. You don't have to jump to your death off the top of a mountain to determine whether or not you can "fly." You can't do something in the present OR the future if no human can do that. But the four-minute mile was "impossible." So was heavier-than-air flight (have you observed a 747 taking off?). What

Columbus did was considered to be, at best, totally improbable. Fred Smith, who originated Federal Express, was told that his idea was foolish, a failure at the outset. It was also "impossible" to split the atom.

Most of what we now take for granted in our lives—things like elevators and telephones—were considered fantasies. Until someone came along and made them happen. Sam Walton was told, several billion dollars ago, that what he wanted to attempt was not doable. Steven Jobs couldn't interest the major "computer" companies in what became the PC, the laptop. The lessons of history are that most of what the experts have considered impossible is now commonplace. In the 1920s, it was declared that no human could perform in the Olympics beyond the records already set. It is clear that what kept most athletes from trying was their belief that this was true. What made it possible for those who broke those records to do so was at least in part their belief that it could be done.

In other words, the "dragons" were internal. And those who achieved goals considered to be "impossible" had simply slain those "dragons" in order to move on and do it.

Leaders are "dragon-slayers." They first slay those dragons within themselves that might keep them from setting out for fear of what they would meet along the way. Those "dragons" are often reasons why something can't be done. In a typical meeting in a typical organization, there are always many more nay-sayers than yea-sayers. These are the people who, when the subject is what needs to be done in the future, can tell you that it can't be done, and why. These are the same people who have nothing substantive to offer about what to do, but can readily tell others why THAT can't be done. These people are not leaders, whatever their role. These are people who have not slain their own dragons, freeing them and others to talk productively about a plan for achieving the "impossible"—that is, something that they have not yet accomplished.

A leader is a person who seems to recognize no impediments to a future mission or goal. There may indeed be some. But those have to be encountered along the way. They cannot be "seen" in some magical way before getting underway. What leaders bring is the need to prepare to meet those obstacles, and the spirit of determination that says we will achieve our aims whatever it takes. What leaders bring is the "whatever it takes"—the kind of determination coupled with the kind of competencies and preparedness that dissolve most of those obstacles. Leaders bring a discipline that makes possible improvising around, over, under, or through those obstacles. Nothing worth achieving comes cheaply. The more "impossible" the goal means merely the more prepared you have to be: skills, heart, and imagination.

It would be foolish to be "Pollyannaish" about all of this. There is a great difference between being fully prepared to carry out one's aims and being merely foolhardy. People don't bring off exceptional achievements because they "want" to. Or because this is their "dream." Or even by being "courageous." There are always risks, no matter how well prepared you are. There are always failures, no matter how determined you are.

And yet, more success comes to those who are more determined coupled with being more prepared. Even luck, it is said, favors those who are best prepared to accomplish what they have set out to accomplish.

So we are not touting the notion that success is a matter of "heart" or of "desire." They count, but not as much as competence, preparedness, and absolute determination. You will recall the old proverb: Necessity is the mother of invention. The "necessity" refers to obstacles you encounter along the way to a destination you are determined to reach. People who are not committed to purposes in life have none of this kind of "necessity." Their "necessities" might come down to getting the VCR repaired by someone else. The "necessity" referred to in the proverb refers to what the person on her quest has to find within herself to deal with the obstacles being confronted. And what can be "invented" is a function of who that person is, how determined that person is, and how competent and prepared to invent solutions that person is.

In other words, a person who is forever doing battle with internal "dragons" is not going to have the time, the energy, or the competencies to deal with the real obstacles that inevitably arise on the path to anywhere worthwhile. That's why most people who never leave their own "comfort zone" can tell you why the difficult thing you propose to do can't be done. It can't be done by them, so they conclude it can't be done.

It is the rare person who emerges from all of this stasis, from all of this comfortable disdain for the pursuit of "impossible" goals. They are the leaders. They lead thought; they lead practice; they lead movements; they lead every aim or purpose that has been deemed "impossible."

That's because they have slain the dragons that would keep them from undertaking even their own dreams or desires. For only then is it possible for them to lead others, to lead the way toward some *collective* aim or purpose.

- A leader is a person who has slain his or her own personal "dragons."
- A follower is a person who wants to go with the "dragon-slayer."

And this raises two additional questions:

1. Why does the prospect of changing oneself loom larger or harder than changing the world—for most people?
2. What, then, is a "hero"?

Private "dragons" are usually more fearsome than the obstacles that we actually meet along the path to our goals. Our imaginations are often more potent than actuality. There will be known obstacles, reported by those who have gone before us, or extrapolated from the past. If our past experiences have consisted of the obstacles we have faced in the pursuit of "impossible" goals, we will know how to prepare for those. If a person has never encountered such adversity because that person has never undertaken to achieve "impossible" goals, then that person will not know how to prepare, or what personal and other provisions might be needed, and will therefore be faced only with his or her internal "dragons." If you have no internal "dragons," and if you have prepared yourself for any likely or unlikely adversity along the way, that adversity does not produce the same level of fear or of helplessness, either before undertaking the journey or along the way. If your "baggage" includes those internal "dragons," you may "freeze," go dumb, unable to cope.

For the person who is determined and prepared, the actual obstacles are merely problems to be solved. They are a challenge to one's capabilities, an opportunity to put oneself to the test, a part of life on a worthy quest. For the person who is not, those same obstacles will either preclude the setting-forth, or will incite retreat or despair. What you can bring to bear on the actual obstacles depends upon how much you have to struggle at the same time with your internal "dragons."

A "hero," then, is not first a person who has achieved something notable in the world. A "hero" is a person who has "overcome" himself or herself. A "hero" is a person who has slain his or her own "dragons."

This is the greater feat. Having accomplished this, that person may then fall into the opportunity of "leading" others. For good or for ill, what stands between us and our goals is . . . us. We can't *know* whether or not something can be accomplished until we have done it. And that requires a kind of passionate abandonment of oneself to one's cause. We cannot abandon ourselves fully to any cause we may have until that cause is more important to us than we are to ourselves.

That is the mother of all "dragons." Most people prefer their own mediocre (at best?) lives to any cause or purpose they may express. They will never fulfill their dreams because they are too consumed with fulfilling themselves. They will ridicule others' goals. They will be the nay-sayers because they have said "No" to their aims by saying "Yes!" to themselves as they are.

The "dragon" has won. There is no "hero." There is a "hero" only when the "dragon" has been slain.

And no matter what else it may be, or where else it may be, the one that stands in our way is the one we imagine will keep us from success in the pursuit of any "impossible" goal.

The lessons for leaders?

- The critical prerequisite for leading others is first "conquering" yourself.
- Whatever you imagine will keep you from achieving the "impossible" goals you set for yourself are personal "dragons." Slay those first.
- What is required is determination, competence, preparedness, and the zeal to encounter the real adversities on the path.
- There is always an "easier" path. That path is offered by the "devil" to seduce you into irrelevance.
- It is not aims or purposes or causes that explain the difference between people who achieve greatly and those who do not. It is indifference to the personal costs involved.
- To abandon yourself to your worthy goals or purposes in life requires an openness to the world that comes from first slaying your own "dragons."
- Extraordinary achievement requires being a servant of your purpose or cause in life, not the other way around.
- The best "theory" about how to accomplish something worthwhile is the one that worked. That can be determined only by looking *back* at the accomplishment.
- Life is not in the destination. It is in the struggle to get there.
- The critical obstacles to real achievement are within. It is their own "dragons" that keep people from setting forth.
- Leaders slay their "dragons." Then they equip others and make it necessary for those others to slay *their* "dragons."

CHAPTER 6

The Way You Think About Things

IT MAY SEEM odd to consider the fact that the way you think can be the central contributor to the obstacles you face. We've observed this before. Now we need to provide more specifics. How you think about what needs thinking about can be your own best ally, or your own worst enemy.

Everyone has "dragons." Slaying them eliminates the most resistant obstacles. The second set of obstacles/barriers to even getting on the path toward great achievement, or the path required to make a great or a high-performance organization, derives from something so common we hardly ever give it heed: the conventional "managerial" mindset. It is a part of our culture. And it is almost universal in most organizations. It is an occupational hazard of moving up the ranks of management in most of the western world.

So what is it about that mindset, which is assumed to be prerequisite to reaching higher levels of management in most organizations, that functions as a bundle of obstacles to extraordinary performance?

Here are several aspects of that conventional "managerial" mindset that invariably work against the kind of thinking required to achieve high performance, or to become the kind of leader who makes a great organization:

Management Is Not Leadership

Managers are not necessarily leaders. Managing is not the same thing as providing leadership. We use that term loosely and are thus misled by it. A person who has "position power" in an organization or an institution is not magically transformed by a lofty title into a leader. It might be a good thing if that happened. But it rarely happens.

Managers are appointed. Leaders have to be permitted that role by their followers. Managers hire subordinates. Leaders have to earn their followers.

Responsibility is not the same thing as leadership. Managers think of themselves as responsible for the outcomes. Leaders think of themselves as responsible for the people who make the outcomes happen. Managers require people to do things right. Leaders lead people to do the right things. Managers devise schemes and deploy technologies to compensate for incompetencies. Leaders, as the old saying goes, do not give people fish. They teach people how to fish.

The list of differences is lengthy. But what's most to the point here is the mistaken belief that becoming a better and better manager will eventually turn that person into a leader. *This will not happen.*

What it takes to be a profit-maker is not what it takes to be a performance-maker. Leaders develop people for purposes of sustainable performance under adversity (which is the only measure of competence). Managers use people to make an acceptable "bottom line." Those who do not deeply comprehend those differences will never become leaders, no matter how good they get at managing.

A manager can be "successful" for reasons that have nothing to do with that manager's capabilities. A leader succeeds or fails on his or her own merits. Managers can often explain-away their shortfalls, attributing them to someone or something else. Leaders fail themselves because it was *their* aim, *their* purpose in life that was at stake. Managers can tell you who was "responsible." Leaders hold themselves accountable.

The "managerial" mindset takes you down a different path. Under the influence of this mindset, you do not think like leaders do. Thus you do not make decisions or take actions like leaders do. If you want to be a leader, that "managerial" mindset will not take you where you want to go.

If you are a competent manager, with timing and luck on your side, you could preside over a successful enterprise—personal or organizational. But to preside over a *high-performance organization*, you would have to be a leader.

Managers organize for what's likely or what's possible. Leaders for what is unlikely or for what is deemed at the outset to be "impossible." Managers chase the possible. Leaders challenge themselves against the "impossible." Leaders have a lust to experience the world of which they have a vision—beyond the possible. Managers prefer the comfort and security of working safely within conventional limits—of measuring against last year's numbers, for example.

Yet, and very important: leaders do not disdain "the numbers." They understand that fiscal health is just as important as personal health to the pursuit of any mission. But they do not permit "the numbers" to define them or to define what's possible. They do not believe that destiny is *in* the numbers. They believe that destiny is what they can make it to be. It is the leader who takes the measure of "numbers," not the other way around.

It is our mindsets that lead us, that take us where *they* go. In this case, our conventional Western managerial mindset can be a serious obstacle to the kind of thinking required to pursue a great achievement.

This is one of those things that makes the process so "hard." You can't get there by conventional thinking, especially if your conventional thinking is bounded by a "managerial mindset," as we will see in what follows.

Being "The Boss" Is Addictive

Every person who has ever been put in the *position* of being the boss has become—more or less—*addicted*.

Addicted? Strong word. Addicted to what?

Well, the boss has power. It may be no more than position power. But people who have not conquered themselves (remember the "Dragons"?) easily become addicted to having . . . power over others.

Becoming something other than the traditional "boss" with the traditional power traditional bosses have is almost certain to provide that person with some anxiety about losing that power. You know how addictions are. Very hard to give up voluntarily. A person might agree that the addiction is not healthy. But would still be reluctant, even resistant, to giving it up—as "managers" are.

So one thing that makes this whole process so hard is that it might take away something that the boss has become addicted to—in this case, the power carried by the position. "Empowering" others requires giving up some power *over* them.

Like power, control over others is addictive. The more people are able to control themselves and their circumstances at work, the less control the traditional manager will have *over* them. To be "addicted" means wanting more and more of what you're addicted to.

Money—at least the buying power of money—is also addictive. If the only way to maximize the getting of money is to be the boss over more people, then the conventional mindset leads many people to be *upwardly* ambitious. They don't necessarily want the additional responsibility. But they'll do what has to be done to get more money. They'll do what it takes to move "up" in the organization because that's obviously where the money is.

What else is addictive for the conventional mindset? Prestige. The prestige that goes with the position can easily become addictive. When you see the arrogance that often goes with position, you can know that the person is addicted. The "perks" that go with the position are also addictive. Are the people who have struggled and connived to get there ready to give up their advantage, those perks?

It is also the case that the sheer *dependence* of subordinates on the whims or needs of the boss is addictive. Universally understood if not always stated: I've been the subordinate and I've been the boss. Being the boss is better. If you're the boss, it is understood that you are "more important" than other people. More relevant. And having people defer to you, as if you were more relevant than they are, can easily become addictive.

What makes the process so hard for traditional organizations managed by traditional managers? What are some of the basic obstacles? Consider thoughtfully this matter of "addiction."

Why are most bosses not great bosses? Because they became addicted to what comes with the position of "manager," and lost sight of what really makes them successful—or not. Lessons?

- Get de-addicted.
- Addiction-proof yourself.
- If you don't, you will not lead yourself or anyone else.

The Conventional Mindset

If you don't want to be tripped-up or blindsided by the most common obstacles to extraordinary performance, it helps to know what to be aware of. Here are some additional obstacles that derive from the conventional mindset of our time, which is itself a product of the popular culture:

1) One of the most basic of these obstacles is our compulsion for short-term thinking. And of all the short-term practices that result. We are a quick-fix society. That has in some instances served us well. But becoming really good at *anything* requires a commitment to whatever it takes—and that includes the investment of time and effort required. "Air Jordans" *will not* by themselves enable a person to jump higher.

- Why is it that we always seem to have the time required to solve a problem, but we don't have the "time" to become competent enough to avoid that problem in the first place?

- Those who live by the quarterly numbers will likely die by them.

2) A similar obstacle that bars your entry to world-class performance is recipe/panacea thinking. This kind of thinking culminates in your belief that somehow, just around the corner, there is a magical solution to your problems that merely has to be applied—the less effort, the better. "Open Sesame." Like predators, whole industries have sprung up to prey upon such gullibility. There is no "painless," immediate ticket to being masterful at anything. No recipe can be better than the cook. The business press may peddle the panacea of the month. But it is only our belief that there *is* such a panacea that they prey upon. If it weren't for our belief that there is such a panacea, they might be forced to sell us some reality.

- No snake oil salesman could sell anything to a person who isn't out there looking for a "magic bullet" or a cure-all tonic.
- An idea, no matter how good, is not an accomplishment. You can buy the best cookbook. But that will not transform you into a great cook. The believers, failing at real cookery, simply buy more cookbooks. Maybe they just haven't found the "right" cookbook. It couldn't be them. Or could it?

3) Closely related is the belief that words can be used to change people. That is, if you use just the right "magic" words, you can change people from being merely adequate to being truly masterful at what they do. If we ourselves "buy" just the right words, we would thereby—shazam!—be great. Or, if you use just the right words on others, they would thereby be transformed into great performers. Hasn't happened yet.

This is what, in our belief in easy magic, we often mean by the term "motivation." Can you somehow simply *talk people into* being more competent, more diligent, more attentive to their work? Leaders have had to learn the difference between enthusiasm and competence. Or maybe you could use money to "buy" the recipe for the performance you hope for. Maybe not. Faust made that deal with the devil. But that didn't make him any smarter.

- If people come to your place because you offer them more money (or other goodies), wouldn't they leave for the same reason?
- If *bribery* hasn't made great performers out of people in their first twenty-five years of life, does it make sense to try bribing them?
- If the words "responsibility" and "duty" don't mean anything to the people you intend to "motivate" by words, what words would you use?
- And when you go to the bank to borrow money to pay people what they believe they "deserve," who loses?
- It isn't technology or ideas that change the course of history or the destiny of any organization. It's people, and what changes *them* is a change in the way they think about things.

4) If you believe that the answer to your prayers is in some recipe for how-to-do-it, then you must necessarily assume that people are interchangeable with respect to that recipe. They are not.

5) If you go with the flow—the conventional mindset—you will see the world as far more "linear" than it is. And you will see human behavior as far more "literal" than it is.

To see things as more "linear" than they are is to attribute simple cause-and-effect explanations or predictions to a world that only rarely works that way. To see things as more "literal" than they are is to attribute more reality to your observations than they could provide, to attribute to others' words more reality than they deserve, and to assume that there is a one-to-one relationship between a word (or a number) and the simple reality it supposedly refers to.

Either way, it is to miss the fact that the world is far more convoluted and full of happenstance than this kind of thinking can capture. You may want to review our discussion of "Cause" in the lexicon chapters.

About what people say: They may not know what they mean. They may not have the words to approximate what they mean even if they do have a grasp of what they want to say. What they offer is at best no more than their interpretation. That is more likely to be an opinion, or even a minor political maneuver. At worst, the world is full of people who cannot lead you, but will inadvertently *mislead* you. People often don't mean what they say, and sometimes this is intentional. Sometimes people are speaking metaphorically. That is, their words or pictures or numbers may be intended figuratively—to provoke in you something other than a picture of any reality except their own.

Whatever else may be said about it, our cultural inclination to look at the world as "linear" and at words as "literal" is an obstacle to any successful pursuit of real achievement.

6) The last of these conventional mindset obstacles we will consider here is this: Across the range of people we look to for leadership, such as the managers of our organizations, there is a significant shortfall of courage, of vision, of passion, of commitment, even of competence.

These are all required for those who would either lead themselves or others. Such shortfalls function as obstacles. Those who can't muster the courage required, the vision required, the passion required, and the competence required will neither find the path nor what it takes to stay on the path to any extraordinary performance.

Some thought-prodders:

• George Bernard Shaw once said, "The reasonable person adapts to the world. The unreasonable person persists in getting the world to adapt to him. Therefore, all progress depends upon the unreasonable person." Can that be reasonably understood?

- Most people are okay with the notion of change as long as it does not involve them personally.
- Most people are satisfied with their mediocrity. In fact, most people will work harder at preserving their mediocrity than at anything else. What "motivates" them to do this?
- People and their byproducts are *perverse*. What sort of logic, therefore, is required to provide leadership to them?
- How do you need to *think* about this?

Chapter 7

The Drivers, Right Or Wrong

WHAT MAKES IT so hard? What are the obstacles that impede the few who try, or discourage the many from even setting forth?

Here are five usually unseen but potent drivers of wimpy behavior, of mediocrity, of tunnel vision, of lack of heart, of reluctance to change—even for the better:

Habits

The biggie, as we have seen, is "habits." People essentially see the world, think the world, feel the world, and behave in the world according to their habits. You are never "free" in the sense that you can see or feel or act in the world according to the way the world "is." You are a victim of your habits. They take you where they would go, not where you would go. If you want to predict your, or anyone else's, destiny, observe their everyday habits. Who is that person? She is the person she is because this is the person her habits make possible, and make necessary. We live our habits, and they live us.

Your habits will serve either to enable you to accomplish your aims in life, or as obstacles to moving in that direction. They make your life possible without your conscious effort. But they serve at the same time to make any other life impossible. If you've wondered where the bulk of all of that "resistance to change" we hear so much about comes from, this is where to look. Once formed, your habits will then persist as drivers of your thought and your actions forever. Some are hard to come by. Have you tried learning a foreign language? But they are even harder to change or dislodge. They are not just "habits." They are who you *are*, a bundle of interwoven habits from the smallest to the largest. Changing them means you can no longer be who you are. Not many sign up for this kind of adventure voluntarily. Leaders do. Because leaders are adventurers, understanding deeply that "getting there" may require them to change—sometimes even their most basic drivers. **Displacing them** would be a better term. Your present habits will take you where they have to go. If you want to go a different direction, you have to displace them with the habits that will take you there. But you can't simply add on habits that are inconsistent with your present batch. Not smoking doesn't work well for a smoker. Scary stuff. The fact that it scares most people off is why this is where that basic set of obstacles will always be found. If you can't destroy the habits that inhibit your future and replace them with habits that enable that future, you will never be the maker of that envisioned future—you will never be a leader.

For your rightful or intended destiny, the wrong habits are "**dragons**." And if you haven't figured out how to replace the wrong drivers with the right drivers in your own thinking, attitudes, and behavior, you haven't much of a hope of helping others make those changes in themselves.

- Leaders are "driven."
- We are all "driven."
- The difference is that most people are victimized by their "drivers." Leaders make their drivers work for them and their purposes, rather than the other way around.

"Routines"

Habits grow into "routines." A routine is best described as the way a person thinks, or, in an organization, the way things get done—essentially "how we do things around here." Routines are habits made tangible, public. The way a person or a group of people habitually do things is a "routine."

When two or more people are involved, those "routines" are a part of the subculture to which those two people belong. It may be as small as a marriage or a friendship, or as large as a civilization. What makes routines so resistant to change is that they are often a part of a culture that is larger than you are. They are then no longer subject to change by you unilaterally. A spouse, for example, may want to change some routine in the marriage that seems not to contribute in a positive direction. But the routine "belongs" to the relationship, and therefore cannot be changed at will by either person unilaterally. A thoughtful person in an organization may see a way to improve a process. But that might put in jeopardy a routine that involves other people. Even though the change may obviously be for the better, there is resistance to it. This is not intentional. It is that those other people have a real and personal stake in the permanence of the existing process.

So a routine, like a habit, is a barrier to changing things—even if obviously for the best self-interests of the people involved. Leaders understand this. Managers may take the resistance personally, or believe the resistance to originate with the individuals involved. They would be wrong. People will struggle to maintain a way of doing things even if they see a personal advantage in the change. This is because they have a vested interest in the way things are being done now.

It gets worse. People develop a rationale—**explanations**—for why they do things the way they do. Unintentionally, they create mythologies that justify their current routines, making those ways of doing things more or less sacrosanct—unchangeable by people because they are a part of the mythology which those people take as "given." Think of it this way: there are people who starve to death looking right at cattle. Why? Because their beliefs—their mythologies—make the cattle untouchable for the purpose of human consumption. Routines in organizations are often "sacred cows."

There is another very important aspect of "routines." It is that a routine enables a person to function on "auto-pilot." That is, they can function without really being engaged mentally or emotionally in what they are doing. Routines thus have the byproduct of disengaging people from their work. Once routinized, you can do much or most of your work without thinking, or with no feeling. There are two dangers here: one is that, in certain occupations, like driving a car, operating a machine, or flying a plane, safety may be endangered. The other is that those who are not vitally engaged with their work are not going to be the ones who see or implement ways of improving the processes by which they do their work.

In other words, ideas like "continuous improvement" depend upon people being engaged in what they are doing. The more routinized their work, the less engaged they are with it and in it. Where Toyota automobiles were manufactured some years ago, more than 5,000 process improvement ideas were *implemented* every day. This required people who were **engaged** in what they were doing, not a "Suggestion Box" and a scheme for rewarding employees for suggesting an idea that might have some economic merit.

Having people in every role who are fully **engaged** in what they are doing is what leaders think through and make happen. They do this by making it impossible for "routines" to take root and thus become a part of the culture. They do this by making engagement with what a person is doing **necessary**.

- People read routinely. They are not really engaged in what they are "reading." Thus the "return" on the investment is negligible.
- Lovers routinize their actions. And "love" disappears.
- People at work aim to get on auto-pilot, so that they do not have to think about what they are doing. The day gets longer, their performance gets poorer.
- Routinization displaces life.

Bureaucratization

Big word. Big subject. HUGE barrier to any extraordinary performance.

In a bureaucracy, as small as a marriage, as large as the largest corporation or government agency, the "rules" for how to do things take precedence over the accomplishment. In a small community or a small organization, the "rules" are imbedded in the practices, the routines, that have evolved over time. They are a part of the culture. But in large organizations, with more people coming and going all the time, managers decided that the way to achieve reliability and consistency was to have a formal set of rules for how to do things, called "Policies and "Procedures."

The problematic is how to control things, so they turn out the way they are supposed to turn out even though the "manager" may be some distance away. They are substitutes for direct "supervision."

Maybe a necessary evil. Until the rules become ends in themselves. People get rewarded—or punished—not for achieving a goal, where "the rules" are only the means to that end, but for following—or not—"the rules." In a bureaucracy, violating a rule, or following a rule to the letter, is more important than what was supposed to be accomplished. Or in spite of the harm done. How often do you hear "It's our policy"? A customer, for example, does not dictate how she or he wants to do things. It is the "company" that decides how things are to be done. I was once told, "That's not how we do business, Dr. Thayer." My reply, in lieu of telling this company where to go was, simply, "Well, that's the way *I* do business." It was like baying at the moon. But isn't it interesting how easily bureaucracy gets in the way of customer service, in spite of how vocal these same companies are about "customer service"? They haven't learned after all these years that following a rule is not the same thing as accomplishing what needs accomplishing.

It isn't that rules are not useful and sometimes even necessary. We couldn't keep all of those aircraft in the skies away from each other if there weren't rules with serious consequences for violations.

The leadership issue is whether or not you have your sights set on what is to be accomplished—or on slavishly following the rules.

- If you have formal "rules" about sex, you've lost what you were trying to gain.
- If you think you can wow customers with the rules you devise to control your own incompetent people, you would be . . . wrong.
- The less say your people have in how they do what needs to be done, the less likely it is that they will experience much "satisfaction" in their dealings with you.
- Again . . . what are "rules" *for*?

"Comfort Zone"

We all have one. It refers to certain habitual, comfortable, familiar ways of thinking, feeling, seeing, acting and reacting. It refers to the fact that we are who we are because we think the way we do, see the way we do, feel the way we do, and act the way we do. If these work, even marginally, we'll settle into our "comfort zone."

Why is this an obstacle? Did you ever try to rock yourself out of your "comfort zone"? Ever try to see the world from some alien point of view? Ever try to think thoughts you never even imagined before? Ever tried to make the opposite out of some really strong feelings you had, and for which you felt justified? Ever tried to act or react so differently that others didn't recognize you? That's what our "comfort zones" protect us from.

Why is this an obstacle? Well, if your comfort zone is going to provide the infrastructure for real achievement, no problem. But not even superior athletes imagine they can compete unless they suffer the pain of staying in condition for competition. If your competitor is better prepared, in better shape, more competent, and better informed than you are, it may be that your enemy is not your competitor, but your own "comfort zone."

It is *dissatisfaction* with the status quo that energizes leaders. And the status quo they have to deal with first is their own comfort

LEADERSHIP: THINKING, BEING, DOING

zone. All of our "dragons" live and flourish in our personal comfort zones. They would keep us as we are—or worse. With comfort comes arrogance. From the point of view of our comfort zones, we can see that there is truth—those who agree with us—and untruth—those who disagree with us. From our comfort zones, we judge others and everything else. We see any change as a threat to who we ARE. We are like pit vipers around anyone who tries to better us. If your comfort zone is at stake, you will indeed bite the hand that might advantage you. Or dismiss it as wrong.

We are *driven* by the need to stay within our zone of comfort. We attempt to ignore or disagree with anything that would rock our boat.

Leaders have had to learn how powerful a driver their own comfort zones are. And this serves as a constant reminder of what they face if they appear to be a threat to anyone else's "comfort zone." They know what kind of fierce obstacle this is. They lead others out of their comfort zones in the same way they had to lead themselves out of theirs.

- Whether or not you have what it takes to lead yourself depends upon how dissatisfied you are with yourself.
- Whether or not you can provide significant leadership at work or in the world depends upon how dissatisfied you are with the status quo.
- If you crave or pursue comfort, you are on the opposite path.
- The less "maintenance" you require from others, the more likely it is that you can be an achiever.
- The reason why most people can't think "out of the box" is that this would take them outside their "comfort zone."
- Why would anyone want to go *there?*

The "Knowing Mode"

Yes, that is an awkward term. But we don't seem to have a word to refer to the fact that most adults are in the "knowing mode." When we were infants, the driver was an insatiable curiosity, an often out-of-control need to learn about everything around us. We were in the "learning mode"—the opposite of the "knowing mode." As we became older, we little by little left the "learning mode" and entered into the "knowing mode." We either knew the answer to everything we considered important, or we sought an acceptable answer. We no longer lived in wonder or awe. We were no longer the active instrument of our learning. We no longer asked questions—silently or not—about everything we came in contact with.

We lined our comfort zones with the bits and pieces of what we knew, and began to fuss with the world if it did not fit our understandings of it. We began to get into all sorts of contests with others about right and wrong, good and bad, or how something in the past "really" happened. We wore our particular understandings like armor. And we fought with any weapon we could find in our petty stash of "knowledge" to wound or destroy others who seemed to disagree with something we happened to know (and then fell in love with—our "beliefs"). We stopped asking and started telling.

Here and there we would add a bit of information that seemed to fit with what we already "knew." But if it didn't fit with what we already knew, it had to be wrong and therefore never found its way into our thinking. We stopped asking and started telling— the beginnings of the cancer-like growth of the "knowing mode."

Obviously we have to know a lot of stuff about all kinds of things in order to get around in our complex world. But we lost sight of the great advantage, which is considering everything we know as *provisional*—that is, as subject to revision or elimination when something better or more useful comes along. We became strange and paradoxical archivists: we wanted to store and preserve all of the knowledge that preceded us. But we wanted to learn only from our own experiences. "New" knowledge was always useful for cocktail parties and for verbal parrying to one-up others. But we were unlikely to internalize any of it for our own use if it didn't fit what we already knew—i.e., our own trivial experiences.

You may recall Siddhartha's dictum: "Wisdom is not

communicable." For a person to "receive" wisdom, past or present, that person would have to be wise enough to see it for what it is. What we pass around to each other is not wisdom. It is gossip, hearsay, "common" knowledge. To most of those in the "knowing mode," a good conversation is one that never touches upon anything relevant to the lives that the conversationalists have. I tell you what I know. You tell me what you know. Most of it is irrelevant to anything vital to our lives. And that is what makes it so satisfactory.

So that is a partial definition of the "knowing mode." Is there another useful term for all that?

The "knowing mode," thus described, is a driver for most people. That is, what drives your knowing is what you already know. What drives your feelings are the feelings you have in your repertoire, the ones that belong to you. What drives your observations of others or of the world are the limited mental models you can bring to bear. What drives your interpretations and explanations are the ones that seemed to have worked for you previously. What drives your life is the way you were yesterday. Their future is a product of what you "know."

To be in the "learning mode" means living toward the other end of that continuum. It means being curious. It means being open to contrary ideas or beliefs. *It means asking rather than telling.* It means growing rather than withering on the vine. It means taking the position that the world will forever be more complex than you can ever be, and thus always beyond your reach.

Our belief, fed by our faith in "science," is that one day we will "know" everything there is to know about ourselves and the world in which we live. Well, perhaps. But if that did come to pass, we would no longer exist as humans (as we understand that term now), for what would we have to do *then,* since everyone would automatically know all there is to know? Is there anyone who thinks that sex is better to the extent that we "know" more about the physiology of it? Are the humans and animals who don't "know" everything about it without feelings for it? On the other hand, don't those products of the "learning mode"—the art and the poetry and the music we have about love and sex—don't they have the potential of elevating our *sense* of the wonder of it all? Is "Bolero" merely a tune? Is the Mona Lisa's smile before or after?

You get the point. The point is that what you know is always an obstacle to what you *can* know. Or, even more critically, to what you *need* to know. The lesson here is certainly not to try to know "everything." It is that one of the indispensable skills for leadership is the virtuosity one can muster for asking just the right question. The purpose of knowing stuff is not to play social or educational games. It is to enable you to ask sharper and better questions. The ones that light the way to your purposes. The ones that enable you to invent a solution to an intractable problem. The ones that give you the rush of learning something that would not have occurred if you had not asked that particular question. The ones that reveal to you (or me) our wrong-headedness or stupidity about something.

One thinker suggested that something is meaningful to us to the extent we could formulate the question to which that something is the answer. The quality of life rests on the meaningfulness of the world. And that meaningfulness is spun out the questions we can put to ourselves about it, and about ourselves. *A competent organization, like a competent person, is the one that asks the better questions.*

How does this provide some invaluable foundation for real achievement? Maybe that rides on the question, "What does real achievement **mean—to you?**" This is probably the best predictor there is for assessing your potential for leadership.

Some thought-prodders?

- Questions are life-giving. Answers diminish life.
- When you are in the "knowing mode," you are part of the problem and cannot, therefore, be a part of the solution, whether in personal or organizational life.
- It is better, as the old proverb has it, to ask a question and appear to be stupid for the moment, than to never ask a question and be stupid forever.
- What is the one question which you could ask of yourself

that would make it impossible for you to continue on as who you are?

- What you know—your habits of thought—are your drivers. Masterful questions are a way of getting better drivers.

These are some of the obstacles and barriers to getting on the path that leads to real achievement—to becoming "the best." There are others, of course. But this will get you started.

Knowing that what you know can be an obstacle to what you want to accomplish may not be the conventional wisdom on the street or in your own thinking. If you intend to be a leader, you can't get hung-up on what you "know." You will pursue with zeal and abandon what you *need* to know. How can you do that without asking the questions that are going to get you there? How can you do that without shaking yourself out of—or being shaken out of—your comfort zone?

We like to know stuff. So we pretend that we already know the stuff we need to know. Learning is hard. Thinking is hard. Leadership is harder still. That's because it hinges on those two prerequisites.

You can't *know* how to be a leader. You can only *learn* how. If you want to know how, you're in the wrong place. If you want to learn how, you are in the right place.

There are, ultimately, no obstacles to your journey but your personal ones. How you think makes all the difference at square one. What you learned here is not given in what's here. It is measured by what you do with what's here.

CHAPTER 8

Under-empowerment

IT MAY BE the case that "empowerment" adds to the prowess and the performance of people. If so, then "under-empowerment," which is the standard in modern America, is an obstacle for the individual or the organization where there is a serious commitment to extraordinary achievement.

I should first caution you about the use of a buzzword like "empowerment." As a synonym for "motivating" people, "empowering" people has the same flaws. People may or may not be capable of "motivating" themselves, or of "empowering" themselves. There are two fundamental reasons for being skeptical of these loosely used terms. One is that people have no need to be "motivated" or to be "empowered" if they are not up to something worthy and long-term. It makes little sense to be a self-starter if you have nowhere to go once you're started. So the need for being "motivated" or "empowered" lies in the significance of the purpose which that motivation or empowerment is supposed to serve. Trivial pursuits don't require much in the way of being "motivated" to achieve them. The pursuit of real achievement—of great performance—does. So if a person is not committed to great ends, there is not much needed in the way of "motivation" or "empowerment."

The other reason for skepticism is that it doesn't make much sense to be "motivated" to do something you do not have the skills to do. And it becomes dangerous for people to be "empowered" to make decisions or to take actions they are not competent to carry out. It may sound good, this myth of "empowering" people. But you cannot "empower" people to do something they cannot do. You cannot "empower" people to do well what they are incapable of doing well.

The issue is not "empowering" people. It is helping them, and making it necessary for them, to become *competent*. *It is competence that is empowering, not the fashionable words of a manager.*

The obstacle is "under-empowerment." The obstacle is a shortfall of competence—or of a purpose in life, or at least of compelling conscientiousness.

"Empowerment"?

The fashionable "how-to" press has taken us down the wrong path on this one. "Empowerment" is not kissing up to employees. "Empowerment" is not a trick to make employees *feel like* they now have a say in things—and, since they think they have a say in things, would therefore feel some "ownership" for the performance of the organization.

The buzzword "empowerment" may have grown out of an earlier fashionable buzzword, "participative management." Although there were some sincere attempts in this direction, most of those who picked up on it as a panacea put on a show of involving employees in strategic and tactical decisions, but it was mainly pretense. The managers who tried this technique for elevating performance and solving some perennial "people problems" may have fooled themselves. But there were not many "employees" who were fooled. After years of trickery in the name of finding a short-term solution for a long-term problem (like competence), employees are increasingly not much taken in by the empty verbiage.

"Empowerment" is not a fringe benefit (some tried it). It is not a way of providing a "feel-good" atmosphere for employees in an otherwise indifferent organization.

It is about responsibility. A person who has even a vague notion of what she intends to be when she grows up may have some small beachhead of responsibility for her own destiny. So the basic fact about "empowerment" is that people can "empower" themselves. But they cannot be "empowered" any more than they can be "motivated." If they have assumed some significant level of responsibility for their own destinies, they have "empowered" themselves. Isn't it clear that this is not something that can be done *to* them?

A person who knows that winning a gold medal at the Olympics is his chosen destiny, and who is dedicated to doing whatever it takes to get there, is "empowered." A person who is simply told she can "be anything she wants to be" is not.

People who are thus "under-empowered" are dangerous—to themselves, to their organizations or communities, to the society. They are dangerous because they have to be dealt with as children—that is, as *dependent on their parents, their bosses, and/or their peers for their own destinies.* They do not "own" the problems of their own lives, and thus do not see themselves as responsible either for what they do or what they fail to do. Getting on the path to real achievement personally requires *ownership* of the problems of one's destiny—and thus everything that happens between here and there.

Getting on the path to outstanding performance as an organization requires at least a critical mass of people who are no longer children—people who have assumed an adequate level of responsibility for themselves, and for how well they perform the role they are in. This is the dilemma of "corporate welfare." Yes, people sometimes need help, and we should help them. But we should be helping them to help themselves. If all we provide them with is a safety net that keeps them comfortably operational, they become dependent upon that help, forever needing more of it.

At its worst, "empowerment" is deployed as if it were a form of corporate welfare, of which we already have a surfeit. If attempts to "empower" people makes them more dependent, then it does them and the organization harm.

- You cannot "empower" people who have not already "empowered" themselves.

- If you could "empower" another, or others, you would then have less power *over* them. Most managers couldn't handle this.
- Like other panaceas, simply professing it doesn't work.

"Empowerment" Isn't Competence

"Empowerment" and competence are two quite different things. While it is the case that increased competence empowers people directly, it is impossible to increase competence directly by offering people "empowerment." It might spark their enthusiasm or their superficial appreciation—that is, they might pretend to like you more. But, as we have seen, a lesson every leader must learn is how to distinguish enthusiasm from competence.

If you have a worthy goal or destiny that is more important to you than your present comfort or your comfortable routines, then you have empowered yourself. If you *have* to get there, and can develop the discipline and the competencies required to get there, then you have empowered your mind and your eye and your actions. The idea of "empowerment" apart from competence just doesn't make sense. If you can't do something, you can't do it, no matter how "empowered" you feel, or how "empowered" you are told you are.

- There is a book about every trick so far created for getting to real achievement in lieu of real competence.
- Actually, we have many, and new ones are being invented monthly, because none of the existing ones "work."
- Are *you* an "empowered" reader? Think about this one. What you understand will always be a function of your competence as a reader.

More Empowerment

People who are (self-) empowered (since there is no other kind) are people who are accomplishment-driven, not event-driven. We have visited this before, and will visit it again, because it is such a central and potent concept.

Most people, and thus most organizations, are *event-driven*. What this means is that their day, then their days, then their lives, are determined by what happens to them, the happenings of the day they give their attention to, get involved in. Since they have no particular destination or purpose of their own, they allow their destination to be wherever the events of the day take them.

Those who do have a purpose or chosen aims in life look at the same events of the day, but interpret them—their importance, their urgency, their value—*in terms of* the short-term or long-term goals to be accomplished. The same events, but different interpretations. The "event-driven" person (or organization) becomes a hapless victim of the events of the day. The accomplishment-driven person (or organization) *either* uses those events to pursue self-chosen goals, or pays them no more heed than they deserve as random (non-controllable) events. People either use events for their own purposes, or they get "used" *by* those events.

- Events are relevant only as they bear upon someone's goals. If there are no specific goals to be served, then what happens makes little, if any, difference.
- Most people's lives (and the lives of most organizations) are determined by what happens to them along the way, willy-nilly. To have a specific aim or purpose in life means making certain events happen, rather than being *made by* the events that arbitrarily happen.
- To choose to have no purpose or mission in life is to choose to be a victim of whatever happens.
- To be "empowered" means to have some power over the events that occur.
- Whether an individual or an organization, being under-empowered will function continuously as an obstacle to getting on or staying on the path to extraordinary performance.

Measuring Empowerment

To be "empowered" means that you know in great detail what constitutes performance in your role. It means that you can measure your performance in that role not only in terms of your growth in competence from month to month and year to year, but you can measure your performance against both the standard level of performance for that role *and* the best performance in that role there has ever been, anywhere, by anyone. It means as well that you know with great awareness what bears upon your performance in that role from within or outside your organization, and what your performance in that role bears upon elsewhere in your organization or in the world.

If that seems like what you mean by "empowerment," then you are on the right track. If that seems like what the people in your organization or your peers mean by that term, then you're on the right track. If not, then you may be falling into a trap.

How "empowered" people are can be measured directly by how well they are performing the role they are currently in, and by the rate of growth in their competencies in that role. We are repeating here: but to be "empowered" is to be fully competent in your role. The more competent the person is, the more "empowered" that person is.

- "Empowerment" is a function of competence, not the other way around.
- To measure "empowerment," measure competence.
- All this provides some clues about how awesome an obstacle "under-empowerment" is.
- Most useful clue? You cannot "talk" your way out of it, either personally or as a leader of others.

Under-developed Conscience

We have to come back to this. Conscience is the great unseen regulator. It lays down the law internally for individuals about what is right and what is wrong, what is good and what is bad, what is useful and what is not, what contributes to chosen purposes and aims, and what does not.

We are not born with a conscience. And it cannot be bought, borrowed, or shared. It either got developed or not. The more developed it is, the more "empowered" the person is. People who are "under-empowered" have a distinctly immature or under-developed **conscience**. As a practical matter, this is where poor quality comes from. This is where mistakes and errors and injuries come from. This is where poor "customer service" comes from. This is where the costs of fixing things comes from. This is where waste comes from, and indifference, and inattention. If the devil is in the details, as the old saying goes, then the devil emerges in all of those under-developed *consciences* there are in your organization. From the standpoint of your aims in life, this is the devil's playground and it will stretch widely and extensively as a persistent obstacle across the path you would take.

In a typical organization (or for the typical person), problems will arise on top of those that have been "fixed" or solved, forever. The reason is that the root cause—the absence or under-development of conscience—continues on unabated.

There is no competence without conscience. Even then, the level of competence will always be limited by the level of conscience. A person may know the difference between right and wrong. But it is only a powerful *conscience* that will make it necessary to DO the right thing. A person who is not competent to do the right thing even if he or she knows the right thing to do—will not be able to carry it out. It takes both. One without the other will diminish performance.

- A person who is not competent, OR a person who does not have an adequate conscience, will not be an exceptional performer—will not be a dependable achiever.
- That person is under-empowered.
- And under-empowerment will always be an obstacle to the achievement of any worthy goal.

Let us latch onto a different kind of concept. It is useful. It is powerful.

A *bricoleur* is a person who accomplishes what has to be accomplished, when it has to be accomplished, with the tools and resources at hand. This means that when you invest in bricoleurs, you get a full return on your investment. Otherwise your investment has to be discounted. A bricoleur is a fully empowered person.

It's interesting that we do not have an English term for this concept. And it is interesting that we do not regularly use such a concept. Is that because a part of our management folklore is that, to accomplish something, we have to throw money or personnel or capital equipment at it? We seem to assume that people must be aided or supported to accomplish something they have already agreed to accomplish. Is that why we buy the most prestigious, highly-advertised paraphernalia for our kids: on the assumption that these amateurs will turn into achieving professionals if we just buy them the best shoes or tennis rackets or ski boots available? Is it that we assume that it is easier to buy people more tools or resources than it is to equip those same people to be more resourceful themselves? Is it that we find it too hard to elevate people's competencies, so we buy them mental or "process" prostheses instead? So, if clerks cannot add or subtract, we buy them a cash register that will do it for them? Or, if they cannot think, we send them to a seminar on "time management"? Or, if they are not accomplishers, we reward them for simply "trying"? Or, that we have despaired of making them truly competent and conscientious, so we devise incentive and bonus schemes to get them to do what they have already signed up to do? Or that if we have a laptop on every lap, the organization will perform smarter?

It's fairly obvious that we do not believe that there are people who can accomplish what they said they would, with the tools and the resources available to them. And that, over the years, we have made this a self-fulfilling prophecy. By assuming that there aren't such people, and proceeding as if people will accomplish what they have agreed to accomplish only with additional tools or support, we have made our belief come true. There may not be many "bricoleurs." And that may be why this is not a familiar term for you.

But if you had an organization of bricoleurs, you would be doing things at far less cost than your competitors, faster, and better. And you wouldn't be spending an inordinate amount of time most days on "people problems." And if you did make capital investments for tools or other resources, you would be getting the full return on your investment. That is, much of that investment would not be going to *compensate* for people's incompetence. *The "return" will always be related to the level of competence in which you have invested*—them *or* you.

It could be time or money. It takes more time to fix stupid errors than would have been required to preclude those errors through competence/conscientiousness to begin with. It takes more money, more time, more involvement to get the same level of productivity out of marginally competent people (the "typical" employee).

To believe that you could ever be the best requires that you become a bricoleur. It requires that you have the level of discipline and of mastery that enables you to *improvise*, to invent a way to your accomplishment when the path you are on seems to have insurmountable obstacles. How well you have mastered your role, and the tools required to perform it, can only be measured by how well you perform under adversity. It is the bricoleur who smashes through adversity. It is the bricoleur who finds a way through, or around, or over or under obstacles that stand in the way. All great achievers are bricoleurs. All great bricoleurs are the pushers and pullers of achievement.

- What cannot be accomplished with the tools and resources at hand is a measure of how robust is the competence of the individual, or the capabilities of any organization.
- A great tool or a great resource is of *full value* only to those who do not need them in order to accomplish what needs to be accomplished.
- Being under-empowered leads to an "Open Sesame!" magic

belief in "more" or different tools or recipes or resources, not in oneself.

- *Somebody* has to pay for those. Will that be you?

Consider, then, these overall thought-prodders:

- People who don't know what they want to be when they grow up usually never do.
- People who don't know what they *ought to be* when they grow up believe that is solely a matter of their "choice."
- People who don't "own" the problems of their own destiny will never understand what it would mean to assume some ownership of the problems of the destiny of the organization (or the team or the society).
- People who are not bricoleurs will never really understand ROI.

CHAPTER 9

"Dumb" Systems

THE WORLD IN which we live—both internally and externally—is comprised of "systems." As a practical matter, all this means is that everything is more or less connected to everything else. In your thinking, for example, everything is eventually connected in some direct or indirect way. In the world outside of us, everything is loosely or tightly connected to everything else.

Why is this important? Because looking at the world this way takes us out of our cause-and-effect, linear mode of thinking, which rarely fits actuality. It is also useful to "see" the world this way because it forces us to recognize that we can rarely ever change one thing without affecting the other things to which it is related. If you change a procedure, it may well make another procedure, keyed to the old way of doing things, fail to operate. People are related to each other. Attempting to change one may be difficult or impossible because of the way that person is related to all of the others. Providing "customer service" may not be easy if the customer has had bad experiences in the past. The present is always related to the past in some way. Trying to change yourself, for example, is difficult not only because of your own habits, but because you are who you are largely due to the image others have of you, and they may be disinclined to change their image of you. You are a part of a whole set of systems—consisting of people, ideas, communication channels, relationships, habits, routines, things, devices, and happenings. So is everyone else. You are who you are because of your *roles* in those systems.

Systems both *enable* and *constrain*. What can be done depends upon what those systems enable—that is, what they make possible, and what they make necessary. What can be changed depends upon what those constraints will permit. Leaders know, for example, that how they can deal with people depends upon the *relationship* they have with those people individually and collectively. And leaders know that people are different people depending upon what other people they are with. We all do it. When with others, we are in different "systems" and will perform roughly in accordance with the system we find ourselves in. You typically will not tell people to their face, for example, what you might say about them to others. You will always behave in keeping with the system you're in. Emailing a person usually brings out a "you" that is different from who you are when you are face to face with that person. When with your boss, you will behave differently than when you are with a subordinate.

The *system* in which you are operating will always provide both enablers and constraints on your aims and purposes. In order to see *them* for what they are, you have to look at the *system* and not the component parts of that system. Thinking psychologically leads you to focus only on the people and your past relationships with them. Thinking technologically leads you to focus on the modes of information exchange. Thinking rationally leads you to attribute more rationality to the event or the persons involved than is ever there. And so on. You will "see" the parts but not the whole (system), and how the *system* works.

For example, you might try to "fix" yourself or another person when it may actually be the system in which you are embedded with them that is faulty. Marriages are often this way. There's nothing wrong with the people, but the way the system is put together is dysfunctional. It helps to keep in mind that organizations and every other human institution in our modern world are *always* more or less dysfunctional. Probably more rather than less.

Most systems are "dumb" systems. That's because the output of the *system* is "dumb." Marriages may not produce a healthy atmosphere, may not be stimulating or produce beauty and happiness for the people involved. Fixing the components doesn't solve the problem. A bad relationship with a customer clouds perceptions on both sides. It isn't the people who are bad. It is that the relationship (the system) shared by both parties is flawed. It is the relationship (the system in which these people are operating) that needs to be fixed.

Poor performance may be a function of a dumb system, and may not reflect the capabilities or the competencies of the person or the people involved. Here is an initial test: If you put extremely competent people in a "dumb" system, the output of the system will be "dumb." (It's likely, of course, that extremely competent people would fix the system in order to avoid this depreciation of their competencies.)

But if you put average performers in a "smart" system, the output of that system will rarely be better than average. What happens in many conventional organizations is that marginally competent people are required to function in "dumb" systems. The output of that system is going to be unreliable, and always less than marginally competent. The performance of any set of interdependent people will vary with how "smart" or how "dumb" the system is. A "smart" system will make anyone appear to be smarter than they actually are. "Dumb" systems will make even competent people appear to be dumber than they actually are. Flight attendants do their work in the context of extremely dumb systems. That's why they so often appear to be without souls. Or brains.

The universal product of most conventional organizations is the careless emergence of dumb systems. People in dumb systems try to fix it while operating inside those dumb systems. The prognosis is not good.

Most human systems—including our organizations and institutions—were not designed to be "smart." They simply emerged over time, and according to the fashions of the day, and therefore became routinized with very little thought given to their architecture, their functioning, or the criteria by which they were to be measured. Paying people to carry out the activities that are listed on their "job descriptions" is an example of a dumb system. It isn't their activities that are of value. It is only their accomplishments that might be.

In fact, most compensation systems are "dumb" systems. They pay whether or not the person actually makes a contribution to the health or the growth of an organization. They even pay people for being sick, which seems not an altogether intelligent thing to encourage in people. CEOs can arrange a contract in such a way that they make more money by getting fired than they could by making the organization more successful. Celebrities are frequently paid not for what they do (or even how well they do it), but for how much money their names can attract. So we have singers who can't sing performing for people who wouldn't know the difference. The money wins. Everybody else loses. Is that a "smart" system?

The business press has a vested interest in your not getting so smart that you don't need more of their stuff. Is that a "smart" system? A politician with principles is an oxymoron. Is *that* a smart system? Crime has to increase to justify more police, more laws, more cells. Is that a "smart" system? More people have to have more illnesses in order for the medical industry to grow and prosper. Is that a smart system? Similarly, for the educational enterprise to grow and prosper, there has to be an increase in ignorance and incapability. Smart? The U.S. government subsidizes tobacco growing while paying for anti-smoking campaigns. Is that a smart system? But before you begin to feel above it all, take a look. You will have in your organization more "dumb" systems than "smart" ones.

But you get the point. The point is that "smart" systems have outcomes that elevate the performance of competent people. "Dumb" systems are great levelers. Their output is "dumb," making everyone who functions in them look incompetent. "Smart" systems contribute to the outcomes intended or required. "Dumb" systems produce outcomes other than the ones intended or required. You may say to someone, "This is what has to be accomplished." Clear enough. But if that person is not capable of accomplishing what you intended, then the conversation is itself "dumb." The system can't be smarter than the people who comprise it. That's why competence is always the critical criterion at every position in any organization. You can compensate to a degree for the marginal competence of the people involved in a system of work by designing an impersonal system that controls their actions and requires them not to think.

But that's always a trade-off. Non-human data systems are ultimately "dumb" because they can only do what they are designed to do. Yet if you need thinking humans in the system, those humans could make poor judgments.

Predictability Vs. Adaptation

This is the perennial dilemma. A robotic system is a purely rule-following system. As long as everything occurs routinely and no thought is required, robotic systems maximize the predictability of the system. Not necessarily the efficacy of the outcomes. Not necessarily even the efficiency of the system. In this case you want reliability/predictability. You want to know that the output is going to be what was intended. McDonald's kitchen systems (by the numbers) would be an example.

But it's actually very rare that things go as assumed. You want some form of human intelligence in there to adapt to the unexpected happenings, to the changes that inevitably occur. You'll recall that Henry Ford wanted to hire "hands" to do the work involved when there was a rationalized division of labor. Things were supposed to go like clockwork. The problem he faced ("Do I have to get their minds when I only want to hire their hands?") is, in a dynamic, ever-changing context, the only possible solution.

You can rationalize the systems involved to an optimum degree. But none of the robotic systems involved in the Apollo 13 return flight would have figured out how to save it. That would have been, for them, "impossible." Humans were required to think about a problem never before encountered (which of course never guarantees a happy ending).

So you can rationalize a system to the extent that it repeats an invariant routine. If the problem that arises is not anticipated by the rule-following robotic system, then human competence is required. A robotic system applied to a unique set of circumstances will be a "dumb" system. Creative people working on a routine problem will create a "dumb" system. A rule-following organization will produce certain kinds of problems (customer complaints, for example). But an organization with few constraints would produce other kinds of problems ("communication problems," for example).

It takes both. You rationalize what is fairly routine, although this has to be designed by extremely competent people. Otherwise the rationalized system is as "dumb" as its designers. And the more freedom there is for people to follow their own interests and inclinations, the more chaos there will be. Either extreme fails at some point.

You have to leave open to human adaptation those problems that emerge uniquely from the sheer dynamics of the human/organizational/economic world. A "smart" robotic system can tell you how to optimize your shelf space. But it can't tell you what product mix should be there to maximize sales.

Since most systems are combinations of data infrastructure and of human input, what's clear—and worth thinking about—is that *both* have to be extremely competent for the system to be optimum. A good way to think about this is to be alert to how your performance varies with the systems in which you operate. That might be a relationship with a trusted lieutenant, a meeting, your reading list, the ways in which you deploy yourself, or a source of advice or intelligence. When are you "smarter"? When are you "dumber"? How much of that is you? How much of that is attributable to the system? In terms of the operant systems at work, when are you at your best? What does it take to overcome a "dumb" system?

To think about:

- How would you design the systems in which you are embedded if you wanted to optimize your performance?
- What would that require of you?

- What would that require of the system?
- Why are the two so cussedly interdependent?
- If you can't put in place "smart" systems for yourself, you will have great frustrations trying to do so for your organization.

"Communication"

We'll sneak this back in here. You can make it a big word or a small one. You can talk about it endlessly or you can pretend it is no part of the problem. But the facts have always been there. They are these:

1. Communication is the universal and indispensable component of any system that involves people.
2. Even robotic systems are, at the core, communication systems.
3. Communication guarantees outcomes or consequences. But communication is a neutral process. It doesn't care whether the consequences are good for us or bad for us.
4. As we communicate, we will create the problems that confront us. But it's the only means we have for trying to solve those problems. So we can't actually have "communication problems." We search endlessly for the external causes of our problems. But they are typically internal—our own stupidity or incompetence.

Competence begins and ends with mastery of the communication process, first for oneself, and then for the complex interdependencies you find yourself in. This is especially so for people who are joined together in a partially robotic system (e.g., wherever there is a rule-following "information" infrastructure).

No IT system can compensate for human incompetencies. The more competent people are, the more they can neutralize "dumb" information systems.

It is only when they are both fully competent, and fully competent in their interactions, that there is efficacy in the system.

Here are some thought-prodders:

- Those who cannot design efficacious systems for their own lives will be unlikely to be able to do so for an organization. If you want to know how competent an IT person is, examine the consequences of the systems they have designed for themselves.
- Great achievers first put in place "smart" systems for themselves.
- Leadership—like all performance—depends upon "smart" systems.

Identifying "Dumb" Or "Sick" Systems

A "dumb" system is a system that is "dysfunctional," to use a fashionable term. That simply means that

a) It contributes to outcomes other than those desired or intended; and
b) It functions as an obstacle to anything worthwhile you may want to accomplish.

So here are some tips about "seeing" them for what they are:

- A "dumb" system is a system that accommodates inferior performance. It impedes rather than contributes.
- A "dumb" system encourages mediocrity, absorbs profits, permits indifference or inattention.
- A "dumb" system inhibits real performance and produces problems that engage people endlessly, but misleads them from identifying it as the underlying problem.
- A "dumb" system is one that rewards "A" while you were hoping for "B."
- A "dumb" system, once accommodated, will be preferred over a "smart" one.
- A "dumb" system is one that is more resistant to change than is a "smart" system.

- A "dumb" system is one in which the persons who ought to own the problem don't, and the people who ought not own the problem do.
- Every adversarial system is a "sick" system. Labor-management.
- The tendency for every system is to become, over time, a "dumb" system. For example, customer relationships seem to deteriorate when the "honeymoon" is over.
- People who are in the "knowing mode" will always support "dumb" systems.
- Any system you cannot make "smart" will be "dumb." Etc.

CHAPTER 10

"Pop" Culture

IT MAY SEEM strange to identify the larger, popular culture as an obstacle or barrier to real achievement. But it seems clear that some cultures have been more prone to facilitate higher levels of performance, and others to inhibit that kind of thinking. In our own (American) civilization, there are orientations and beliefs having their source in the "pop" culture that actually run contrary to commitment or competence, or even diligence in support of a chosen, worthy goal in life. We like our celebrities. But we prefer to attribute their success to something other than choice and hard work. That would leave the rest of us with no excuse. There are negative epithets for anyone who takes work or achievement seriously. "Geek"?

There has never been a human culture or civilization that both encouraged and facilitated excellence. Perhaps some of the Native American Indian cultures were an exception. They had very few possible roles, as we have seen, and virtuosity in those roles was simply expected. Our own contemporary culture is a very "mixed bag": we seem to have a penchant for heroics, and we love to consume sports and other competitive excellence in books, magazines, and television programs. And yet we are inclined to attribute superiority (which we dislike) to "talent," to "luck," or to knowing the "right people" or "kissing-up" at the right time in the right place. We seem to be disinterested in the fact that even those with "talent" have to work hard, discipline themselves, make social and personal sacrifices, and practice, practice, practice. We may dote on the finished product, but we don't want to hear about what it takes to get there.

There are two lessons to be learned about all this:

1. One is that, at least in our own culture, we prefer the idea of achieving greatness as a sort of "immaculate conception"— that is, those who achieve greatly got there because they couldn't help it—it's just the way things happened. In order to get ourselves off the hook, we attribute the great achievements of others to everything and anything other than the effort and the discipline and the commitment that was required to get there—whatever advantage they may have had at the outset. So the notion that an "ordinary" person could re-engineer herself to achieve extraordinary goals *on purpose* is not something that "makes sense" to most Americans. So ours is a culture that may promote "excellence." But we mystify and denigrate any long-term way of getting there. It's as if achieving some on-purpose goal is a little bit like winning the lottery. It's a matter of "luck" or happenstance, so it is not something you might actually work at. If you *do* work at it, you are likely to be laughed at or "put down" by others as a "dufus." So, yes, there is a fundamental obstacle right there.

2. Second, there has never been a culture that made the process easy. So what makes the process so difficult? Other people. The society. The culture. We may be our own worst enemy, but we will not be aided and abetted any such endeavor toward greatness by our peers, our communities, our culture. The closest we can get to the work and the effort and the years of practice required to be a top athlete is "Just Do It!" . . . Right.

It is not that others directly oppose your efforts or your dream.

The more immersed other people are in the "pop" culture, the more likely they are to react to your commitment in one of two ways: by ridiculing you behind your back, or by actively disbelieving you. It's not an easy environment for achievers.

So what are some of those aspects of the "pop" culture that function to preclude an orientation to real achievement?

Victimization As A Way Of Life

There was a time when parents and communities largely determined the values and beliefs of succeeding generations. But the more people surrender their consciousness to the pop culture— peers and media—and the more there are who do this, the dominant players in our values and beliefs have become the themes and ideologies explicit or implicit in media fare. Being "sexy," for example, drives our images from underwear and make-up to clothes and cars.

There are many pop culture beliefs we could choose from. In the aggregate, they define who we are as a people. But let's focus in on those that function as major obstacles and barriers to real achievement or great performance, the targets of this book. They would thus be crucial to how you think.

Perhaps the most ubiquitous pop culture belief is that of "victimization." Because the media (and our peers) are saturated with what we might call "psychologism," we are increasingly a civilization of victims. This is simple enough in its origins. To appear to be scientific, all of the popular branches of psychology assume that whatever happens is "caused" by something beyond a person's control. There are, as we have seen, acceptable reasons for being depressed. We are victimized by our parents, by our teachers and the physical conditions of our lives, by our teachers, by our friends, and by the organizations we work for. People who want to know "how" they have been victimized can tune into a talk show like "Oprah."

It isn't how all of this works that is of interest to us here. What is of interest and of value to your thinking is how this and other orientations end up changing the laws and regulations, and the availability of "helping" institutions of all kinds. We noted previously that a student's inability to learn led to an army of "special education" teachers and programs. The child is taught— reinforced by peers and the media—that any shortfall on her part is not her fault. She's merely a "victim" and the rest of the world is responsible for protecting her and somehow compensating her for not being able to learn. Smoking-related illnesses are no fault of the person. Smokers were "victimized" by the manufacturers. If you spill hot coffee on yourself, you're not to blame. The restaurant is. Obesity is a "disease" for which you need special protection. You have been victimized. You cannot be stupid by choice. You have to be a victim.

A person who works at your place and who is militantly incompetent can sue you for saying so, or doing anything about it. Those who can't or won't are merely victims. They must be protected by government regulation. Women are "victims" of sexual harassment. But never by other women.

You're the one responsible for the ineptitudes of anyone on your payroll. There are laws protecting them from you, but not you from them. That's the way it is. Try *The Excuse Factory* by Walter Olson if you haven't yet lost at this game of protectionism.

- The point is that people are victims of forces beyond their control. They are not responsible for what happens to them.
- So you are.
- That's what they learn from their peers and the media. That's the obstacle. That orientation never made a great anything. The leader has to invent a way of overcoming it.
- Real achievement can't be pursued with a victim mentality.
- To your peers, you may be a "fool" for simply trying to do your job well, or to pretend to own your own destiny.
- If you achieve through no fault of your own, you may be

okay. Getting something for nothing, in school or in life, makes you a local hero.

If you intend to pursue real achievement, you have to be crazy enough, and committed enough, to crash through all of that. Or be impervious to it. If you can't, those "obstacles" will bring you down to where "everybody" else lives and thinks.

- If something or someone denies your right to choose, and if something or someone else has the right to explain your emotions and decisions, you are a victim.
- And, apropos the previous chapter, when you take away from people their *ownership* of their own problems, you typically create sick systems. The problems that emerge there will be largely insoluble.

Where Life Is

"Pop" culture includes popular songs, however distributed, whether by CDs, concerts, radio or television. It includes popular images (for "style"), whatever their source or means of distribution (e.g., magazines, commercial advertising, how your friends dress and comport themselves). It includes popular ideas and ideologies, popular understandings, feelings, explanations, etc., however they circulate. And in a "modern" culture, they *will* circulate, since much depends on being in fashion, keeping up with the fads of the day.

So the "instructions" for how to be, how to do, what to think, what to have, and what to say (and how) will be explicit or implicit there.

Let's consider one of the most relevant examples. Most Americans have "a job." For most, this "job" is not an essential part of who they are or how they live. It is incidental. A means to an end. A "job" is what a person does to earn the money required to buy what they feel they deserve. Or what they feel they need to create or maintain an identity they desire.

Work is not a central aspect of life in our civilization. "Life" is what can be *bought* with what you *earn* at "work." Most "work" because they *have to*. Their lives are mainly what they can *buy* with what they earn at "work." What leaders face in their organizations, as the saying goes, is that people don't live to work, they work to live. What this means is that

- Most people will not be interested in your (or anyone else's) ideas about any great achievements. They will be interested in the paychecks and other benefits you provide them. But if they can't get their quasi-welfare at your place, they'll get it someplace else. That's the leader's challenge.
- "Work" is something they *have to* do; play or leisure is something they *get to* do. Life is pursued in leisure activities.

In order for anyone to pursue a goal such as being "the best" at anything, that pursuit has to be the driving force of their lives. It cannot be a hobby or an avocation. It has to be the core, the very trajectory, of their lives. In other words, if the role one has "at work" is not a vital part of one's life, there are two terrible consequences to think about. One is that the person has to accommodate to the fact that he or she is simply blowing off the major part of his or her life. They "put in their time." They go to idle while waiting for their real lives to begin. The quality of their lives thereby suffers. The media advertisers offer the solace of buying something—a "vacation," some cosmetics, some booze, better sex, more stuff, etc. And this is what people are offered in exchange for selling the bulk of their waking hours for years. Faust sold his soul. Many people sell their "time." But isn't it the same thing?

The second consequence is that the organization for which such "normal" people "work" can never be the best no matter what the top person buys to try to make this happen. The reason is that you cannot make a robust, prepared, extremely virtuosic organization when many are just putting in their time at work.

People at work who are not wholly awake or engaged at work will not contribute to causes that are larger than they are.

This circumstance stands as a formidable obstacle to any attempt to make a great organization, or to pursue any real achievement. Think on these:

- It isn't until one's "work" is a vital and central part of one's life that a person has a twenty-four hour quality of life.
- It isn't until people have a life at work that they put life into their work, one of the many challenges of leadership.
- When "life" begins after "work," as the beer commercial has it, the hours at work are merely thrown away, doing whatever is supposed to be done, but without anyone's "heart" in it.

ME-ISM

Let us not overlook the fact that the media and the pop culture that provides its content do not "cause" people to be the way they are. They merely refract the kinds of trends and movements in the most popular ways of doing, being, saying, having, and knowing they can detect. It will always be the case that a seducer requires a seducee.

We now inhabit a me-first (last and always) culture. A culture of radical individualism. Meaning essentially that my concerns and interests come first. And maybe there are no others that concern me at all. "Spoiled" children who complain about their families apparently have never learned that if they want a great family, it is their responsibility to make it so by sometimes putting the collective interests of the family before their own. Most native Americans had learned that the tribe comes before individual interests before they had learned how to talk. Our "me-ism" and our ferocity about immediate gratification may seem "natural" to us because that's all we have ever known: self-indulgence. More? Lasch's *The Culture of Narcissism*.

But this is not a book of social criticism. It's a book about leadership thinking. And what leaders have to be able to think about is how to mold a set of interdependent people out of a bunch of radical individualists. With psychologism came the focus on "self." And with affluence came the means of gratifying every self need. We live in a therapeutic environment, where much of what goes on in the culture is geared to providing solace and therapy to the individual selves that pay for it. As the commercial has it, "You deserve it." Apparently, we believe we deserve whatever we want or need at the moment. And, as long as we have the means, we'll buy it because there will be enterprises of all sorts stumbling over each other to minister to our momentary needs and interests.

It has to be the other way around in a high-performance *organization* (whether that is a community, a family, a team, or a civilization). A leader who can't turn that orientation around will never be able to pursue any real achievement.

Relativism

You may have noticed that many young people believe deeply that there is no authority higher than themselves. It's an orientation (attitude) that is widely and deeply nurtured by the pop culture.

Derived from some popularized "theories" in physics, this is basically the notion that any perception, any opinion, any explanation is as good as any other. Just because someone is far better informed, or is wiser, or is in a position of higher "authority" doesn't make that person's judgments any better than that of a person who isn't.

One corollary to think about. One consequence of this pervasive attitude of "relativism" is that of making everyone and every idea equal. Just because you're the "boss" (or the parent, or the teacher) doesn't make your opinions (even in math class) any better than mine. It's a way of raising "my" voice above all others by bringing theirs down.

It's subtle. But it's powerful. A leader who cannot neutralize or co-opt this attitude will fail. The contrary, of course, is not necessarily true. Parents and teachers and bosses can be as stupid as they are sometimes accused. But a failure to establish and abide by *some* standard of right and wrong makes losers of us all.

- The best "standard" for leaders? The fact that different interpretations have different (better or worse) outcomes. People may have a "right" to overeat their way to obesity. But we'll all have to pay for their "right" to self-destruction, including them.
- If such "rights" don't end where a person's obligations begin, it's merely a slide to the lowest common denominator. There was never a great organization or a great achievement that came from there.

Nonresponsibility

There are exceptions. There have always been exceptions. There will always be exceptions. But what we're trying to capture here are some deep tectonics in our culture (which is, indeed, the "pop" culture). Trends. Growing and spreading inclinations. Like an epidemic. It's not as bad as the worst-case scenario. But, without changes of direction, it will be. They are what future leaders will, increasingly, be faced with.

Increasingly, people are into personal "freedom." They don't want to be committed to anything that might seem to them to reduce their absolute freedom to do whatever they want to do whenever they want to do it.

So they are more or less likely to see "responsibility" as a quaint notion that could possibly reduce their "freedom," whether that responsibility is to themselves or to something or someone else. That attitude might be characterized thus: Don't tell me what my "responsibilities" are. Let's talk about my "entitlements," my privileges, my "rights." After all, those are owed to me. And I don't owe anybody anything.

Those who share this kind of attitude are aided and abetted by certain political ideologies. And ideologies always have ideologues—people, in this case politicians, though it might also be CEOs—who confirm the correctness of the attitude and cater to it. Witness ever growing-government regulations.

Young people, who are the heaviest consumers of the "pop" culture and its styles, seem to understand "freedom" as freedom from any constraints. And perhaps even more insidious, freedom *from* any responsibility for their actions (or their failures to act). Thus "nonreponsibility." They simply decline any responsibility for anything, in order to keep their "freedom."

This is seldom merely a passive attitude. Those who are seriously infected will be actively and even aggressively anti-accountability. Where they are concerned, they want no measures of performance but their own. They scoff at the idea of account-ability. "Duty" is not even in their lexicon.

Maybe all of that is a bad thing. Maybe it's okay. It is what is occurring.

The point is not to pass judgment on them, or even of the "pop" culture where they nourish and justify themselves. It is simply and emphatically that there is no real (intended) achievement without accountability. There is no high performance without responsibility. At minimum, responsibility to something bigger and better than oneself.

To claim certain "rights," but to disown any ownership of the consequences of exercising those rights describes a very sick system. You cannot build on it.

More thought-prodders?

- A person who has no particular purpose in life (except to avoid having one) will never understand why you have one.
- Being nonresponsible is the ultimate self-indulgence. It gets you off the hook, no matter the circumstances.
- The "pop" culture sells envy as the prime "motive," and consumerism as the answer to everything.

- In this kind of culture, those who do not cater to your whims are undesirables, to be avoided when denigration is not possible.
- The answer to nonresponsibility is victimage. And the answer to being victimized is to be actively irresponsible. Nice "catch."
- If you don't own the outcome, you can see no connection between what you do (or don't do) and how things turn out.
- Advertisers know how to target these people. Can a leader do less?

Protectionism

- If people are to be protected from those who would prey upon them, who will protect us from our protectors?
- Good intentions have consequences that are not necessarily good for those who are supposed to be helped by government regulations, by unions, by therapists, by any who would save us from ourselves.
- Seeing the world as adversarial makes one adversarial.

The good leader takes the position that the measure of his or her leadership lies in how well people are able to lead themselves. Do we have enough protectionism in place to make that impossible—in *your* place?

- Think on these things?
- A mediocre performer at work potentially jeopardizes the present and future well-being of every fellow-worker. Who protects *them* from his incompetence?
- Protectionism encourages victimage.
- Where leadership is most needed, it is probably most constrained.
- Competence is more in need of "protection" in our culture than is incompetence. Will the weeds protect the flower?

"Entertainment"

All of this probably brings to mind a whole long list of the obstacles to real achievement that are recycled and elaborated endlessly by the popular culture. Books have been written about them.

Here we might consider one more, knowing that you can, and will, extrapolate, bringing into your own thinking the obstacles from the popular culture that bear most directly or most heavily in your situation.

It is that the "pop" culture is mainly devoted to "entertainment." Nothing wrong with that. Until it becomes the predominant mind-food. Then a strange thing happens. The more one lives in the pure entertainment world, the less one is able to think for herself. The reasons are obvious: the images, the plots, and the themes are all built from one formula or another, with only minor variations. For example, all commercial advertising "works" because the premises hit their consumers' hot buttons. So the premise that "whiter teeth" will lead to more joyful romance is easy to swallow (pun intended). Or that you drink to "have fun" with your friends. Or that buying "Air Jordans" will enable you to jump higher. You get the point. If you comprehend any commercial ad, it is because its premises "work" for you.

You don't have to think about this. All the thinking required has already been done for you. "Entertainment" is a consumer sport. Ultimately, it eats away at whatever capability you had for thinking on your own.

So. Again, without passing judgment on whether this is a good thing or a bad thing, but is just the way things are, what all of this means is that the people who may need to be able to think at your place may not be able to do so. It isn't that they don't want to. Or don't claim to. It is that they *can't*.

Something to think about:

- People who can't think can readily be replaced by an impersonal system that can't think either, but is not nearly so high maintenance.

- The inability to think is not a "psychological" problem. It is a basic shortfall in simple but needed competence.
- How long does it take for a person to lose that capacity to such a degree that it cannot be rekindled?
- Investing time in people who can't, or won't, think is a waste of time. The ROI in people is the leader's most critical decision.
- Beginning with himself or herself. If you are one of them, how can you lead them?

The journey to real achievement is a way of life, not a destination. Those who have a contrary way of life have made the obstacles and barriers to real achievement into a way of life. The struggle for the hearts and minds of people is universal. In this our "pop" culture, as a leader you are up against some formidable opponents in this struggle, including the people themselves.

But that was the lesson from the story of Moses, wasn't it? If you have overcome these obstacles in yourself, you might then be able to figure out how to help others to overcome them. The journey to real achievement is the best journey they could ever take. Taking that journey with you is the best win-win others will ever encounter.

Chapter 11

Perversity

"PERVERSITY" IS AN obstacle to real achievement? That may seem perverse to you at the moment. But when you have finished with this chapter, you may be wondering why you wouldn't consider "perversity" as the toughest of all the obstacles you will have to deal with.

If you look it up in the dictionary, you will find that "perversity" refers to the illogic of what goes on in the world. In brief, it refers to the common experience of living in a world that frequently does not coincide with your expectations about it. It is what happens rather than what you hoped or expected was going to happen. It refers to the fact that people are inconsistent, always improvising, changing their minds, putting a spin here and there on what they heard or what they saw. "You" would be one of those "people." It refers to the fact that you apply your hypotheses about the world in that world as if there were some necessary connection between actuality and how you perceive it or expect it to be.

So "perversity" arises in the disconnect between outcomes you are certain you're going to get, and the actualities that produce contrary outcomes.

"Perversity" is what can be said to be at work behind every situation where your reaction is, "I can't understand how that happened!" It has three fundamental sources:

1. Neither other people nor the world you cohabit with them is obligated to be the way you think they are, or to behave in the way you expect them to. Your mind is not reality. It is only your take on reality.

2. The way other people see the world and think about it, and the way other people make decisions and take actions in the world is neither something you can control or predict with much accuracy. That's because those people have minds of their own and, like yours, those are flawed but independent of your reach. The short version? People are perverse *because* they think.

3. The world you live in with them is forever generating happenings and outcomes and effects other than what you intended. The three or four volumes of "Murphy's Laws" capture some of the perversity you will encounter. Add the electronics and other information and communication devices, and you'll have a surfeit of "perversity."

People Are Incompetent And People "Lie"

There can be no news there for you.

The catch you may not have thought of is that people lie to themselves all the time about their competence. And will therefore lie to you. Intentional lies can sometimes be detected. But the lies people tell themselves about themselves come into the mix looking just like facts. That kind of perversity is deep-rooted. Fixing it requires fixing the person's interpretations of who he thinks he is and what he "knows." If it's long-standing, it may not be fixable.

A person who is barely competent to do what has to be done will not have what it takes even to see what is in their own best self-interest. So large numbers of people pursue ways of being and doing that are not in their own best self-interests. A variation on an ancient Greek adage would be, "You cannot confer a benefit on a person who is incompetent to see the benefit in it." Now *there's* a leadership challenge, since leading people toward their own best self-interests is *the* dilemma for any good leader.

"Most People" . . .

If you have to deal with "people" (and who doesn't?), there is a fundamental dilemma. Most people are enough like other people that they can be put in the category of "people." But every person is different. The challenge is to know when to apply the "most people" category, and when to look for what makes a particular person an exception to the rules of how to account for "people."

About "people," there are some generalizations that hold reasonably well:

- Most people prefer a problem they can't solve to a solution they don't like. Many problems recur in organizations because the people who have them prefer them to the solution. Incompetence is a good example. Most people prefer the problems that occur as a result of their incompetence to the effort and changes required to become competent.

- Most people will promise you future performance, if they imagine they can gain something by doing so. Leaders make this impossible by measuring performance solely by performance. As Harold Geneen put it, " . . . words are words, explanations are explanations, promises are promises—but only performance is reality."

- Most people will end up being like and thinking like most people. They didn't set out to be "average." But that's where their comfort zone is. That's why most people are scornful of those few who try to be "better" than they are.

- Most people do not want to be accountable for the consequences of their actions or inactions. They'll abandon their responsibilities to anyone who will be responsible for them.

- Most people don't know what their best self-interests are. That's because they have no cause or aim in life. So they'll take immediate gratification over their own best self-interests anytime.

- Most people know some stuff. Most people assume that what they know is what they need to know. If they have no aim or purpose in life, that's good enough.

- Most people don't want what they need. They want what they want, whether that is good for them or not.
- Most people can prove to you any given day that in any conflict between emotion and intellect, emotion will put up the better fight.
- Most people behave in a way that confirms the proposition that no good deed (where they are concerned) will go unpunished.
- Most people can't understand something if their paycheck depends upon their not understanding it.

Leaders don't take any of this personally. It's just that "most people" are that way. People may be perverse. But their perversity is also the leader's reality.

If you want to have an understanding of what "most people" are like, you have to listen to the people-watchers. The more intelligent and the more insightful the better. You need to pick your intelligence sources very carefully, because there is no possibility you will ever get your own arms around "most people." You have to be a student of those people-watchers who have figured out what is common to large numbers of people, and what is more individual. Scott Adams ("Dilbert") would be a good example. P. J. O'Rourke would be another.

However, if you want to understand a particular individual, then it's up to you. You have to ask the right questions, make the right observations, and collect the evidence yourself. And how you understand another person as an individual will depend upon the *relationship* you have with her or him. How that person thinks, talks, or behaves for you will depend upon who *you* are. (Keeping in mind that we are who we are in relationship to others. You are not someone independently of the others you associate with. And vice versa.)

So when you are taking the measure of someone else, you need to remember that what you see there is as much a function of who you are as it is of who the other person is. That's why leaders take the caveat of "Know Thyself" seriously. They have to know what part of what they see is them, and what part belongs to the other person. A greatly underrated competence by executives and poor coaches.

Is there perversity even there? For sure. The other person may listen to you. But not to what you meant by what you said. They listen to what *they* meant by what you said.

Most people don't do what they *should* do. You need to be able to recognize the person who is an exception to this rule. Most people who buy lottery tickets don't seem to know that they are more likely to be struck by lightning than to win the lottery. If you come across a person who seems to play by the real probabilities rather than his own faulty take on the world, you know you may have a "keeper." If a person wants to know what you mean by what you say, there's an exception that may turn out to be very valuable. Most people are perverse in common ways. A person who is individually perverse may be more challenging to get along with. But it may indicate that the person has a mind of her own—a rather remarkable characteristic these days.

But most people are not as perverse as pop psychologists are. And then there are individuals who are not as perverse as pop psychologists are because they aren't regular consumers. It may seem to be easier to deal with "most people" because of their herd behavior. But you can't pursue real achievement if you are either a part of the herd, or the herder.

Here are some thinking challenges:

- Social movements—like unionization—don't originate in bad times. They originate when things are good and getting better. It's perverse. But is there a lesson for leaders here?
- Why do most people avoid living until they are told the end is in sight? Perverse, for sure. As the leader, how would you enhance people's lives at work, given this?
- Your rational arguments are not going to move people who waste their lives, marry the wrong person, have work they don't like, etc. What will?

Coping With Perversity

You may meet a person or two who believes you can cope with perversity by this or that strategy, all being very rational in construction. Well, they would be wrong. The logic of "perversity" is unlike any logic used by mathematics or by science or even economics. It is the logic of everyday life, which emerges out of our perversity. Computer programmers, who are themselves often very perverse, write code that is for the most part thoroughly linear and rational. For them, the occupational hazard is putting their minds to work in a logic that is alien to the logic of the human and social worlds. This may be why they are frequently not very good at human and social relationships. And if they are, then they may not be as good as other programmers.

How to cope with "perversity"? You may not like the answer.

The more conventional your thinking is, the more you will be victimized by all of the perversity that emerges from conventional thinkers as they engage each other in everyday life. People say what people say, and people do what people do, not because they are saying or doing what *you* think they should. But because they are saying and doing what *they* think they should—if they have even thought about it at all. What's "perverse" is what you do not, can not, control. Perversity, once again, lies in a disconnect between what happens and what you thought would happen, or should happen. Perversity thrives in how people deal with themselves, and with each other. You are, I am, one of those "people."

In the beginning, we are told, god created humans. She instructed the first human not to eat of "the fruit of the tree of knowledge." In the version I have of that story (which exists primarily as a teaching-learning instrument), that's what the two of them did. Never mind that there was some encouragement from the "serpent." That will always be the case. They did precisely what they were instructed not to do. That's perversity. You would think, wouldn't you, that if you didn't want people to do something, it would be easy and far cleverer to make their doing it impossible.

Maybe by putting the tree (or the humans) somewhere else. But if god can't get something done by instruction, having actually created the humans involved, how likely are you to be able to avoid such "perversity."

But, back to that other point. If you are absolutely "had by" a purpose in life, you be looked upon as not "normal." But it would be mainly your blindness to being so perverse as to have a "calling" in life that would produce followers. All great leaders have been "perverse." This is why other people follow them. Without *their* perversity, there would be no leaders.

What's reasonable is what makes sense to you. What is "unreasonable" to you is something that doesn't "make sense" to you. But where do historical change and progress come from? This is how George Bernard Shaw put it: "The reasonable man adapts to the world. The unreasonable man persists in getting the world to adapt to him. Therefore, all progress is due to the unreasonable man." Man or woman, it is the unreasonable person who makes a difference. That's what leaders do. If the level of your commitment to your vision does not appear "perverse" to the average person, then you don't have the level of commitment required to be a leader.

Perversity yields only to superior perversity. It does not yield to rational argument. When faced with stupidity, the best leadership strategy may be responding with something that will appear to those other people as really stupid. You win. Stupid people are not moved by intelligent argument or action. Have you tried it?

Perhaps the most potent perversity of all is that of not understanding something, or of misunderstanding it. The mistake that many managers make is taking the position that they "understand" everything. You can't fight perversity by feeding your ego. That only increases it. There are things that you will legitimately not understand. Push your non-understanding. It will minimally help others to clarify what they are saying (or doing). But you may need to do more than this. You may need to *not* understand what people say to you or what you observe going on. Randomly, unless you can figure out just the right tactical maneuvers for this, you may need to not understand. Or even to misunderstand. This forces other people to be less perverse.

It's perverse. But perversity yields only to superior perversity. You have to be capable of that superior perversity, as Sun Tzu and Machiavelli said long ago. If you're not, you will be victimized by it.

- Meet ignorance with ignorance.
- Meet intelligence with intelligence, strategy with counter-strategy.
- Meet indifference with indifference.
- Meet emotional arguments with emotional arguments that trump them.
- The world is not obligated to be like you see it. Or to function according to your needs or intentions.
- To the leader there is no "perversity." There is only the reality that challenges his or her competencies every step of the way. No time for frustration or commiseration. What the leader is learning is how to outwit the unexpected—that is, to *be* the perverse element.

Paying Heed

It's old, old wisdom. But if there is something you must achieve, then there are things that happen that deserve no attention. There are others that require some minimum attention. There are others that deserve your fiercest attention and the unreasonableness (or ruthlessness) with which you have to deal with them. It is those you must prepare for.

The Most Perverse Person. . .

The most perverse person in the world . . . is you.

Your life has to be relevant to your cause. Your cause has to be relevant to the people in the world who are capable of achieving your cause. That's why the order of things for leaders is *thinking, being, doing*.

If you can't overcome your own perversities, you cannot lead others out of theirs, no matter what recipe you use.

Most people don't know what their own best self-interests are. They may not even care. That's why there is a role for leaders. Leaders provide people with a glimpse (at least) of what their own best self-interests are. People will resist this. Leaders make it necessary. If you think in the conventional mainstream, if you *are* a part of the mainstream, then that's the only place you could lead people to. Leading them out of their perversities will require superior perversities. If you made it, then it required your superior perversities. Even a habit will win unless you can attack it with overwhelming perversity.

So, some thought-prodders to pull us on?

- If you are not capable of meeting the perversity of the world you live in with superior perversity, you will be a victim of that world.
- In order to make that world a "victim" of the best self-interests of the people in it, their leader has to be more powerfully perverse than it is.

Or, for fun, some variations on "Murphy's Laws"?

- When you are served a meal aboard an aircraft, the aircraft will encounter turbulence.
- Everything takes longer than it should, except sex.
- You cannot tell for certain ahead of time which side of the bread to put the butter on.
- Any change you impose will bite you back.
- If there is a wrong way to do something, then someone will do it.
- "Gwen's Law": Do not join encounter groups. If you enjoy being made to feel inadequate, call your mother.

Or, perhaps, by challenging a real achiever.

PART III

THAT WAS A longggg wind-up. But a necessary one.

It is not your "understanding" of something that counts when your leadership is called for. It is the *depth* of your understanding. It is your habits of thought that take over when the heat's on. So all of the preceding is intended to provide you with some *habits* of thought, and some ways of thinking about certain key factors that will add to your mental horsepower and thus your performance . . . as a leader.

All of this wind-up may have strained your patience. But far better that than being in a critical leadership situation and not being able to call upon the mental resources you need. The better you can think about the things that need thinking about *out of habit*, the more compelling your leadership performance will be.

Now if you're mentally provisioned, we want to move on. What we want to get immersed in now are the strategies and tactics for real achievement. If you want to achieve something really worthwhile, or if you want to lead the making of a high-performance organization, you will need all of the leadership you can muster. What's just ahead is a clear description of what's required, of the tools you will need if you are to become a compelling leader, and if those you lead (including yourself) are to be successful in the pursuit of real achievement.

When you are standing there one day in the future, your leadership called for, and all around you are people waiting for you to provide the needed leadership, it's too late to consult the instructions. What you have not previously made a fundamental part of your thinking can play no part.

What follows will be optimally useful to you if you have seriously and with effort thought through the foundations offered up in the pages that have preceded this. Your capacity to understand and to use the tools that follow depend upon it. That's why that came first and what follows can be fully usable only now.

The next two chapters—sort of the "heart" of this guidebook—are about "what it takes" to successfully pursue a mission, a great achievement, or a high-performance organization. You won't get far without *what it takes*. So equip yourself with what it takes. Or locate the problem where it exists—in any shortfall you may have with respect to what it takes.

CHAPTER 12

What It Takes

HERE'S A RATHER remarkable fact that may deserve your attention.

It is that those who have most frequently risen to the top ranks of leadership in past history have done so without a current recipe book to guide them. Neither Genghis Khan nor Tecumseh ever attended a Maxwell seminar or read a Tom Peters article on the subject of "leadership." How was it possible for them, and hundreds of others, to provide the kind of leadership they did without our store of "knowledge"?

At the same time, there seems to be little evidence that those who take courses and attend seminars or read books on the subject of "leadership" ever gain much of a reputation for having changed the course of history—in large *or* small ways.

What's the lesson here? That those who made their mark didn't have the advantage of our 10,000 or so books on the subject but did so anyway? That those who have available the world's accumulated "wisdom" about leadership don't seem to be able to make much of a difference *with* that hyped advantage? If we really "know" so much about leadership after all these millennia of practicing it, why do we need so many books, so many articles, and so many seminars about it?

How can we understand this? People who never knew what we

presume to know about this subject excelled as leaders. Most of those who have 10,000 books on management and leadership available to them don't seem to deliver that much more or that much better leadership for all of the time and money spent on acquiring the "secrets" of how to do it. How ought we understand this?

The lesson may be this: If you're standing at the site (in the middle of the circumstances that require a leader), and there is either no one else to do it—or perhaps the others seem less qualified—you're it. There are two prerequisites. One is that there has to be an opportunity for the kind of leadership you could uniquely provide. The other that all of the other possible candidates for the role would have to be viewed by potential followers as less desirable than you are. In the opinion of the followers, the person chosen to be the "leader" is the least-worst candidate. That's the reality. *Leadership is a role*, not a person. You have to be chosen, first by the circumstances, then by your followers.

What's important here? You will not be "chosen" as a result of how much you "want to" be the leader. Or as a result of how much you know about "leadership." If there is a need, and there is no "better" choice, you will get the role. Then it's a matter of how good a job you do in the eyes of the followers, given their interests, as they understand them. If this is not crystal clear to you, you may want to revisit the story of Moses. Or of Churchill.

There is more to consider here. Most of the people who are in charge of other people are appointed. They are not selected by the people they have "authority" over. These people are therefore not "leaders." Not yet. They are at most "heads" of some hierarchical arrangement which puts them at the "top" and others "below" them. They get there for many reasons having little to do with their competencies. They may have "subordinates," depending upon whether or not those "subordinates" want to play that game. But followers are not appointed. They are earned. And a "superior" who does not have followers is not, by definition, a "leader."

Being placed in a position of authority does not guarantee anyone's ability to provide leadership. In fact, the ways in which people get to those positions guarantees that a great many of them will fail as heads of whatever they are "heads." They fail for the reason that when their leadership was required, they didn't have what it took to provide the leadership needed. Not that they weren't sincere or didn't really "try." As Charlie Brown put it: "How can we fail when we're so sincere?"

Chief executives conventionally give themselves too much credit for their successes, and not enough for their failures. A lofty position does not qualify you or anyone else as a *leader*. A "desire" to achieve something cannot underwrite your getting there. You have to have *what it takes* when the time to perform arrives.

With that in mind, let's move on to consider "what it takes."

"Luck" And Preparation

Strange bedfellows those two, right? You can't really prepare for "luck." And you can't depend on luck to substitute for preparation. But you're probably not going to like this anyway. You've been exposed to gargantuan doses of fluff and folklore and "new think" about leadership. A little reality may not go down as easily as some of that fairy dust may. But this small dose of reality will serve your purposes far better when the chips are down and it's time to perform.

Consider, first, the fact that you have to "get lucky" to be needed as a leader. Churchill was a fairly mediocre government functionary, and never had great success as a politician. But it's hard to imagine that anyone else could have carried the Brits through the early part of WW II the way he did. Consider too the fact that we will never know if someone else could have provided far better—or far worse—leadership. That is always determined from historical retrospective. There is never a test in advance of what the outcome might have been with different leadership.

So he was "lucky" that the Second World War came along when it did. Otherwise, he would have been a minor government administrator, never remembered. A lot of things had to fall into place for him just to have the opportunity to provide his unique brand of leadership. A lot of things which he had absolutely no control over. That's one aspect of the "luck" part.

General Swartzkopf might well have retired unknown to the American public had not the Gulf War occurred when it did. The circumstances and the timing have to conspire for there to be any historical leader known to us. Somewhat like Caesar, Napoleon was a great field general, but a lousy politician. For every composer who "led" music off in a different direction, and for every artist who "led" art off in a different direction, there were countless composers and artists who are mostly unknown to us today. There may have been better business leaders than Jack Welch. But they did not serve as CEO at GE during the same period of time that he did. They may have lived and died when their unique capacities for leadership were either unneeded or unrecognized.

Going by history, this means that if you intend to be a great leader, you have to be in the right place at the right time. You have to have "the right stuff" (what is needed by the situation and by the people in that situation). And you have to be recognized by the observers, the pundits, and the historians as a leader who made a difference. The point is that you have to be "lucky" in three ways all at the same time.

Even though it is frequently pitched to you that way, there is no such thing as "generic" leadership. There is not some set of "secrets" that will enable you to be "the" leader no matter the timing, the circumstances, or a widely-enough recognized need for "your" leadership. Leadership is a *role* that emerges from a need for your brand of leadership that is widely recognized by those who would be the followers.

This changes the whole idea of "preparation," doesn't it?

In our time, in our culture, you've been led to believe that you can have far more control over outcomes than you do. It's been made easy for you to believe that if you read about the "seven" secrets or 21 "laws" of leadership, you'll thereby be able to make things turn out the way you want them to. That would be nonsense. Believe it or not, the world does not conspire to make you successful just because you paid money to be privy to certain "secrets" or "rules" that are going to make you successful no matter what happens in the real world. Every investment guru has had a "theory" about the stock market. Sooner or later, they were all wrong. So are the "secrets" mongers. Every leader has been who he or she was. Sheer luck has to get the credit when a person is simply playing out who he or she is on the world's stage. The *preparation* part of it occurs when you undertake to make yourself into the kind of person who is going to be needed by a particular group of people, by a particular situation, at a particular time. The leadership provided will always be unique to a particular person. Abraham Lincoln wrote: "I will study and get ready, and some day my chance will come."

The person is not interchangeable with other persons. The circumstances are never the same elsewhere or at a later date. Followers never seem to want the same characteristics in their leaders as they did last year. What you prepare for is the emergence of the need for the kind of leadership you can provide. In an organization, you can help this along—immensely. But you cannot force people to follow you. Knowing you as you do, would *you* follow you? Not perfect, but still a good litmus test. If you wouldn't, why would they?

You have to be prepared *if* you are called. This book is about how to prepare yourself to answer the call to leadership. There is no such thing as leadership apart from the role. This will become more and more obvious to you as we move on.

Sorry. I said you might not like this reality check. You can go on believing the hype, or you can "get real." And, just so you will know, no significant leader in history ever bought the "hype" about leadership. They understood that the only test of leadership is the reality test—the outcomes of your performance in a leadership *role*.

"Being Had" By Your Cause

On the list of what it takes, the second most challenging for leaders is this: It isn't "having" a vision or a mission that is compelling to followers. It is your *being had by* a vision, mission, or goal that appears worthy to those would-be followers. Joan of Arc would be a good example. As would Bill Gates. Or Shaka Zulu. Or any other of our great historical examples.

There is a significant difference between merely "having" a purpose and being had by a purpose. Most people abandon their espoused purposes in life, as everyone knows. Talk is cheap. If the road is a tough one, and if it requires real effort or sacrifice, most people won't follow the talk. They'll follow the walk. The more you are had "by" your cause, the more *necessity* there is for you to see it through. A follower has to determine two things: Is this the person we need? Does this person have *what it takes* to get us where he or she intends to go? Much of that "what it takes" comes from being in the thrall of a purpose or cause which seems to other people more important to that potential leader than does his or her own life. You are compelling to others because they cannot imagine you could escape your duty to your own cause.

So if you are not "had by" a cause or purpose which is bigger than you are, what can you do? You can do what leaders have always done: *perform* it. It is your performance that matters, not your intentions and not your feelings. It is only your performance that others can see. They will infer all the rest of you from your performance. Everyone wins. If you turn in a convincing performance of being had by a cause that is bigger than you are, you will in time be had by that cause.

- A professed purpose is nothing but a tenuous promise.
- People have been taken in by promises before. Why would they believe you?
- If you're willing to stake your life on your cause because you seem to have no choice, others may be willing to follow you.
- Being "had by" your cause is part of what it takes.

Enthusiasm

Unflagging enthusiasm for your cause and your path and your days of struggle with your followers. Required.

Leadership is not a rational enterprise. It changes the status quo, which is where rationality has its stranglehold. So rational enthusiasm is not going to capture people's hearts. Irrational enthusiasm for your cause—no matter what the present circumstances—is what's required.

If you haven't got it, perform it until you do.

- Enthusiasm begets enthusiasm.
- Have you ever come across a great leader who expressed to his or her followers doubts about their joint cause?
- If you are totally had by your cause, you will be enthusiastic about all the right things.
- Enthusiasm: attack, attack, attack!
- What you are not incorrigibly enthusiastic about won't gather much enthusiasm.

Who's Going To Make It Happen?

About this you have to be perfectly clear. And your clarity and single-mindedness about this must be inescapably obvious to everyone else.

The distance between your vision and future reality is the greatest distance there is. If you think that you are the one who is going to make it happen, that you are single-handedly going to make your cause a reality, you have just punched the ticket that guarantees your failure. It is your disciples, your followers, who have to make it happen.

With your leadership, of course. But leadership doesn't do anything in the world. Leadership is about people, about strategies that people can put their hearts and their minds to. Unless your enterprise is entirely dependent on you (as in individual competition in the Olympics), it is everyone else around you who have to make it happen. Actually, even in that situation, it is how capable you are of being led by yourself that counts. Not you with the purpose. But the person inside you who does whatever it takes to carry out that purpose.

- If you are competent to attract, select, and cast the people who can and will make it happen, it can happen.
- Even the Lone Ranger needed Tonto to make it happen.
- Patton never won a single battle by himself. The leader's work is not fighting the battle.
- The leader's work consists of surrounding herself or himself with the people who are capable of, and totally committed to, making it happen.
- What it takes is whatever it takes.

The Four Covenants

Between you and these key people, there have to be in place four covenants—four agreements that are indispensable to what it takes.

1. The first of these is that each of those key persons has to be dedicated to being the best there is at what they do. This means that they study their role and its context, and that they improve their performance in their role everyday . . . forever. This has to be necessary for them—either because of the way they're built, or because they are given no option by you, their leader. If that person is not the best there is in that person's role (at least in the industry if not in the country), it has to be because they are not *competent* enough to get to that level. Or because there simply was not enough *necessity* to do so, personal or imposed.

- Leadership lesson? There can be no other reason for shortfall.

2. The second covenant is that they are committed to learning how to provide compelling leadership to others. They do this by the surest route there is—by being the best followers there have ever been. The best leaders will come from the pool of the best followers.

- The critical *followership* lessons?
- Learning when to follow, when to lead, and when to get out of the way.
- Making your boss successful—no matter what.
- Carrying out your role in the mission, whatever it takes.

3. The third "covenant" is that each of those key persons must function at all times as the *chief steward* of your mission. This means that each of those persons owns 100% of the responsibility for making it happen. No finger-pointing. If there are four such key people, each does not own 25% of the responsibility. Each owns 100% of the responsibility. If someone drops the ball, another picks it up and runs with it. There is no time for editorializing. There is no one in the bleachers or the press box. They are all on the field, and they're either playing the game to accomplish what needs to be accomplished or they are not. The only judgment that counts is the one they make of their own performance. And then what they do about it.

- There is no way to build a "team" when each does not own 100% of the responsibility not only for her own performance, but for the achievement of the whole.
- This is not "delegation." This is *ownership*.
- If they don't own the outcomes, you do. And you can't.
- It isn't your reality that is going to make it happen. It is theirs. If they haven't got what it takes, it isn't going to happen.
- Max De Pree refers to this as "abandoning yourself to the strength of others." As if you had any choice.
- Your task: to make sure they are the people who have what it takes.

4. The fourth covenant is this—each of those persons who has a role in making it happen has to equip and prepare himself

to take on a role like yours and perform it better than you do. That might well be in your organization. But you would never get into the maneuvering involved if they're after your job. The issue is whether or not they equip themselves to outperform you. In order to do this, they have to see your world as you do. They have to see your world well enough to make you successful in that world.

This is how people develop themselves. They look for the best role models in the world and go to school there. If that is not you, it should be. But if you're not the best there is in your role, and they use you as their role model, the future of your organization is already in doubt.

You want them to *compete* with you and your performance in your role. You do not want them "climbing *your* ladder." You want them to compete with you as one of the best there is in your role anywhere. To do this, you have to be one of the best there is in your role. Those pushes and pulls are all a part of what it takes.

- What you can't teach, you can't learn.
- You will know how capable they are of keeping their covenant with you by the quality of the questions they ask—of themselves, of each other, and of the best there have ever been.
- How well they keep this covenant with you will be a measure of how well they are going to make covenants with their own people.

The aim is the performance of the organization. You cannot get that without the "multiplier" produced by this way of doing things.

And If You Don't Have . . .

If you don't have or can't muster these prerequisites of what it takes, here is how you should assess the problem:

- That you were not capable of recruiting, selecting, casting, or seducing people into the joint pursuit of your cause.
- If you have to abandon your cause for want of competence to make it happen, you should move aside and put someone in your role who can.
- If your people are not capable of fulfilling their roles in the pursuit of your cause, that's probably because you are not capable in yours.
- For people who don't have the heart for real achievement, there must be some form and some level of necessity for getting there anyway. That applies to you first. And then to them.
- And if they finally can't or won't, get someone who will.

Much of this is about "commitment." The lesson for leaders is this:

- In reality, there is only one measure of commitment. And that is *performance.*
- In reality, that is the only measure of any promise, any "words." *Performance.*

This is a brief look at part of what it takes. Unlike other books you may have read, these requirements are not merely helpful things to *do.* If you don't put in place these conditions, it's likely you won't have what it takes.

And always remember: *hope is not a method.*

CHAPTER 13

More Of *What It Takes*

YOU'VE BEEN TOLD over and over again how easy it is. All you have to do is buy this book or take that seminar, and it's a done deal. A few "steps," a few "secrets," you're practically there. But you may have noticed that there are very few people (or organizations) seriously committed to becoming "the best" (one perspective on what we're up to here). And fewer still who have stayed the course.

We've examined some reasons for this—all of the misleading myths and panaceas peddled by those who prey on our (your?) wishful thinking. If it were all that "easy" to become "the best," you would already be there.

It might take 20 years for an apprentice to really learn his craft, and that's working at *learning* it every day. Concert pianists have not read a book on "learning to play the piano like a virtuoso in 24 hours." It's hard work. It requires diligence, total engagement, and awesome work and effort. What we're talking about here is far more complex and dynamic than being a concert pianist or a basketball star. Look at the best at doing anything in the world. Then multiply what that required of them by a factor of ten or more. That's what would be required just to have a shot at it.

It takes courage and commitment. You have to develop, day by day, what it takes to perform with the best. No one has ever overestimated the difficulty of what has to be done, of what it takes. You're not going to be told how difficult it is by the celebrities.

Difficult beyond imagination doesn't sell books. "Easy" does. "Leadership for Dummies." Would you buy that? If you put a spin on reality, it's no longer reality.

So here we are. Looking at more of the indispensable aspects of "what it takes." Reality bytes.

Reprise

What have we unpacked so far?

- The need for a leadership *role*, and the possibility that you might fit it. You have to be at the right place, at the right time, with the right "stuff."
- Putting together (including yourself) the competent and passionately committed people who can and will make it happen.
- A compelling cause that has them all in its thrall. They are "had by" the cause to which they are dedicated.
- If you have the four "covenants" working throughout your organization, it will perform well in any posture: bottom-up, top-down, side-to-side.
- There is no fairy dust . . . that works.
- If you imagine you are interchangeable with anyone else who might take up the current panacea, you probably are.
- On the other hand, if you think you already know it all, you probably don't yet know what you *need* to know.
- *Methods don't do anything.* In the same way that "Talk does not cook rice."
- [Your turn]

Moving on . . . >

A Robust Plan

What else does it take? It takes a "robust" plan. Not a financial forecast. Not a plan for the next quarter's (or the next year's) numbers. But a plan for how you and your followers are going to get from where you are to where you have to get to.

So what does it mean—a "robust" plan? This is what it means:

- It means you must have a clear and comprehensive understanding of exactly what it's going to be like when people get there.
- It means that you must be able (might as well do it) to write the story (in detail) of how you got from where you were to where you got to.
- In doing this, you will have identified the key roles that were required to make it happen.
- And in doing *that*, you will have identified the competencies and other qualifications required to carry out those roles that made the story turn out the way it did.
- This story, with the people, the circumstances, and the plot and themes that accounted for how you got from where you were to where you had to get to constitutes the bare bones of your robust plan.
- You "flesh it out" by putting in place the business plan that is going to pay for and otherwise underwrite your pursuit of real achievement—a high-performance organization.

Merely being successful (i.e., "making money") is a conventional aim that goes nowhere. It isn't until you have a unique destination that you put yourself on the path of real achievement. You differentiate yourself by competing with and outperforming the best organizations there have ever been. If that is not your aim, then you don't need a plan. All you have to do is ride the currents like everyone else.

A "robust" plan means that every person and every system in your organization is healthy, competent, capable, and prepared for what is expected and for what is not expected. In terms of competence, it means that you have excess capacity at every position in your organization. It means that you actually believe in "continuous improvement," which can be sustained only if every person, every system, and every process performs better today than it did yesterday. At any age, in any role, it means that if there is not significant learning today, you will be falling behind tomorrow. It means, simply, that every day is like a "dress rehearsal," deliberately preparing for a perfect performance tomorrow.

It means that everyone knows what the plan is, what part of it they own, and why their fulfillment of their role is necessary. Otherwise, they have to get off the train and make room for someone who can, and will.

In a robust plan, there is no place for an irrelevant or unnecessary role. And there is no place for mediocrity.

Your plan has to seem to your people like *the* plan that is actually going to get you from where you are to where you are going. And, as we have seen, *you* have to be seen by your people as the only person who could pull this off—their *leader*.

- Canned plans, no matter how expensive they are, don't (and can't) work.
- You have to *invent* the plan that fits your story, that fits you, that fits those who are going to make it happen, and that fits the only world in which it has to happen—the "real" world.
- A "robust" plan is one people have to invent for their circumstances, which they can then improvise on to keep the story going in the right direction.
- What you can't imagine you can't realize. The plan is what has to happen to get you from your vision to its realization.

Your plan is part of *what it takes*. You will be no more successful than your plan is "robust."

On Telling The Story

People have to *experience* (even if only vicariously) this place where you intend to go. That requires a story. *Star Trek* takes you where no one has gone before. Your story has to be at least as compelling. And you?

What enables truly great leaders is their ability to tell the story of how something that has not yet happened—is going to happen. A compelling story of how remarkably better for everyone who makes the journey it is going to be. The story of how—together—you and they are going to bring this off. Chamberlain's talk to the "mutineers" near the beginning of the film *Gettysburg* is an example. Columbus's speech to his men aboard ship when they want to mutiny is another (the film is *1492*). Jack Welch was a story-teller, but was probably outdone in the long-run by Nucor's Ken Iverson.

If you are had by a great and worthy cause, people want to be a part of your story. And they want to be responsible for bringing it off by telling their part of the story.

- Stories are powerful stuff.
- We live by them—you, me, all the rest of it.
- Everything depends upon whose story we are in.
- Stories are compelling if they are told by compelling leaders. A compelling leader is the one who will make the story "come true," whatever it takes.
- These people you need will either be in your story or some one else's. If it is to their benefit, it should be yours.

Power

You gotta have power.

No matter how much "charisma" you may have or persuasiveness you can muster, it is not enough. You have to have the prerogative to say what will be, and who the players will be. You have to have the power to organize the place—the people and the processes—as you deem necessary. You have to have the power to change things—according to you as the primary author of the story that will be told. Of course people may have their say. And the more competent they are, the more you need to pay heed to what they say.

But there can be only one leader. If that's not you, then you don't have one. Other people must be capable of leading themselves, and of leading those who are going to make their part of it happen. But they don't want to follow a person who will automatically defer to them in order to be liked—as may be the case in poorly-instrumented "participative management." They want to follow someone who is more passionately determined to achieve than they are. They want your strength, your certainty, your dedication, your decisiveness, and your relentless determination. They want to go, not with the person who can "see" the future, but the person who is going to make the future. Paradoxically, they want to follow the person who has the power—and the will—to include them or exclude them. The person who knows what roles are needed to make it happen, and to cast them in just the right role.

All that takes power.

How will they know you are the right choice for them? By whether or not you exercise over yourself the kind of power that makes a difference. This is what they sense they lack. When they see it in another, they are ready to follow. If you are the one with the loftiest and most worthy cause, that had better be you. Otherwise, they will follow the loser.

Nothing guarantees your success. The best you can do is to surround yourself with the people who are competent enough, and determined enough, to provide *whatever it takes* to carry out your cause.

- Being "had by" a great and worthy cause empowers you.
- Demonstrating invariant self-leadership seduces others to your cause.
- It is power over themselves and their destiny that empowers others, never your power *over them*. Making that happen is fundamental to a robust "plan."
- The best leaders *always* have the best followers, and vice versa.
- You may need to use your power to get there, but it is when those other people have the power, the competence, and the will to make it happen that it begins to happen.

Staying The Path

Making change is easy. Making the right changes that are then sustained is far more difficult. Ask those many who have failed. Or those few who have succeeded.

Basically, what's required is that the people who are going to make it happen have to *own* the problem(s) of making it happen. They have to *own* the accomplishment, not just the activities. If they don't own the outcome(s), the effort will not be sustained, and those outcome(s) will not be maintained.

To stay the path, the problems encountered there and the outcomes of how they are dealt with have to be "owned" by the people who are making it happen.

Leadership is not owning the problem. It is owning the problem of casting in the right roles the people who have to own the problem.

That's what your power is for. Not to wallow in. But to enable you to become a wise and prudent radical decentralizer. That is, make sure that the person or the people who ought to own the problem do, in fact, own it.

Perseverance

If you don't persevere, you will never know what could have been accomplished.

All of your explanations of why it didn't happen are as fanciful as they are irrelevant.

The only measure is what you accomplished. If you let yourself off the hook, others will follow your lead. If you have an explanation which is better than real achievement, you are not a candidate for the kind of leadership we're talking about here.

[I once met a CEO who was convinced that his whim of the day was a good enough plan. Well, it was. It was good enough to make his organization the worst performer in the industry. Of course he blamed his people. Lesson? If you're shooting yourself in the foot because you don't have what it takes, don't persevere.]

Communication

It may sound like a ho-hum subject. But it turns out to be the core subject, the one that is *always* involved. Here's why:

- The way your mind works determines how you think.
- How you think determines who you *are.*
- Who you are determines what you will do, and how you will do it.
- And how you "communicate" determines the way your mind works.

That fairly well covers it. But some more detail may be useful.

- There is something about the way your mind works that leads you to pay attention to certain things, and to ignore others. What you pay attention to, and how (your interpretations of those things), will constitute your picture of reality. Your eyes and your ears work for your mind. Not the other way around.
- Or, you may seek to gather certain information about that "reality" by asking questions or by inquiring into things that do not come running to you. Through questions and critical observation, you may elicit some "intelligence" that reconfigures your understanding of what's going on.
- Both are forms of communication—the critical factors in how you "communicate." You will never be better informed than your routine strategies enable you to be. Your "picture" and your assessment of the reality around you will be a function of how well you can inform yourself.
- On this side of things, a great communicator is one who continuously restructures his mind to fit the real world

rather than trying to restructure the world to fit his "minding" of it.
- It matters whose *ideas* you expose yourself to, and it matters even more whose ideas you fall in love with. These will be the architectural framework for the way your mind works.

That's merely the "input" side. Not only does how you think direct you to what to pay attention to. The way you think will also determine how you interpret everything you observe or everything you hear or read. Shortfalls of performance are always ultimately traceable to inadequate or faulty thinking. What determines the kind of leadership you might be able to provide is how you think about the things that need thinking about.

How you think is a cumulative consequence of how you have "communicated" in the past. Your ability to think in the future will be a cumulative consequence of how you "communicate" today. That should make it for you the core subject.

In spite of all the flap-flap that we get engaged in every hour of every day, most communication—at least most of the communication that makes a real difference—is what goes on when you talk to yourself. Keeping in mind that most people pay more attention to what they say to themselves than they do of what you or others say *to* them. And that what they will protect with all the defenses they can muster is their view of reality. Their view of reality is not your view of reality. Productive communication is what goes on when you're out to figure out what the differences are and why your own view of reality may be wrong. "Intelligence" lies in knowing what other people view as reality, not what you view as reality.

Because that's a matter of persuasion or influence. Many people think that is what communication is mainly about—persuading or influencing someone else, or trying to convince them that what you know is what they ought to know. It's far more about having the capacity to be influenced by the world or by certain others. It's far more about having the capacity to be advantageously influenced by the world, or by others.

There is, of course, that other side of things—trying to sway other people in the direction of their own best self-interests, whether they know what those are or not, or even whether they care or not. But the ability to persuade others, to influence others, to take up a just cause the results of which are in their own best self-interests, this can be readily dealt with, as follows:

- Your heart must belong to your cause.
- Your words must come from your heart, whether you are talking to other people or to yourself.

Since "communication" is always an issue, it will appear again and again in these pages. But let us consider here two further ways you may want to be able to think about communication.

One is the simple fact that *what you can't understand, you won't understand.* What this means is that the limits of your mind are the limits of your world.

Each of us has to understand the world the way our own mind makes possible and necessary. The world is what it is. What happens is what happens. People are who they are, and they do what they do. All of this we have to see, or hear or read about. But our individual understanding of all these things comes down to the interpretations we make. You will always and inescapably function as you interpret the world, not the world itself.

That's why the leader's primary instrument of leadership is his or her own mind. The more capable your mind, the more successful your leadership. It is made of communication. It comes down to how good you are at informing yourself, how good you are at acquiring the "intelligence" and the interpretations you need to underwrite your success.

The other is the flip side. What other people can't understand, they won't understand. That's always square one. Their interpretations of what you say are enabled and constrained by *their* minds. Being able to influence others requires you to start with the workings of those minds on which your words will fall. What you cannot ask will produce no answer useful to you.

We all have two enemies. One is the way our own minds work. The other is the way others' minds work. They're either working for you or against you. Where words and communication are concerned, there is no neutral ground.

Some thought-prodders:

- Here's an old saw. You must say what you mean and you must mean what you say.
- That requires you to understand what you mean—not in terms of the words, but in terms of what is to be accomplished.
- And that requires a tacit understanding on your part and the part of others that there are significant consequences for any failure to accomplish what is explicit or implicit.
- Communication doesn't *do* anything. It should never, ever be taken as an end in itself. It is the consequences or the outcomes that matter. Not the words. Not the agreements or the disagreements. But the consequences.
- Leaders focus on the outcomes, the accomplishment, not the words, not the chatter.
- If people don't say what they mean, or if they do not mean what they say, they cannot be a part of your endeavor. That would be especially true of you.
- If you want to know something, you may have to ask the person who knows, and who has a great and worthy purpose that absolutely depends on knowing that.
- What people mean by what they say is what they *do*. That includes you.
- Every human enterprise has to be conducted by communication.
- Verbiage is verbiage. The reality is in the consequences, the measurable outcomes.
- A mind is an ongoing product of communication.
- Words that do not come from your heart will never engage the hearts of others.
- If you are not a servant of your cause, you will be a victim of whatever words are aimed at you.

- A person's mind and the way a person communicates are two aspects of the same thing. Consider what this means to you.
- Choose your mental diet carefully. That's who you will be.

In communication, there are two basic maneuvers: making a statement and raising a question. Asking the right questions will take you further—and with more compatriots—than will telling, no matter how much you know. Isn't that consistent with *your* experience?

And a question permits you to try again to figure out what you want to say. A statement closes everything down, except for explanations and arguments about who is right or wrong.

Sometimes words are more or less adequately *referential*. But words—and every other mode of communication—are always *consequential*. Leaders play for the required or desired consequences. Never for the opportunity to play yawp-yawp with people who do not have their eye on the consequences.

The conditions of real achievement always come down to matters of communication. Your competence at gathering the intelligence you need to pursue your aims. Your competence at processing that intelligence (your ability to think about what needs thinking about). And your competence to draw others to the level of performance necessary to achieve your mission. If you don't seem to be getting to where you need to go, check first how good you are at those three things. You can't fix the world. You can't fix other people. But you can fix your own shortfalls. For example, if you "need to have a meeting," what's caused the "problem" is most likely some failure or incompetence in communication. Can you fix that in a meeting? Or does that have to be fixed in some other way?

There are many paths to "success." But there is only one way to be the best at what you do. And that is—by unwavering commitment to be the best.

And by having what it takes to stay the path of getting there. For those who pursue real achievement, what it takes is whatever it takes, beginning with the ability to *think* precisely about what it takes, and then to *be* what it takes, so as to be able to *do* what it takes.

It seems that the only thing that holds us back is not having what it takes, right?

What leaders know: The "meaning" of anything whatever—a thought, an idea, a question—can be deduced only by the consequences. Only what people did about what was said. If you want to know what you mean by what you say, look to the consequences. Communication takes us where it goes. Better to be the master rather than the victim, wouldn't you say?

PART IV

Some Tools For Making It Happen

The two indispensable tools for making it happen we have dwelt on at length in the preceding pages are:

1. How you *think*. If you can't think the way you need to think in order to put together all of the pieces of this puzzle, you'll never get it put together in a way that will actually get you where you want to go.
2. Who you *are*. Who you are is the second most necessary tool you have available to you. If who you *are* isn't the kind of tool you need to make it happen, you need to change that first.

Most people skip over these "soft" issues as if they weren't very important. That's one of the reasons why most people fail at this. These two—how you think and who you are—hold up all the rest of it. These are the master tools. If they are not right, you cannot make any of the other tools work like they need to work. No tool is any better than the person who wields it.

Too many people are eager to begin with what to *do* and the tools and techniques to do it with. But no tool or technique is optimally effective without the master tools—how you *think*, and who you *are*.

The "Right" Tool For The Right Task

A Phillips screwdriver won't work on a slot-head screw. It's tough to drive a staple with a hammer. A master carpenter has a tool for every purpose. An amateur has a few standard tools and tries to make them work them work for every purpose.

So it is with amateur managers. They pick up a few tools from their limited "experience," or from a casual reading of a business magazine or from attending a seminar, and try to force them to fit every new situation they encounter. If dentists did their work the way amateur managers do theirs, they'd have a couple of all-purpose drills and maybe a pair of pliers.

Amateur managers define the problem in terms of the tools they have personally but accidentally acquired in the past. Leaders acquire or invent the tools they need to fit the circumstances. They let the situation or the problem define the tools or techniques needed, rather than defining the problem by the tools they happen to have available. They look at "problems" as an opportunity to learn something, rather than merely as an opportunity to apply something they already know.

Whether a tool or a technique will work in a present situation is not guaranteed by the fact that it worked in some situation in the past. The amateur manager looks for why the present situation looks like a previous one. The professional manager looks for what makes the present situation *different*. Amateurs fail by applying a "success paradigm" that seemed to have worked for them before.

So a leader is a tool-*finder* as well as a *tool-maker*. She realizes that unconventional situations require unconventional tools. Amateur managers let the tools they happen to have define the situation. Leaders want the situations to define the tools required.

A perverse situation may call for a perverse technique.

A virtuoso at what he or she does is enabled by virtuoso tools, and vice versa. A tool does not make a person competent. A tool is the "right" tool only in the right hands. A master carpenter and the tool he is using are interdependent. They each enable the other. That's the way it needs to be with leaders.

There is this sense of seamlessness with their tools. The aim is not to "use" the tool properly. It is to accomplish something that would be difficult or impossible for the amateur by bringing together the right tool with the right person. When you are witnessing virtuoso performers, you cannot separate the dancer from the dance. And they make it look easy because it is . . . for them.

And they pick their mentors, their exemplars, carefully. Trying to gain wisdom from amateurs would be a bit like trying to climb a mountain by walking downhill.

By itself, a hammer does nothing it was designed to do. In the hands of an amateur, expect damage. In the hands of a master craftsman, expect superior results. No tool or technique—including high-tech gadgets like computers—can compensate for the inadequacies of their users. We are led—easily on our part—to believe that we can buy smarts—or at least buy something that would compensate for our own or others' incompetencies. You cannot, I cannot. No one can.

The "right" person is the person who is fully capacitated—fully competent—to combine with that tool or technique in what can be achieved when each is "right." So the potent tools and techniques that follow will range from "don't work" to downright dangerous if deployed by semi-competent persons. Powerful if deployed by masterful leaders.

Think on these, and then move on to meet them:

- A poor tool in the hands of a fully competent person will produce results far superior to a magnificent tool in the hands of an incompetent person.
- Who is the "right" person? The one who is fully competent to make use of the right tool.
- *Any* shortfall in competence lessens the value of the tool.
- "Computerization" has contributed little to productivity. Why?

Chapter 14

The Basic Tools

WHEREVER AND WHENEVER performance matters, there are fundamentally two kinds of "tools":

- Those that contribute to making that level of performance **possible**; and
- Those that contribute to making the required performance **necessary.**

The main reason people don't perform as required (or desired) is that they *can't*. They are not competent to accomplish what needs to be accomplished. Given the "people" problems that absorb excessive amounts of time and attention daily, it seems that we need to be reminded of this simple fact repeatedly.

You will recall the second reason why people don't perform as required (or desired). It is simply that they *don't have to*. They didn't come with the necessary "fire" in their bellies that might drive their extraordinary performance. They may have loved adolescent irresponsibility, since that was the only life they had known, and wanted to stay in their comfort zone. It was never necessary for them to set goals and then be accountable for achieving them. In short, they never learned how to perform because they never had to. If so, then some of the necessity that drives outstanding performance would have to be imposed by others, by a performance culture, or by systems that make the required performance possible, but also necessary. Nucor would be a good example. As would the U. S. Marines or Special Forces. Or the University of Connecticut women's basketball program.

The more difficult the goal, the tougher the preparation for pursuing it has to be. Young people escape the necessity of this logic by having easy, or no, goals in life. But if you have a real aim in life, you have to equip yourself (and your organization) with the necessity for achieving it.

- What drives exceptional performance is *necessity*.
- What drives mediocre performance is the absence of the level and kind of necessity it takes.

Preparedness / Readiness

So the indispensable or essential tool is **preparedness, or readiness**. Pilots do this *before* they get into the cockpit. Surgeons do this *before* they enter the operating room. Warriors do this *before* they enter the arena. The best organizations do this *before* they confront the need to perform at extraordinary levels.

"Prepared . . . for what?" Well, for one thing, if you don't know exactly where you're going, you're simply going to end up where you're headed. No need to prepare for that. No way to prepare for that.

But if you have a cause or a mission, you have to prepare yourself to carry it out. You have to prepare yourself for what you are likely to encounter on the path from here to there. You have to prepare yourself for what you may possibly encounter in your efforts to get from here to there. And you have to prepare yourself for the unexpected. If the telephone rings in "Customer Service," the person who answers doesn't know in advance what the problem or the inquiry will be, but has to be prepared for it whatever it is. You don't actually know how the customer is going to decide when there has been tough competition for a complex sale. But you have to be prepared regardless. You don't know what kinds of strange turns the economy is going to take. But you'd better be prepared anyway. Being prepared is, simply . . . being prepared. You have to be prepared for the unexpected. If you are not, you will be victimized by those unexpected happenings.

This is one of those master tools. It requires planning. It requires the ability to improvise and keep things on track. It requires great competence—not just being good at what you do, but in seducing others to go where you want to go. It requires the kind of "intelligence" you can use to strategize on the move. And it requires the resilience and the forethought to win in spite of "losing." Without this master tool, you may end up being at sea without a paddle.

Some thought-prodders:

- What you don't prepare for, you can't be ready for.
- A mission is not a "statement." It is what you have to be prepared to achieve, whatever it takes.
- You cannot prepare for a journey you are not committed to take.
- A purpose is the tool for setting direction and maintaining course.
- If a purpose has no starting power, it is worthless. If it has no finishing power, it is just idle talk.
- What you are not prepared to understand, you will not understand.
- What you are not prepared to accomplish, you will not accomplish.

Accountability

In any organization, any problem or failure on the part of the organization can be traced to a shortfall of competence in one or more roles. The consequences usually suck in the time and attention and effort of other people—people above, below, and on all sides. Probably more than 75% of all "meetings" are called to solve a problem which can be traced to shortfalls in competence. The consequences for the organization of these shortfalls of competence are the largest single cause of *waste* in an organization. We seem to have time to talk endlessly and get involved in these consequences. But never seem to have the time—or the will?—to preclude them by fully capacitating every person in ever role. And capacitating every system.

"Talk" is not an accomplishment. It is in lieu of an accomplishment. The more accomplishment-minded people in an organization are, the less they have to talk about it.

- The less purposeful people are, the more "need" they feel to talk about it.
- Communication fills the void left by having no clear purpose.
- Much communication in organizations is in lieu of accomplishment.

Accountability means "owning" the outcome. Not the talk. The person who is regularly involved in an exercise program has little to say about it. The person who talks endlessly about his or her need for it is not doing it. This is not perfect, but is extremely useful to your thinking: the more people talk about stuff, the less time they have just to *do* it.

Accountability requires the competencies required to accomplish what needs accomplishing, and for avoiding those consequences that ought not to occur. Many people these days won't understand what you mean by "accountability." They've never been required to be accountable to themselves, or to anyone or anything else. Accountability may strike many marginally competent or incompetent people as being somehow evil. You are challenging their reality.

But to develop a high-performance organization, you will have to wield this tool. You are, and the people in your organization are—

- Accountable for statements made. If those mislead, the person who made the statement—if only to herself—is accountable.

- Accountable for the promises that were made to anyone inside or outside the organization.
- Cashing your paycheck carries an implicit promise—that there is no one else who could do your job better than you, or for less pay.
- Every accomplishment you sign on to, explicitly or implicitly, makes you accountable for the outcome.
- You are accountable for developing all of the *competencies required* to accomplish what you have signed on to accomplish—your role and all of the performance goals or assignments that you take on.

There is no "accountability" where there are no *consequences* for failing to accomplish what was agreed to (even if the agreement is with oneself). An excuse is the opposite of accountability. If people are pretty good at lying to themselves (which is what a well-worn excuse is), they will feel no compunction about lying to others. To you, to your customers, to their fellow-members. People who do not have personal integrity (which is accountability to themselves) will diminish the health and the performance capabilities of your organization from the inside out.

Every hour of every day there are "Moments of Truth" in every organization, as Jan Carlzon (SAS) wrote some years back. Every transaction that occurs within the organization or with customers or suppliers is a "moment of truth." Add all of those together at the end of the day and that provides you with a picture of the state of the organization. In the outcomes of those "moments of truth," there is either accountability or there is not. Making it necessary for people to be accountable is simply indispensable to making a high-performance organization.

There's hardly a person I know who is pleased with his or her treatment by airline personnel. "Have a nice day" is a statement made in lieu of real performance. *Shouldn't* those airlines be in bankruptcy? Isn't it about time for a comeuppance?

If you were to add up the performance of every person and every piece of the organization at the end of the day, as Carlzon said, you would have a picture of that person's or that organization's destiny. That's where "accountability" lies.

Here are some thoughts to ponder:

- What *cannot* be done *will not* be done.
- Outcomes that are not *necessary* will occur only as a matter of chance or of good or bad "luck."
- Becoming "the best" at anything on purpose has nothing to do with "luck."
- It has to do with competence and necessity—accountability.

Capacitation

By this point, you have noted that there are two concepts that pervade everything else. They are *competence* and *necessity*. People simply have to be *competent* to perform at the level (or in the way) required. If they are not, it isn't going to happen.

And it has to be *necessary* for them to perform at the level required. That necessity may be internal (the best kind), external, or some combination. People may be competent and very conscientious. But unless they *have to* perform to an extraordinary level, they won't. Occasionally, you could be surprised. But it's better to be surprised than it is to fail.

Another concept (and all concepts are "tools") is "capacitation." It is perhaps more encompassing than "competence." You take the measure of "competence" on persons. A person is either fully competent to accomplish something or he/she is not. Capacitation refers to designing or equipping a team of people or a work system involving several processes so that the larger system can accomplish what needs accomplishing.

IT, for example, doesn't increase anyone's competence in the short-term. But if the system designer thinks in terms of *capacitating* the whole system, the performance of the whole could be improved. Capacitation refers to what might be needed by any component of the overall system, or the way in which it is integrated via some infrastructure.

People can be more or less competent. A team or a work system or an organization can be more or less capacitated. For example, no one person controls the outcomes of an organization's performance in the real world. But everything that an organization contributes to that outcome can be reasonably controlled, by design and by capacitation. The way an organization is put together (given the outside conditions) can either capacitate it to perform, or incapacitate its performance.

It is reported that Southwest Airlines hires only one out of fifty applicants. They are looking for that one that adds, doesn't subtract, from the already successful capacitation of the organization. A person is likely either to fit into the existing "culture" or not. If GE eliminates the bottom fifteen percent of middle managers every year, it's because they don't want to invest in people if there is unlikely to be much in the way of payoff.

For the leader, both are tools: competence *and* capacitation.

Inescapable Logic

One of the most reliable of ancient wisdoms is this: Don't challenge the inevitable. If there is a logic to something, go with it. Don't go up against it.

Inherent in every situation, from those involving the machinations of the organization to those involving the machinations of the marketplace, there is a "logic." You can use it as a tool for your purposes by recognizing and acquiescing to it. Or you will simply be a victim of it.

Organizations may "succeed" for many different reasons. But many organizations fail for the reason that they did not adapt to the logic of the situations in which they found themselves. The "logic" of situations, from the interpersonal to larger economy, is always implicit—hidden, tacit. You have to figure it out without having the code book in your hand. It changes, never asking your permission. If one of your lieutenants is gung-ho for your mission, and another expresses overt hostility to it, the logics of the two situations are quite different. If you play them the same, you may lose both. Each game of poker or bridge has a certain logic to it. If you can "read" it better than your opponents, you might win. It is the same for every competitor in every marketplace.

The "logic" of the situation will always win. It pays to be on the side of the forces that are going to win.

Three ponderables:

- How good you are at what you do is revealed solely by how well you perform *under adversity*. Make the logic of adversity your ally.
- What doesn't make you the best at what you do makes you ordinary. What makes you ordinary can never make you the best. You can't beat that logic. People have been trying to do that for years.
- There is no necessary correlation between what people say and what people do. That's the logic. You can play it the other way. If you do, you will lose.

"Casting"

The most important decision you ever make is who to hire. This is the person who is going to make you successful. Or not. The higher your aim, the more critical the decision.

Every organization has a history that is its "story." The people who have roles in that story make it turn out the way it does. If you want that story to turn out as you intend, then you have no choice but to create the roles that are indispensable to that story, and then to find and put in place the right people to perform those roles. They are accountable for performing up to or beyond those roles, as we will consider in more detail ahead.

You need to have just the right roles to make the "story" of your organization turn out the way you intend. And you need to cast just the right people in those roles, and hold their feet to the fire. "Casting," whether for a movie or a symphony orchestra or an NFL team, is crucial to the outcome. It is even more so for an organization dedicated to a cause, to real achievement, to extraordinary performance.

We've been here before and we'll be here again. But let's take another look at one of the fundamental obstacles.

People think of what they do in organizations as "work." And "work" has a negative connotation for most people. People do not come to your place primarily to develop their competencies in the role they're in. They come to your place for *their* reasons, not yours. Before they arrive at your place, it's likely they were looking for a "job." A "job" to them is an arrangement that enables them to obtain the money to pay for the things they want to buy (or assume they deserve). They want to be at your place as a sort of reward or recognition either for past accomplishments, or just for being willing to put up with you and your organization's silliness. They are there to get some "bread." They are there to carry out, less or more conscientiously, the *activities* vaguely described in a "job description." They typically expect you to be responsible for their capabilities, their safety and security, and their "job satisfaction." The problems of the organization, even if they cause them, are usually not matters of much interest to them, except as a way of "spending" the day. They expect you to be responsible for their performance, and to be generously grateful to them for being willing to spend that much time at your place, engaged in activities that interest them.

Overdrawn?

The bottom line: Most people do not come to your place with any longer-range ambitions than today (or perhaps payday). They do not sign on with you with the intention of being world-class at what they do. Only those who are compelling leaders, and who have the power to do so, can change those circumstances. And only the very courageous, very ingenious, leader of an organization who is able and willing to go up against those seemingly overwhelming forces can seriously expect to make an organization that has worthy and lofty aims.

What has to be altered is obvious. Mere "work" has to be made as richly challenging and as richly rewarding as any other aspect of life. People who are enervated have to be awakened and brought back to life. Having a "job" won't do it. People have to have a relevant role in some worthy quest. The answer to "getting a life" is finding the right role and becoming forever better at it. You now know this. They probably do not. Of necessity, leaders lead people to a higher quality of life, even though those people may resist it every step of the way. It is a unique role performed superbly, in the context of a larger cause, that provides people with a real sense of life. That's what high-performance organizations provide, and that's what leaders make possible—and necessary.

- If you intend to pursue real achievement, like a high-performance organization, you have to take a different path.
- You have to have some tools for being different.

Tools For Being Different

To be able to use the tools for being different (like being "the best"), you have to be different yourself. In the following ways (as we have seen):

> **IF** you are had by a great and worthy purpose . . . and
>
> **IF** you have a potent and compelling strategy for getting from here to there . . . and
>
> **IF** you can tell the story of getting from here to there in a way that seduces others . . . and
>
> **IF** you have the right roles to make that story come true, and the right people cast in those right roles . . .
>
> **THEN** you may be the right person to wield these tools for being different.

If you aren't, these tools will under-perform. There is no tool that can be better than the person who uses it. Make sure that you can optimize these tools, and that any person who intends to use them in your organization has the above qualifications at his or her level.

Role Descriptions

The first of these basic tools we want to deal with here is that of "role descriptions." A role description is **not** another name for a "job description." In fact, it is how different they are that you want to come away with. A "job description" describes, more or less ambiguously, the *activities* that a person carries out in her "job." Using "job descriptions" almost guarantees that the status quo will be maintained. That the organization will recycle itself on a daily basis, becoming more and more like it is. And that its destiny is given in the *activities of the day*.

A *role description* describes unambiguously what a virtuoso in that role would be able to accomplish regardless of any adversity. A role description does not describe a person nor the activities that person might engage in. A *role description* is a description of a role to be performed with great mastery in order for the organization to fulfill its intended destiny. A "role" is one of several indispensable roles for making that "story" turn out as intended. The people are "players" and they have a role to perform to make the story unfold as envisioned. A role description describes what the incumbent of that role has to *accomplish* in order for the whole to evolve as intended.

A "job description" lists *activities*. A "role description" sets forth the *accomplishments* the incumbent has agreed to become capable of delivering under adversity. The significant and very consequential difference is that job descriptions generate the present out of what worked in the past for a particular person. A role description, by contrast, outlines the contributions required of that role for the organization to fulfill its cause or mission (its "story"). The incumbent of a role description performs the *role*, not the skills or experience they happen to have. The envisioned organization doesn't yet exist. It is the right people performing extraordinarily in the right roles that bring it into being.

Most people have not lived under the influence of a cause or mission in life, and therefore never had—because they never needed—a role description designed to get them there. Every person at every moment of the day is performing a role. But for most people most of the time, they are not conscious of what it is. They may have thought about the future but didn't like thinking about the role description required to get them there. (Too demanding, too much accountability.) And most of the time their roles are in the "default" setting—meaning that their old habits and other people are pulling their strings.

It's a waste of time to get involved in designing role descriptions into which people are to be cast if they do not have "teeth" in them. If failure to live up to a role description has no serious consequences, it's all an exercise in futility. A violinist who can't perform up to the level of his or her role in a world-class symphony orchestra won't get, or won't be retained, in that role. It's simple. It's powerful. But if the CEO can't or won't live up to *his/her* role, there is likely to be loosey-goosey acceptance of mediocrity throughout the organization.

For all of these reasons, learning how to think about and craft role descriptions is a capability few people have. Yet it is a basic tool, having many of the pushes and pulls in it that are required to elevate performance continuously.

There are no "neutral" roles. Roles either contribute positively to the outcomes as intended for the organization, or they contribute negatively. If you and the incumbent do not perceive any role as being as important as every other role in pulling the organization into its intended future, eliminate it. It's waste. And waste is trouble. Broaden the roles required, both laterally and vertically, to the fewest roles required to carry the organization to its cause. This is not the new "lean." This is old, old wisdom. Increase the requirements of the role to have fewer with more requirements, not more roles with fewer requirements. This is the only way everyone wins. Enrich the role. Don't impoverish it to make employment for more people.

Start at the top. It's a perspective that helps to see how the pieces should fit together. Keeping in mind that this is a key tool only if you intend to pursue real achievement—like a high-performance organization—begin with these kinds of questions:

- What is this organization *for*? Why does it exist? What is its rightful destiny? What is its legacy to be?
- What is its role vis-à-vis its stakeholders: employees, customers, suppliers, owners, the industry, the community, the economy, the nation and its cultural environment, history itself?
- What part of the larger architecture of economic, political, human life will it occupy? How will it adapt to the world? How will it need to make the world adapt to it?
- How will it *do* all of this?

It is the organization's *role* in the world (not its "mission," myopic and inadequate) that reveals what is important and what is not important, and for what the organization itself is to be held accountable. If the criteria for its accountability are not clear, it becomes impossible to make anything else about "the organization" clear to people—inside or outside the organization. *If the CEO doesn't understand what the organization's role is, his own role will be ambiguous, fuzzy, without real accountability.*

It is clear, comprehensive answers to the questions above that establish the core criteria for the CEO's role description. And that's the way it has to work from the top to the bottom of the organization. What needs to be accomplished at every position is what is required by the level above that one. So, given the comprehensive answers to those questions, the CEO has his (or her) basic role description. Then the question is, what roles are needed to carry out those accomplishments, and what are the criteria for those roles—the accomplishments required by those roles to achieve what is specified by the organization's "role" in the world.

We'll see what that might look like. But first, more caveats:

- Given the real achievement envisioned, you are free to put into the role description what, in your wildest dreams, would make your dreams come true. It doesn't have to fit a person. It has to provide a set of accomplishments for a person to equip herself to carry out in that role.

- Always in terms of accomplishments (not "activities") in the long-term, and always objectively measurable. (This means only that any reasonably intelligent person could measure the accomplishments.)
- Every part of the organization could have a "role description"—every department, every unit, team, work group, project, person. Whatever or whoever is critical and relevant to the pursuit and accomplishment of the organization's role needs a sub-role to play, spelled out by a role description.
- Every role description is provisional, meaning that it could be improved upon tomorrow. Its purpose, collaborative or not, is that of *aligning* everyone and everything to the organization's chosen destiny. The words are important only to help the leader and subordinate involved to explore together what those words *mean*, so that the incumbent can devise a plan to fulfill every required accomplishment and both can track progress toward the accomplishment.
- The more conventional the title and the description, the more likely the outcomes will be mediocre. They are for the purpose of creating an organization that does not yet exist. They have to be at least creative enough to light the way to that happening.
- You want everyone to be in the same "business"—to be as much as possible on the "same page." To do this, every role description needs to have the same first line.

There's more to the design and construction of this core tool than that. But here's an example that shows how to accommodate all of these provisos. Here's a very generic role description for an "Executive Assistant," just to give you an idea of how it's done:

Role Description: Administrative/Executive Assistant (CEO Enabler?)

My role: To make XYZ Corp the best in the business by any measure, by—

1) Developing my competencies to ensure that the events that ought to happen, happen, and those that ought not to happen, don't.

2) Enhancing the performance of anyone who needs (whether they know it or not), requests, or expects my resourceful support.

3) Knowing the who, what, when, and where that others need to know to fulfill their roles superbly.

4) Achieving all performance goals with zero errors, and in increasingly less time and others' involvement.

5) Making certain that all aspects of my goals are fulfilled whether I am physically present or not.

6) Establishing and maintaining a world-class, always current repository of the intelligence required for every process and every request.

7) Being the spiritual leader of this organization's mission.

8) Routinely improving the administrative infrastructure of this organization through my innovativeness and by continuous improvement.

9) Becoming the key source of intelligence about what is going on, what ought to be going on, and what ought not to be going on in this organization.

10) Distilling and distributing that intelligence in order to create the most well-informed executive team in this or any other industry.

11) Providing real-time monitoring of specified performance data with variance analysis and projections.

12) Adding measurably to the performance of the CEO.

Not perfect. Never is. But as a way of grounding an ongoing dialogue between the executive and this assistant, this tool will do its job. You can see the posture. The people involved must agree about how each accomplishment is to be tracked and measured, about what's missing from a complete description of what a real virtuoso would accomplish in this role, and about the incumbent's plan for raising her/his competencies to the level required. If a person could walk in and fulfill the role, the description is not demanding enough. The role description needs to reveal how the incumbent would have to develop herself/himself over the long-term. It is also a grounded blueprint for the capabilities that have yet to be acquired.

The CEO? That one might begin this way:

Role Description: CEO (Chief Steward of the Organization's Destiny?)

My role: To make X institution the best in the business by any measure, by—

1) Designing the organizational architecture needed to carry out our mission, identifying the roles required for our story to be told as envisioned, and casting the people in those roles who can and will make it happen.

You see how this tool gets constructed. But tools as such don't accomplish anything. If the role incumbent can't or won't pursue the accomplishments expressed and implied, he or she needs to make room for someone who can, and will.

How about these?

- If role descriptions don't have "teeth" in them, they are little more than bureaucratic exercises. Real achievement that isn't necessary won't happen.
- A plan for every entry makes the accomplishments *possible*.
- But if they aren't *necessary*, the time involved is wasted. This applies throughout. But the leader is the model.
- A tool that is not going to be used for the purpose for which it was designed, by a person who knows how to use it, won't do much good. Can do some harm.
- Great role descriptions make explicit *who* owns *what* problems required for the organization to pursue real achievement.

Chapter 15

More Tools

MORE TOOLS. EVEN though we have to deal with them sequentially, they are all equally important. Different circumstances call for different tools, the right one for those circumstances being, for that purpose, the most "important" one. What is more important than anything else is that you have the right tools in your toolbox.

Performance Goals

Every role in the organization—from that of the organization itself through to every division, department, team, project, and individual—has to have a set of "performance goals." Where do these P/Gs come from?

1. **From the needs and interests of the organization.** Real achievement—like making a high-performance organization— requires that the organization out-perform the best, especially competitors. Not "bench-marking." That will ensure you will be more or less average, since everyone else is using that as a standard. But knowing what and where the best performances have ever been, and beating those in significant ways. This means that the organization has to be better than any others at everything that matters (contrary to Crawford & Mathews, *The Myth of Excellence*). This will

provide the minimum set of P/Gs for the organization. These need to be distributed appropriately and strategically to one or another of the organization's operating entities. Ownership has to be throughout the organization. If each role delivers to the P/Gs thus distributed, the organization will then achieve "its" P/Gs.

P/Gs may be mildly financial. But they work best when the *drivers* of the bottom line are identified and used as the locus of performance measurement. For example, increasing competence counts for more in the long run than increasing revenues.

2. **From the specific requirements of the sub-unit of the organization.** Like the organization itself, every part of it must outperform its counterpart at least among its competitors and comparable organizations generally. So those are added to that part of the organization's P/Gs it now owns.

3. **From the explicit or implicit accomplishments designed into every individual role description.** Every person who has a role in the organization must minimally outperform his or her counterparts in the competitors' organizations. But any other person who might take on their role as well. The organization competes, every component competes, every person competes—to outperform all others. P/Gs are there to make clear the criteria on which all others are to be "bested."

4. **From your wildest hopes and dreams.** What does it take to outperform all others? Coaches know. And they establish performance goals to be surpassed, both individually and collectively, until those levels of performance become habitual. Then you are prepared. Until tomorrow, when you raise the bar, because yesterday's performance will *always* enable a high-performance organization (or person) to outperform you. This is not a resurrection of the once-fashionable "Management by Objectives." Performance goals are not "management," but *performance*, tools.

The **purpose** of performance goals is to develop throughout the organization the *capacity* to devise viable *plans* for meeting specific goals. Implicitly, the purpose of P/Gs is to make *necessary* the *development* of all of the human and other *resources* required to carry out the plans devised to achieve them. Achieving those goals is obviously vital to the existence and the future health of the organization. But even more important over time is developing the internal capabilities of the organization for devising and carrying through plans for achieving objectively measurable goals on a time-line, no matter what gets in the way.

The ultimate achievement here is the full capability and readiness to achieve goals, no matter what happens. This process will never work perfectly. And no one controls the final outcome. But the ownership of planning and execution throughout the organization (not just at "the top") is the key to real achievement.

Performance Goals are necessary to the present—to spell out what's required—whether that is productivity, Return on Time, margins, quality, customer care, or just plain competence. P/Gs are necessary for preparedness. P/Gs are necessary to remind their *owners* of what they might otherwise forget. P/Gs are necessary for raising the level of performance at every touch point in the organization, continuously. P/Gs illuminate the path. What isn't owned won't be done. What isn't necessary and what doesn't have consequences won't be on the front burner. That's what great P/Gs are for.

Performance goals are relatively worthless—

- If they have no "teeth" in them. That is, if a viable plan and its implementation are not **necessary.** That is, if people don't believe there will be serious consequences for failure either to devise a plan or to carry it out, then they are no more than a bureaucratic exercise. A great tool abused.
- If they don't contribute mightily to getting you where you want to go. They may be "perfect" in some other sense. But the "performance" of P/Gs can only be measured by the contribution they make to the movement of the organization from what it is to what it is intended to be.

If the organization's role is its ultimate goal, then performance goals are all of the intermediate goals required to get there—daily, weekly, monthly, quarterly, yearly. They represent all of the tactical plans throughout the organization for carrying out—measurably— the organization's role(s).

Learning Plans

Another tool. Every person in the organization who has a role must have a "Learning Plan." A L/P is a set of personal P/Gs that address a person's shortfalls—skills, conceptual skills, perceptual inadequacies, attitudes that hinder performance, follow-through orientations, habits, etc.—with respect to that person's Role Description and/or P/Gs. These need to be treated, by the person and his or her leader, merely as problems to be solved. Not as shortfalls of the *person*. But as specific shortfalls in that person's present performance or that person's preparedness for future performance. For example, most of the errors that occur in the typical organization are a result either of shortfalls of competence, or of a failure to be totally attentive to what one is doing. People can change themselves to avoid either cause. A learning plan sets forth how, when, and what the measures of changed performance will be.

It may be a shortfall of understanding. Or of the mental or emotional wherewithal to perform at the level required. "New hires" have shortfalls. But so do CEOs and long-timers. A role without a learning plan is not as lofty or as demanding as it must be.

All this raises the question of assessing performance. Who does it? Both the person(s) involved and the leader. What's required in the way of performance is spelled out and agreed to in the R/Ds and P/Gs of the people involved. Since the measures of performance are objectively measurable and on a time-line, any shortfalls are as obvious to the incumbent as to his or her leader. All that's needed is some interpretation. They do this together. Who *owns* the problem? The person(s) who own the shortfall.

N.B. Leaders ("bosses") are not there to pass judgment. They are there to help people continuously to improve their performance in their role. So they have to function as coaches, to make self-leaders of their people. They are there, as all leaders are, to set "impossible" (to those people) goals, and then to help those people capacitate themselves to achieve those goals. The aim is the performance of the organization, not games of dinking around with the problems of the day, or of who's the "smartest."

Thus, a learning plan, devised and implemented by the person who owns the role and the P/Gs that accompany it. Don't aggregate the problem. Organizations can't learn. Only people can. And real learning is a change in the person's ability to measurably perform his or her role. "Organizational Learning" is just pop hype.

There is such a thing as "learning mode," as we have seen. The opposite of the "knowing mode," where people compete to see whose opinion wins. Both are matters of habit. There are habits of performance. And then there are habits that lead in the direction of shortfalls. A person in the "learning mode" is a person who is looking diligently and continuously for ways of improving his or her performance in his/her role. People in the "knowing mode" assume they already know what they need to know—and their performance slides over time until it becomes inadequate.

So, what the Learning Plan says, implicitly, is "get thee into the learning mode." Key driver for raising performance to the next, and then the next, notch.

Since the way *you* think is the indispensable tool, you might want to keep in mind that—

- Most people are lazy, quite self-satisfied, and in their "comfort zone" where their everyday performance is concerned.
- Most people are not going to be diligent about the hard work and effort required to improve their performance at anything beyond perhaps their hobbies or leisure time activities.
- If they don't have to change, they won't.

- Improving performance is the only kind of change that matters in the long term.
- What people and organizations don't get better at, they will be "bested."
- Learning is *the* "tool" of life, and the more life an organization has, the more formidable its performance will be.

Measures

You're familiar with the old saw, "What gets counted gets done." This is intended to suggest that people and organizations will do what "gets counted." Revenues are counted, and thus are deemed very important, even though they may not be achieved. If you go to school or "have" a job, attendance may be counted, and punishments or rewards are handed out for "attendance" or the lack thereof. So what gets counted does not necessarily drive *achievement*. It merely makes clear what is considered important by the society or by the teacher or the boss. We pay attention to what gets measured. But we may be measuring the wrong things.

There's also the old saw, "What is counted is not necessarily what counts." So it seems to have been long understood that "counting" begins with what is easy or conventional to count. But what we count may not be the most important things we need to pay attention to. Accountants count what is typically counted. But what they count may not account for what most needs counting.

As a good example: We count certain things (like income and expenses) to arrive at a "bottom line," which we take to be a good measure of the economic health of an organization. That it may be. But what you are "counting" here is a byproduct of other things that may be more important if you want to enhance the performance of the organization. The "bottom line" does not drive performance. It is a thin, historical measure of past performance. What gets ignored is what *drives* the "bottom line." Competence, for example. What accountant measures *that*? Or zeal. It affects the bottom line significantly. Is it measured? Or simply doing what one has signed up to do. Who measures *that*? Which comes first in the typical organization—performance or paycheck? Are we counting what drives performance in order to get more of it? Or are we counting dollars, assuming that by counting dollars we'll get more of them?

Can you get better outcomes merely by measuring outcomes? Or do you need to measure the performance of the organization by measuring the performance of each of its components?

The destiny of the organization is determined at every moment of every day by how competently people perform in their roles. (Assuming, of course, that the right roles have been conceived and the Role Descriptions comprehensively identify those competencies.) Many try to see what is going on through certain financial and other "reports" prepared *after the fact* by those who are sometimes called "bean counters." But it isn't these "beans" that make a difference in the performance of the organization. It is—

- How masterful people are in their roles (which is measured by where they are on the learning curve of their role descriptions).
- How diligently and creatively they are implementing their plans for achieving the goals set forth in their performance goals.
- How competently and creatively everyone in the organization is dealing with the shortfalls and problems that emerge.
- How much intelligent *zeal* there is behind the pursuit of real accomplishments.
- How adequate the systems are for pushing and pulling real achievement.

These are what drive the "bottom line." They are therefore what most needs counting. Measure everywhere the *performance* you need to get you to where you intend to go. If you do, the "bottom line" will take care of itself. It is the *result*, not the *cause*, of performance.

Decide what's needed, put that into the role descriptions and performance goals, and then measure (objectively) progress and performance. Simple and obvious. Maybe that's why it is so rarely done to great effect.

- Without measurement, there is no accountability.
- Goals that are not measured will be achieved only by accident.

Problems

It may seem odd to consider problems as "tools." They can be.

It may be (old wisdom) that you are given the problems you confront in order to learn what *your* shortfalls or inadequacies may be. You live in a culture where it is most often assumed that problems are "out there," and independent of you. That may not be the best perspective to take if you intend to be a leader, if you intend to be instrumental in the pursuit of real achievement. We continue to try to make the world acquiesce to our egocentricities. It can be done. But building a huge dam is not the same kind of accomplishment as making a great organization. The concrete does not need to collaborate with the engineer. Great organizations, by contrast, require widely distributed and decentralized ownership of the performance of the whole.

So a "problem" can best be enlisted to tell us what's wrong with us—not what's wrong with the "economy" or with the technical details of the product. If you can learn from your problems how you need to change, you will move ahead. If you can't, those problems will become a recurring part of your environment.

The price of not seeing problems as "mirrors," as telling us more about ourselves than they do about our environment, is one that we pay over and over again as new problems arise from the old ones. (We see this everywhere. Look at medicine, or at the legal system.)

So the leader sees problems as challenges to his or her growth and development. A "tool" for making himself or herself a better leader, and thus a "tool" for enabling the organization to "learn" what is required to better perform.

- A "problem" can be a turn-off or a turn-on. That's the "mirror" part.
- If it is a turn-off, nothing much ever changes and the same old problems return again and again.
- If it is a turn-on, what we get turned-on to is our own faulty perceptions, ineptness, and incompetencies. Fixing those provides great ROI.
- That's what "problems" can tell you if you let them. Leaders let them.
- There is no performance of any role that could not be improved upon every day forever, if the problems encountered are seized upon as tools of changing . . . of improving the performance of every role.

"Composing" Organizations

How the organization is "composed," how it is put together, is another tool for altering, in this case for optimizing, its performance. By optimizing the performance of all of its parts as they work in concert.

"Structure" is far too wimpy a word for this purpose. It is much more like "composing" a symphony that will be dramatically unfolded by its virtuoso players than it is like a building or a bridge or even a spaceship. There is a "score." The score is all of the plans of the role incumbents to achieve their performance goals. But it is only in concert with all of the players that the overall effect is achieved. The score helps to keep everyone on the same page. Competence in role moves in two directions. The first is the performer's mastery of his or her role. The second is the competent performer's ability to listen at the same time to all of the other players, and to contribute as much to those others' performances as they contribute to their own.

And all of this while the concert is in progress. And what is the "conductor" (the "leader") doing all of this time? First of all, he or she is the only virtuoso on stage who is in a position to determine what the whole thing *should* sound like—the performance of the whole and how the audience experiences it. And he or she is the only virtuoso on stage on whom all the others depend to influence their individual performances for optimizing the performance of the whole. In other words, he or she "leads" them from where they are to where they ought to be.

This is but a metaphor. The more you appreciate its implications for yourself and your organization, the more value is has. You have to "compose" the organization. This means determining in advance how it is supposed to work (how it gets from here to there through the masterful performance of people in each of their roles). Note that there are as many "symphonies" as there are great composers. And there are as many different performances as there are great conductors and great orchestras. How you "compose" the organization will always be less important than how well it can be made to perform. The design of the organization does not by itself drive performance.

What this means is provocative. It means that a great orchestra can make a poor score sound good. A mediocre orchestra can make a great score sound mediocre or worse. There is always this underlying interdependence.

The best of all possible organization designs will not work with incompetent performers in *any* role. A conventional organization design can be made to perform exceedingly well if there are outstanding performers in every role.

So we're back to the original logic. If you want a high performance organization, you have to have people in every role who are on the path to becoming the best in the business in their role. If you want top performance out of the virtuosos in every role, you have to design the organization in such a way that they *can* and *have to* perform. You cannot get optimum performance without leveraging both at the same time.

In addition: In the same way that the best symphony (or other) performances will emerge in response to the best audiences and the best competition, the performance of your organization will always depend upon how good your suppliers are and how good your customers are. ("Good" here refers to performance, not likability, to demanding-ness, not comfort.) So you always have a vested interest in whether they contribute to your laziness and complacency, or whether their own aims keep you continuously challenged (in the right direction, of course).

So you have to "fit" and "compose" your organization to the circumstances of the existing marketplaces and other conditions of all of your stakeholders. If the labor market is tight, design to it. Do what you have to do to overcome that constraint in the pursuit of your own aims. Don't just talk about it. If it enhances *their* performance, design around or even *into* your customers and/or suppliers. If market or technological intelligence is critical, design for it.

If you want to be different, design differently. Fashions in organization design come and go. You may be tempted. Don't be. No one has your particular cause, or your players. No one else has *you*. Design to where you want to get to, not to what is fashionable. What is fashionable is conventional. And no conventional design will provide you with a competitive advantage.

- Composers "hear" the performance internally and then write the "score."
- What would the "score" look like that would get you to the performance required by your organization's role?
- What is your role as leader before, during, and after your organization's moments of truth?

"Smart" Systems

In an earlier chapter, we explored "dumb systems" as one of the obstacles/barriers to high performance, to real achievement. "Smart systems," the other end of the continuum, are tools for enhancing and elevating the performance of the organization.

It has long been known to field generals that the advantage always falls to the organization having the best information systems and the timeliest information. It isn't that "information" in and of itself improves performance. Which it does not. It isn't that "technology" improves performance. It does not. There is no substitute for competence. There is no substitute for great goals, zealously pursued. There is no substitute for an organization that "works" the way it needs to work in order to outperform all others. There is no substitute for the "right" design. There is no substitute for leadership.

There is no substitute for systems—technological, cultural, mandated—that function to make consistently outstanding performance possible, and *necessary*.

"Smart systems" provide the "intelligence" infrastructure for what has to be accomplished. Smart people who are masterful in their roles can make good use of smart systems, as we have seen. Inadequate or marginally competent people will only be enslaved by them.

Smart systems make it possible for people who are already masterful (in their roles and in the hand-offs between and among roles) to "see" relevant facts more quickly, or more meaningfully, than they would otherwise. A smart system enables you to "look" at what is going on from different perspectives, in different combinations, along different trend lines or time frames. A smart system enables you to simulate various scenarios, to assess different outcomes of a different mix of actions. A smart system enhances your grasp of what is going on and what you might do about it by providing you with the intelligence you need—whether or not you knew you needed it.

Data-basing and shuffling "information" around is a game IT people play. But if the system isn't "smart," which most are not, it isn't going to help you very much. What you can't do without them, you generally can't do with them.

Smart systems are designed to underwrite the *role descriptions* and the *performance goals* that constitute the current operating fabric of the organization. They do not provide performers with what's available. They provide those people with the intelligence and the perspectives they *need* in order to fulfill their roles, and to exceed their performance goals, while providing synergy with other roles, and vice versa.

Smart systems are just now on the horizon. They are not an extension of your average IT. They are a paradigm or two removed. But neither are high-performance organizations merely an extension of mediocre ones. They are a paradigm or two beyond.

You can't devise smart systems apart from having a cause that cannot be achieved without them.

- *If* you know exactly what you want to accomplish and you have a compelling plan for getting there, the intelligence systems by which you determine where you are and what needs to be done will be apparent.
- If you don't, you'll have to be content with the conventional information technology that you can afford, promising much but delivering little.
- Why? Because mediocre tools serve mediocre performers.
- And because smart tools cannot be designed by people who aren't.
- No tool is better than its user, including the tools used by IT designers to design systems for your use.
- No matter how much you pay or where you get it, you will never be able to import something that can compensate for incompetence.
- The higher the level of the role, the more true this becomes.
- By and large, government regulations are not designed to contribute to enhanced performance. Neither are most "information systems."

Consider the average retail clerk, held up and down and all around by various "systems." Could the average person potentially do all of these—

A) Know where all of the merchandise is, including colors, sizes, sources, uses, related items, etc., etc.?

B) Know how to order and stock and do all of the paperwork (or electronic entries) required?

C) Know how to display and "market" the goods, including "upselling"?

D) Actually be able to deal with customers and to help customers solve their problems?

E) Astonish everyone down line with their performance?

The answer is . . . absolutely. So could the average manufacturing or commercial employee. But most systems are designed for people who are no better than marginally competent. And now we're stuck with people who can't or won't perform because the systems they use will not permit them to be anything more than marginally competent. Their "jobs" require some few minimal *activities*. The *accomplishments* are presumably to be provided by the system. Or the "manager."

One more example, of a different kind of "system." We pay certain people (salespeople in some businesses) to do their "job," and then we reward them with a "commission" or a "bonus" for doing what they signed on to do. Similarly, we've come to pay chief executives an astronomical level of compensation, and if they fail or get sticky fingers, pay them more for leaving than for staying.

Those strike me as being *dumb* systems.

Any way of doing things in an organization, if it becomes MO (the way things are done because they're done that way) engenders a *system* by which things are done. The *system* is now in charge. People can't grow in competence and performance if they are working for the system. The system should be working for them. But this can happen only if it is **necessary** for people to capacitate themselves to be "the best" in the business in the role they are in.

- The systems that enable every role and connect all of the working parts of your organization can be dumb . . . or smart.
- The systems that interconnect your organization with its customers, suppliers, and other stakeholders can be dumb . . . or smart.

- The systems you put in place for measuring, for compensation, for rewards and punishments, can be dumb . . . or smart.
- A system is smart if it is measurably moving you from where you are to where you want to be. If it doesn't, it's a dumb system.
- Your call.

CHAPTER 16

More, Power, Tools

THEY'RE ALL "POWER" tools, of course—when used by a powerful person in just the right situation in the most powerful way. What makes them powerful is the level of mastery with which they are understood and employed. It is not even necessary to be able to talk about them. To make them work for you because you are so good at putting them to good use at just the right time, in the right way—that's the measure of their worth in your thinking and in your *performance* as leader.

The leadership tools that follow by no means exhaust the list of tools you need in your toolbox. One is more important than another *only* because that's what the situation calls for. Some are more universal than others—that is, some may be more pertinent than others to most or all situations.

For example—

"Communication"

We're revisiting here, but doing so in order to make some different, highly valuable, observations on this most fundamental of all subjects. If you get involved with yourself or others about anything whatsoever, you're awash in the process and the products of communication.

- It's difficult to live with the facts, even though you know what they are. Fact: there is not a world out there which you and I perceive more or less as it is. What we make of that world, and how that world grasps and informs us, always depends on the workings of our own minds.
- The way you perceive and interpret the world depends upon the meanings you *have* to give to it. What you "see" and how you think about it is both enabled and constrained by what you have to do so with—your own mind.
- What you say or do is interpreted by others, in the same way that what they say or do is interpreted by you. Whatever something means is a product of someone's mind.
- Try as you will, there's no way around all of this.

That's the crux of "communication." But there are lessons here that are not so obvious, but of immense practical value.

1. With what we've got to do it with, you and I have to build up a picture of the way things are and the way they work. There are no "theories" *in* the world. All those are ours, imposed upon the world we "see" and as we understand it.
2. Like all the rest of us, you observe, you take account of what certain others say or do, and you yourself say stuff and do stuff. All this has to be interpreted by you and others. If we observe what goes on in nature, we see immediately that the part of "communication" that is most important is what other critters gather, not what they "send." Making sense of the world is an inescapable condition of our lives. That's a given. What is not given is what it is we need to know in order to avoid predators, to find or avoid a mate, to find food, and when and where it's safe to sleep. These are all metaphors of real practical value to any leader. Competition, alliances, margins, and financial security. Everything depends upon how you take the world into account. All the rest of it hinges on that.

3. We think it's mostly about telling ourselves and other people stuff. It's far more about the quality of the "intelligence" we can provide ourselves about the world we want to maneuver in.

4. You can't pay attention to the world when you're talking. The "opportunity costs" are huge and play out way into the future. That's why the most useful form of communication begins with a question.

5. There is no safety in numbers. Large numbers of people have *always* been wrong, in science as well as pop silliness. That's the lesson of history. Neither the number nor the celebrity of people who believe something has ever obligated the world to conform. "Truth" cannot be trumped by any humans you know. It is what it is. It does not "communicate" itself to us. Nor can we "communicate" it. Whatever is meaningful is made so by humans.

6. So you have to pick the people who inform you carefully, beginning with yourself. "Communication" is indifferent to the outcome. It can as readily sink you as save you.

Remember the bit about a tool cannot be any better than the person who wields it? Here we have the fundamental example. No communication is any better than the person who engages in it. Just because you believe what people tell you does not make it "true." By listening to the wrong people, you may fail at any endeavor you might undertake—from life to leadership. An organization that fails is not one that has "financial" problems. It is one that didn't have the right handle on what mattered in the world in which it operated. It was first about communication. The "financial" part is a result of poor or inadequate communication. The organization didn't "know" what it needed to know in order to survive and thrive. Leaders succeed or fail for the same reason.

The tool here is to be especially skeptical of all you know, and to be skeptical of what others say that for any reason is easy for you to believe.

- The "snake" in the Garden of Eden was not in the tree. It was in Eve's mind. She was talking to herself.
- The "snake" that misleads us still exists, for all of us.
- To "know" something requires you to assume you know it because it is "true." An assumption doesn't get to be "true" just because you believe it.
- What takes the measure of any belief or assumption are the *consequences*.

"Truth" is a red herring. That's never the real issue. The real issue is where you are taken by what you know. Not whether it is "true" or not. Every leader is saved by this realization. What are the consequences if you believe what someone says to you? What are the consequences if you interpret what is going on this way or that way? What are the consequences if you listen to yourself?

The "tool" here is *how not to be duped*. Ultimately, you can only be duped by yourself. And you can limit that. In any struggle between doubt and certainty, cast your lot with doubt and then proceed with certainty, rather than the other way around. The only test of how valid your (or others') view of the world may be will come only with the consequences. Tough. But pragmatic.

- Communication is only academically (and thus trivially) about "content." It is mainly about the consequences.
- Your mind is your master tool. It mediates the world for you whether "inputting," "outputting," or just talking to yourself. Get your thinking right and the rest will follow, leaders say.

Powerful tools, *questions*. Asking just the right question at just the right time in just the right way of just the right source will serve you better than anything you can do. A virtuoso question-asker can generate more pertinent intelligence in just a few minutes than a person of little curiosity, with comfortable certainty, can generate in days, weeks, or years. That's why great leaders are great question-askers, a key lesson most people are too lazy and too full of themselves to learn how to do.

Other lessons for leaders?

- Whether valid or not, most people will not divulge their candid perceptions if they imagine revealing those might jeopardize their interests (usually status quo or interpersonal "politics").
- A good and potent question always trumps present understanding.
- Given a choice, great leaders will choose a potent question over a comfortable statement of "fact," especially when they are talking to themselves.
- Most managers make four statements to every question they ask. Leaders ask four questions to every statement they make.
- Defeat or failure can almost always be traced to a question not asked.
- Being "smart" in the real world is not measured by how much you "know," but the rate at which you can learn by asking the right questions.
- Not being able to figure out what question to ask is like not being able to figure out what key to strike next when playing the piano. Think about it.
- It is not mainly what you don't know that can thwart your endeavors. It is what you know that just ain't so.
- Leader, lead thyself. (By, perhaps, asking a question?)

Communication *Systems*

Don't confuse any of that with communication *systems*.

A communication *system* is what connects or networks people. It can simply evolve from frequent use, or it can be "engineered." A communication system that connects people who think alike will ensure that they do not change unless they change together. The "glue" that holds them together is that they want to go on being who they are, and they want the others to go on being who they are. They will share fashions of being, doing, saying, knowing, and having collectively (which is the only "safe" way). Belonging to any communication *system*, from love affairs to occupations, will influence you in ways that endorse your "membership."

Managers converse most easily with other managers, assemblers with other assemblers, secretaries with other secretaries, engineers with other engineers. People can't "talk shop," even if it's only television fare, with other people whose worlds do not overlap theirs (whose minds are not similarly furnished).

- Communication always takes the path of least resistance. The more used communication channels are, the more they are likely to be used. Observe your own patterns.
- "Politicking" thrives as a driver of all communication systems. Gossip always has political undertones.
- Communication is readily used as the primary means of maneuvering and manipulating. Everyone is a victim of whatever is going on in *any* communication *system*.

Meetings, for example, are quasi-impromptu theater. The only way to know the plot is to participate in developing it. Otherwise, you will be no more than a spectator. "Meetings" are also ad hoc communication systems. The reason they are so notoriously inefficient and unproductive is that the participants usually have their own agendas, and no one of those is the official agenda.

Meetings over coffee or over a beer work better. That's because there is no "official" agenda. It's only when the participants are regular members of the same communication system that "meetings" work as well as they do. If a meeting is not required because people talk to each other productively all the time anyway, they might then be modestly productive.

The communication systems that interconnect an organization with its stakeholders (e.g., customers, suppliers, etc.) are fraught with difficulties. The way customer behavior is interpreted, for example, is created more in the internal conversations about that customer than by anything that actually happens. Did you ever notice that the image flight attendants have of "passengers" never seems to fit *you*? Or that the image passengers have of "flight attendants" is a matter of indifference to those folks, who are busy talking to each other in order to maintain their shared stereotypes of the passengers, and the passengers are doing the same with respect to their shared stereotypes of the flight attendants?

Perceptions and beliefs about customers, for example, are not created by what customers do or do not do, but by what "we" *say* about what they do or do not do. Most basic ideas, attitudes, stereotypes, etc., that people take for granted are actually products of the communication system(s) they "belong" to. That's why it is so difficult to change people. They're going to be the way they are as a result of the communication systems they participate in. So you have to change or modify those systems.

- A communication system is a system. It can be "dumb" or "smart."
- "Smart" communication systems are a prerequisite to preparedness and of exceptional performance anywhere in the organization.
- Leaders who can create and engineer smart systems *for themselves* might therefore be competent to design communication systems throughout the organization.
- Those who can't create smart communication systems for themselves will bring their faulty communication systems to bear on all the rest of the organization.
- So what's the key to designing "smart" communication systems?
- Competent people in every role. They will make it happen.
- All any leader has are interpretations (explanations, descriptions, etc.)—whether his own or those of others.
- Everything has to be interpreted in terms of *something*.
- The "tool"? Interpret *everything* in terms of your goals.
- Make it possible *and* necessary for everyone around you to do the same. "Smart" systems are built that way.

Doing More With Less

You've heard much in recent years about getting "lean"—lean manufacturing, lean thinking, you know the drill. If you've done your homework, you also recognize that most of all that un-lean outpouring is merely old wine in new bottles. The idea of doing more with less has been around literally forever. Henry Ford could outdo any of the "lean" authors. So could the 18th-century industrial innovator Robert Owen. And every medieval craftsman understood "lean."

You don't need an elaborate corporate program for pushing and pulling the idea of doing more with less. You have to practice it yourself, and preach it. Get more done with less talk. Accomplish more in less time. Reward people who accomplish what needs accomplishing with the tools and resources at hand. If you reward people on the basis of how big their empire is, that's what you'll get—more people accomplishing less.

There's a bit of logic here worth thinking about. The more you divide up tasks (once known as "division of labor"), the more coordination is required. Costs increase exponentially, simply because "coordinating" things is always more expensive than the cost of doing those things themselves.

Doing more with less is about three things—

1. Continuously elevating and enlarging the competencies of every person in every role in the organization.
2. Making it necessary for every person to measurably enhance the performance of everyone above, below, and each side of them.
3. Recognizing and rewarding those people who make themselves wholly dispensable by getting their roles performed so well without them they are no longer needed. Give these people "tenure" and a little time to find some other role they would like to take on. Then you win twice. So do they.

"Lean" is about eliminating waste. The two greatest sources of waste in the typical organization are those of wasting people, and wasting time by talking too much. "Talk," as the ancient wisdom has it, "does not cook rice." Talking about something is not the same thing as doing it.

Yes, you can take out all of the non-value-added activities. But competent people will do this for you because they won't put up with it. Competent people know *you* represent "overhead." They know that eliminating overhead is fundamental to doing more with less. Are they willing, through their own efforts, to cover your compensation and perks? If not, you're not the leader they need and want.

Doing more with less starts at the top. If you are in it to amass material goods and the glitziest new things—from cars to management panaceas—you've set the tone.

- If you don't do it, then it's likely it won't get done.
- How many people does it take to get your job done? How many hours a week? With how much in the way of resources?
- Think about it. But only to the ends of accomplishing more with less.

Here, some practical tips about doing more with less:

- Want your organization to be more effective? Tell people to stop talking about it and go do what needs to be done.
- Want to save some money? Cut the number and the length of "meetings" by 50%.
- Observe the increase in productivity and cut them in half again.
- Tell people to engage their minds before engaging in *any* communication. If they haven't got what it takes to get engaged, fix that first.
- The aim of communication is consequences. People who don't know what these need to be are wasting everyone else's time.
- Forty to sixty per cent of the operating costs of the average

organization are the costs of "communication." Begin with your own?

- The next time someone tells you how much things are going to improve by adding people or a computer program, let him bet his job on it. He's asking the organization to bet on it.

The effectiveness of a telephone conversation is usually inversely related to the time spent on it. E-mail? That's a place where people who can't communicate go into hiding to hassle other people who believe that computers improve their mental capabilities.

The more masterful people are at what they do, the less they waste time, effort, materials, or other people's lives.

- Start there.
- And don't waste time looking for substitutes.
- There aren't any that are even 10% as good.

Words

Let's try some "more with less" here. Just to show ourselves and the rest of the world that we can do it.

Some lessons:

- Words (or any other form of mental "representation") are the tools of thought.
- If you think it a bit odd to look at "words" as tools, try doing anything with yourself or other people without them.
- The right word in the wrong place is a waste. The wrong word is always waste.
- People without the right words waste themselves and others. Look no further than your own experience.
- As tools, words are no better than the person who sends them or receives them.
- People who don't have the words to influence others when it would advantage the performance of those others or the organization—waste.

- People who are not capable of being influenced when that would advantage their performance or the performance of the organization—waste.
- Not having the right tools in your toolbox when you need them—wasted opportunity.
- People who speak or listen only in clichés lay to waste everything they encounter. That could be you. Or them.

Power

Power is an indispensable tool. If you don't have power over yourself, you can't make much on purpose of the raw material that is you. Waste. If you don't have power in the eyes of others, they'll conclude they could waste their time and effort in better places. If you don't have the power, ultimately, to make happen what has to happen, it's unlikely to happen.

Power isn't something you came with. It's given to you by others. If you don't use it for the reasons they granted it to you, it will evaporate. Power is as power does. If you do good with it (in the eyes of others), you will have more of it.

As a tool, power can be no better than the person who wields it. So it's what you accomplish together that counts. A carpenter builds a great or a shoddy house depending on how competent he is at making use of the tools at his disposal. The same with leaders. They can build great or shoddy organizations depending on how competent they are at making use of the tools in their toolbox. Especially their (always temporary, always provisional) power.

You have to know when to use it, and how. The best use of power lies in influencing the world (and the people in it) so you don't have to use it. The nail knows the kind of power the carpenter has. So the carpenter never has to talk about it. Never has to threaten the nail with it in order to get the nail to do its job.

Here's the "bottom line":

- Leaders are frugal. They seek no more power than they need.

But they do not attempt great achievements without the power needed to achieve them.

- The path to real achievement can make huge demands on power, especially will-power. And on the kind of "power" required to seduce others to your cause.
- If you haven't got the power to see it through, get that first.
- How do you measure your power? By how far you and your people will go to transform your mission into reality.

Just a couple of thought-prodders for the flavor they might produce:

- For most people over history, it has been powerful gods who have been behind both permanence and change in the world.
- Having abandoned that explanation, we now look to our leaders to provide what was once provided by the gods.
- Without the power of that expectation, you can't make it happen.

Dissatisfaction

Without dissatisfaction, there is no change. Without dissatisfaction with the present, given some imagined future, there will be no significant change. People don't undertake significant change unless they feel the necessity to do so. And that necessity will come from a persistent sense of dissatisfaction with their present state.

When Henry V addressed his troops at Agincourt, he created an imagined end to the day that was far different from what appeared to be certain: annihilation. When Columbus addressed the mutineers on the voyage to a new land no one (including Columbus) was certain could be reached, he played upon the uncertainties of their position. If they journeyed on, they *might* all die for lack of food or water; but if they turned back, they would all *surely* die. When Joshua Lawrence Chamberlain addressed the

Union deserters he was to guard, he gave them a reason for fighting on, making their present situation a source of dissatisfaction. It isn't enough to paint a compelling picture of the future. You have to make people dissatisfied with their present circumstances. As I'm sure you know, most commercial advertising is based on just those premises. Followers want someone who will take away their dissatisfaction with things as they are.

The leader may have to create that sense of dissatisfaction. Or it may already exist. Either way, the leader's mission is to take people out of their (sense of) dissatisfaction to a world that promises to be far more satisfying to them.

- If you are not driven by your dissatisfaction with the present state of things, there's little hope that you will ever be called to lead anything.
- If your would-be followers are not dissatisfied enough to put up with the ordeal of change and to bring to bear the efforts required for achieving some other conditions of life, you won't have followers.
- The whole process is not a rational one. It is an emotional one. You have to "lead" with your—and your followers—feelings.
- There is a leap of faith required. People have to be seriously dissatisfied to make that leap in your direction.

Seductiveness

Awkward term. All it means is that all leaders are "seductive"—that is, that there is something about who they are that captures the imagination and fires the hearts of those who would be followers. The bigger the leap of faith required, and the more uncertain or difficult the path ahead with the leader seems to be, the more the would-be followers have to be seduced by how that leader *thinks*, who he *is*, and how he *does* what he does.

Seduction always involves consent and collaboration. This is the leader's aim: to gain the voluntary followership of others. When

Martin Luther King, Jr. was speaking so eloquently of his "dream," he was aiming to seduce his listeners to a cause he believed to be a just cause. This is what all leaders do.

If you do not have the stomach for or the skills for seducing others to your cause, there will be no cause, there will be no leader, and chance will lead.

- Leaders are seducers. They have been seduced by their cause. For there to be such a cause for others, they have to be seduced.
- The problem is not that there are seducers. Always have been, always will be. The "problem" is, whose ideas ought you to be seduced by? The "problem" is, are the potential leaders who would be good for you the ones who have the most potent skills for seducing you?
- A variation on the old saw, "Lead, follow, or get out of the way"—"Seduce and be burdened with followers, be seduced and suffer the consequences, or get out of the way!" Those are the "tools."

Unreasonableness

Being "addicted" to his or her cause, the leader has no choice but to be unreasonable. People who have never been "had by" a cause will perceive that leader as being unreasonable. They would be using the wrong criteria. To a person who has to achieve his or her aim, whatever has to be done is reasonable, no matter how "unreasonable" that may appear to aimless people.

All great leaders have been *capable* of great wrath. That may be the tool that gets the key message across—you are either with me or against me. There is no neutral position. If you don't "kill" complacency, it will kill you and your cause.

Those who intend to be leaders will be unreasonable about incompetence, about laziness, about indifference, about self-absorption, about dereliction of duty, about carelessness and waste, about negativity, about analysis-paralysis, about stupidity, about lack of attention or zeal, about sycophancy or other forms of kissing-up, about politicking, about the inability to set goals and devise plans for achieving them, about duplicity, etc. Whatever doesn't contribute to the cause works against it. Compelling leaders are so unreasonable about immaturity and about lack of character that they do something unreasonable about it every day.

- Real achievement requires unreasonableness.
- If you are not "ruthless" about what really matters, about what *will* you be "ruthless"?
- There is no change without unreasonableness (as G. B. Shaw said).
- If you are not as unreasonable as your adversaries, both within and outside your organization, you will be their victim.
- Having the "courage of your convictions" may mean being strategically unreasonable about them.

Reputation

There is who you "are." And then there is who people *say* you are. As a tool, the crafting of your reputation can be just as important as your crafting of yourself.

Best example: If you have a reputation for being ruthless with respect to your cause and others' performance in their roles, then it's unlikely you will ever have to *be* ruthless. If there are things you don't like doing, or aren't very good at, then craft your reputation in such a way that *you* don't have to do it because your reputation (which always precedes you in the perceptions of others) has already done it for you.

As Gracian wrote: You must not only *have* certain characteristics to be an effective leader. You must be *seen* as having those characteristics.

- Sharpen that tool diligently and daily.
- What you have to *be* in order to lead others in your cause exists in two places—in your eyes and in the eyes of your followers. It takes both.

- If you had to choose, your reputation will always be the better real-time tool.

"Luck"

Have we said enough about the role of luck in all human endeavors? If you actually picked your parents, then you probably don't need to think about "luck."

If you didn't, then you'll know that things turn out the way they do for reasons you cannot control. Whatever you want to call those other uncontrollable forces are what we are calling "luck.

Those who are not prepared cannot be "lucky." And those who aren't prepared will be deemed "unlucky." As Jean Cocteau once put it: "We must believe in luck. For how else can we explain the success of those we don't like?"

Leaders have long known, for example, that there is as much luck in not getting what you want as there is getting what you want. So they are very prudent about taking credit—or blame—for outcomes which they cannot control. Stephen Leacock said, "I am a great believer in luck, and the harder I work the more I have of it." That's what achievers think of "luck." It's all of the hard work you put in to prepare yourself.

- If you want to be seen as "unlucky," then when things go your way you would have to attribute that to getting "lucky," wouldn't you?
- If a person who cannot count finds a four-leaf clover, is that person "lucky"?
- Leaders make themselves an ally of "luck."

We've let George Bernard Shaw into our arena before. Let's give him a shot at this one:

> "People are always blaming their circumstances for what they are. I don't believe in circumstances. The people who get on in this world are the people who get up and look for the circumstances they want, and if they can't find them, make them."

Leaders may fail. But they fail in an all-out attempt to accomplish something that has them "by the skin and the hair." They never fail by being "victims" of circumstances. Unacceptable. They succeed because they risk everything to avoid being merely victims. Victims *can't* succeed. That's why they believe their fate turns on "luck." For the compelling leader, "luck" turns on taking their fate into their own hands. They are not caused. They *cause*.

- The prepared mind is prepared for whatever happens.
- Great leaders, as we have seen, take the randomness out of events.

There are of course many, many other "tools." In fact, all of the particulars of your thinking are tools. They will serve you well. Or ill. Who you are is an ever-present tool. So, too, are others' images of you. And how *they* think. What you do not bring into alignment with your cause and the journey to it will bring obstacles to carrying it out. You will be dealing with the symptoms of a much deeper problem. If you don't fix the problem(s), you will forever be plagued and harassed by the symptoms.

The ultimate "tool," then, may be your capacity for distinguishing symptoms from their source, and your capacity for aligning all of those sources to your cause. For example, if you know how to make an organization that is actually *good* for people, people who want a higher quality of life and know what that requires of them will be attracted to your place. Great coaches don't need to spend nearly as much as poor ones on recruiting. Great leadership provides its own self-fulfilling prophecy.

PART V

WHEREVER THERE HAVE BEEN people engaged in some mutual endeavor, there have been "codes" of conduct. Whenever any person today engages in any human activity, he or she is guided by a "code" of conduct, of which they may be blissfully unaware. But behavior is guided and channeled. And such "codes" of conduct, once internalized, serve that purpose.

In addition, the values and beliefs that comprise the core of who people are and how they think and feel also play a usually hidden, always *tacit* role. The leader who does not know how his or her own beliefs and values color what they see and what they say will be a victim of how others use those to resist and manipulate the leader. The values and beliefs that are necessary for the pursuit of the leader's cause have to be in place. But tacitly. Values and beliefs that are not a part of the people involved do not play a role. What you post on the walls of your place, no matter how elegantly framed, are merely words on the wall. They don't *do* anything.

Every leader needs to align these. In addition, there are a few "core" stratagems that need to be a part of how the leader thinks, who the leader *is*, and thus how the leader "leads." That is what's ahead in the next three chapters.

CHAPTER 17

Codes Of Conduct

EVERYDAY BEHAVIOR—AT work or at play—is *all* guided, invented, carried out, and evaluated on the basis of *some* "code of conduct." What this means is that people have at least some vague, usually implicit sense of *what* they are supposed to do in the situations they encounter. How they are to conduct themselves in those situations. They have a similar set of assumptions about how others should be conducting themselves in those situations. When people, intentionally or not, venture outside of those understood "codes" of conduct, they will at least be misunderstood by others, or be ostracized or chastised by others. Or they may have a sense of shame or guilt at having breached what would have been "appropriate" behavior. Or all of these.

There are "rules" of engagement. Without such "rules," implicitly observed, human interaction would be chaotic. It wouldn't make any sense. You couldn't make sense of it. Thus such "rules" of conduct, which constitute a sort of internalized "code," are fundamental to making sense of your own and others' behavior.

The important point here is that these implicit codes of conduct will take you *somewhere*. There have always been rather explicit codes of conduct for warriors like the Samurai, for military units, and for any organization that has a cause—like the Mafia or the Catholic Church.

The next most important point is that the "codes" of conduct most people in the modern world bring with them into your organization are very unlikely to provide adequate support for what you want to accomplish.

Thus—and this is the crunch issue—you may have to formulate a "code" for the conduct of the people in your organization which *will* underwrite your cause and the journey required to pursue it.

But let's be clear. The "codes" of conduct that actually guide and inform people's behavior (and hence attitudes) are unrelated to anything you might have printed up and posted in conspicuous places on the walls at your place. The only "codes" that function are those that have been internalized by people. Only those that have become routine habits for people. The "code" that makes a difference is the one that has become a part of who those people *are*. You can pretend. But "company policy" is not at all the same thing as a code of conduct. People might "obey" rules imposed upon them. But their hearts and minds won't be in it.

So the challenges to leaders are always these two:

1. How to formulate a code of conduct that, widely internalized, will be what is needed to get you where you want to go.
2. How to get that code of conduct widely or broadly internalized.

Here's How

First, there is no reason why you would want to concern yourself with a "code of conduct" at your place unless you are committed to achieving extraordinary performance. You can take people as they cross your threshold and devote much of your time to the problems that come from the fact that most people have no aim in life—"Whatever happens, happens." But if you do have that kind of commitment, then you will need to concern yourself with a code of conduct that may be necessary to underwrite extraordinary performance. This is the idea behind the "Code of the Samurai," with which you are probably familiar. Any great achievement that requires the interdependent performances of many people has to be underwritten by a code of conduct. Why don't troops under fire break and run? Code of conduct. Why are some people diligent about their commitments? Code of conduct.

A code of conduct that has no consequences for shortfalls is not in fact a "code" that will make any difference to people. The consequences, whether applied by the person to himself or applied from outside, must be in keeping with the significance (to the mission) of the shortfall.

Second, the "code of conduct" you want to be internalized throughout your organization has to be evident and exemplified in every encounter people have with the leaders and executives in your organization—beginning with you. You have a code of conduct when anyone who visits your place could accurately infer what it consists of from the way every key person comports himself or herself. This is not quite "Monkey see, monkey do." But if the top people can violate it at will, then everyone else has an excuse for doing the same.

Third, you have to recruit and select people (or retain them, or not) according to how close their personal code of conduct already is to the one you want everyone to adhere to. Or, that these are people who can readily adopt the code of conduct you see as necessary to your journey to real achievement. This may appear to you altogether obvious. But most organizations hire for "experience" or for other credentials when it is this "right stuff" that counts in the crunch.

Fourth, you need to invent and customize the systems by which your organization operates so that they provide just the kinds of pushes and pulls required to get the code of conduct in place and to keep it in place. This includes compensation systems. If you "reward A while hoping for B," you won't get B. The systems by which you account for things and make persons clearly "accountable" have to be thoroughly consistent with your code of conduct. If you make it possible—and *necessary*—for people to work diligently at becoming virtuosos in their roles, you have to have systems that provide the right pushes and pulls for that to happen. For example, if it's the only way people can get recognition and reward at your place, they will climb your "ladder" to get it, and no real gain in performance will actually occur. Competence in role counts.

Fifth, it is a struggle at the outset. And everything has to be exaggerated to be noticed. But once there begins to be a critical mass of people who have internalized the code of conduct needed to support the journey to great achievement, the culture of the organization will kick in and make the "code" appear to be "natural" (because it is embedded in the culture) and inescapable, since the culture envelops everyone.

Worth thinking about—

- The codes for becoming mediocre are ubiquitous, easy to adopt, and have been adopted by most people. That's why, in an open struggle between mediocrity and achievement, mediocrity will usually win.
- If the "code" required to become "the best" were that prevalent, people who wanted to be mediocre would be struggling against the current.
- Once the culture of your organization takes over from a critical mass of people, what once appeared to be extraordinary performance will simply be the standard level of performance. Productive perversity!

So What Is A Code Of Conduct *About?*

A code of conduct is "about" the human criteria you believe are critical to getting on and staying on the path to the real achievement you have envisioned. It is what informs and drives the everyday ways of thinking and action in your organization that you believe are necessary to make progress on your mission every day. It is "about" those personal traits and generic orientations you believe your people would have to internalize in order to achieve any or all of the goals of the organization.

Just a reminder: the actual code of conduct that is behind the everyday thinking and actions of your people is what could reasonably be inferred by observing them. When people in your organization observe you, they infer your code of conduct. Is the one that guides your present thinking and behavior going to get you to where you intend to go? If not, designing and exemplifying the one that will . . . is a basic tool for making it happen.

It will become clear to you if we go to example. What follows is a sort of generic list of the kinds of orientations that would be required to move an organization in the direction of real achievement. This list is not intended to be either comprehensive nor exclusive. You may think of other criteria that would suit your situation better. And none of the following criteria is intended to exclude any other possibilities. We'll look first at the themes you may need to drive your story going forward. And then we'll circle back to put some "meat" for deep comprehension and implementation on these bare bones.

A generic code might have the following themes. They are not a description of how you are now. They are intended to describe how you and your people need to *be* to get to where you are committed to going.

- We will become virtuoso **communicators**.
- We will be **courageous**.
- We will become an organization of "**bricoleurs**."
- We will become heroic, world-class **inventors** of a better way.
- We will become a **humanizing** organization.
- We will become an organization of **learners**.
- We will become an organization of **leaders**.
- We will become a **community** of **interdependent achievers**.
- We will make **great lives** by doing **great work**.
- We will kill **complacency** and **mediocrity**.
- We will be joined in **common cause**.
- We will become an organization of **dragon-slayers**.
- We will relentlessly equip and prepare ourselves to do our **duty**.

If you achieved all of this—or any similar list—you would clearly have an outstanding organization. Even if you did no more than try to instill this code in every member of your organization, you would stand apart as unique and extremely capable. You wouldn't have to worry about things like "customer service." Your customers and clients would be astonished by their treatment every day in every way by the people who had internalized this kind of internal guidance system.

But getting there: that's the rub. It's all in the implementation. So you first have to make certain that you understand every one of these themes deeply, for two reasons: one, so that you exemplify the terms of this "code" in everything you do and say, and second, so that you can "explain" what each of these topics means to the person you're talking to, no matter how skeptical or reticent that person might be.

Explaining The "Code"

"Explain" first to yourself, until you and the theme are indistinguishable. Then you can "explain" it to others and answer any questions others may have about it, because you are now the "source" of it. That's how well you have to understand what you are talking about when you talk about a "code of conduct." Challenge yourself with as many of the toughest questions as you can imagine might be asked of you. Nothing less will serve you when you are being grilled about the "whys" and the "hows."

Using the same list as above, here are some ideas that might serve as starters for explaining every major theme (to yourself or others):

- "We will become virtuoso **communicators**."

    A. We will say what we mean and mean what we say.
    B. This requires becoming virtuoso thinkers about anything we want to talk about, and fully engaging our minds in every encounter.

C. We will become virtuoso question-askers—ever more masterful at acquiring the intelligence we need to fulfill our roles, and at providing the information or intelligence others need to carry out their roles whenever, wherever, or however our performance or that of any of our customers or our suppliers is at stake.

D. We will study and practice and raise our competencies as communicators every successive day.

- "We will be **courageous**."

    A. The depth of our commitments to ourselves and our mission will provide all of the courage we need to do the right thing, every time.

    B. Attempting the impossible involves risk and failure. We will recognize that what is inexcusable is failing to push the envelope, whatever the tasks—individual or collective.

    C. We will recover from our mistakes with speed, without compunction or blame, and move boldly ahead.

- "We will become an organization of **bricoleurs**."

    A. As "bricoleurs," we will accomplish what has to be accomplished with the tools and resources at hand.

    B. Our daily purpose will be to outperform ourselves as we outpace all of our competitors, actual or potential.

- "We will become heroic, world-class **inventors**."

    A. We will invent a better way of doing everything we do, *before* it becomes necessary to do so.

    B. Tomorrow we will re-invent better ways of doing things, better products and services, better systems. We will get better at everything we do.

- "We will become a **humanizing** organization."

  A. We will perform our roles in such a way that every person who comes into contact with us during the course of our workday will be the better for it.

  B. We will never expect less than the best of ourselves, and we will equip ourselves to be invaluable resources to others along the same path of growth and development.

- "We will become an organization of **learners**."

  A. We will look at life as an opportunity for continuous, lifelong learning, because we will understand that growth through learning is the source of life and of the qualities that make life meaningful and exciting.

  B. We will forever be in pursuit of what it takes to be the best in the business, and we will never cease learning how to deliver it.

- "We will become an organization of **leaders**."

  A. We will demonstrate this by leading ourselves in extraordinary ways.

  B. We will provide invaluable leadership to our customers, our suppliers, our competitors, and all of our other stakeholders.

  C. Where our mission is concerned—which is everywhere at all times—we will learn to lead, to follow, or to get out of the way.

- "We will become a human **community** of **interdependent achievers**."

  A. We will do that by putting the needs and interests of the organization first, the needs and interests of our fellow members second, and our own needs and interests last.

B.   There is no other way to create a community of interdependent people.

C.   If there is a better way of creating the kind of totally effective and engaging organization we all want and need, we will invent it.

D.   We will become the model for all those who seek a better way of doing things, and a better way of life while doing it.

- "We will make **great lives** by doing **great work**."

   A.   There is no other way.

   B.   We will know that the better we are at what we do, the more engaging it will be and the more gratification there will be in doing it.

   C.   Creativity is a function of discipline. We will have so much of the latter we can enjoy all we wish of the former.

   D.   "Work," as one wise man said, "is love made visible." We will show the world how much we care about ourselves and others by the excellence we put into everything we do. We will show others how much we care about ourselves and about them by the rate of growth of our performance.

- "We will kill **complacency** and **mediocrity**."

   A.   We will actively resist the forces of mediocrity in ourselves.

   B.   Having succeeded in that most difficult of tasks, we will help others to do the same.

- "We will be joined in **common cause**."

A. We will have a deep sense of interdependence in the mutual pursuit of our common cause—our mission.

B. Those outcomes of all our doing and saying that move us along the path toward our mission we will recognize as contributions.

C. Those outcomes that do not move us along that path we will recognize as discontributions. Our common cause will judge each of us on our contributions.

D. There are no "observers" or critics in an organization that has a great mission. There are no neutral thoughts, actions, or attitudes in an organization committed to real achievement. Everyone is an indispensable player.

- "We will become an organization of **dragon-slayers**."

    A. Wherever there is a belief, a myth, a practice, or a habit that impedes us on our path, we will slay it.

    B. Every explanation of why something can't be done is a loathsome dragon. There is no "can't." There is only inventing a "how" to accomplish what has to be accomplished.

- "We will continuously equip and prepare ourselves to do our **duty**."

    A. Whether to our fellow members, to our customers, or to ourselves, we will never fail to carry through the duty we have signed on to fulfill.

    B. We will never fail to *see* what our duty is in any situation—present or future—nor will we fail *to equip ourselves* to fulfill that duty, whatever it takes.

If you're thinking these seem to be fairly lofty goals, yes they are. These days, the common inclination is probably to smirk. That's because mediocrity loathes every form of excellence that offends it, or any serious attempt to rise above mediocrity. There is more comfort in being in the middle of the crowd than in the much smaller company of achievers.

Yes, these are "lofty" words, *ideals*. If a code like this were the core of your organization's culture and thus of your people's consciences, you would likely achieve your mission. But if the ideals of such a "code" as the one above make *you* uncomfortable, it may simply mean that you have not personally escaped the clutches of the most irresistible dragon of all. That would be the dragon that comes of knowing that if you are not compelled by a cause, you will be approved of by the majority of people (who are mediocrities) rather than by the small minority of people who are achievers. Reaching for something significantly above where most people are will take you out of your comfort zone. If you can't get out of it, real achievement may be out of your reach.

- If you have "lofty" goals, these can be described, understood, and held in mind only with such "lofty" words.
- But nothing much happens if you don't have what it takes to make reality out of such ideal blueprints.
- No matter how hard you try, you cannot achieve something great out of commonplace (un-lofty) thinking.
- The aim of a "code" of conduct is to give voice to who you *intend* to be.
- Without it, you will forever be who you are.

Here's what it might feel like to add one to the mix. For example—

- We will each perform our roles with the **sense of urgency** that says we may not be here tomorrow if we don't.

Indeed, we may not be here tomorrow if we don't. Those are the words. What kinds of pushes and pulls would you have to provide as leader in order to make that orientation the order of every day?

There is no "common cause" without a shared code of conduct. It's what makes a team out of a group of individuals. It is what's needed to make a coherent organization on its way to real achievement out of a bunch of "employees." You want people who exemplify what it takes to get where you intend to go. That's what a "code of conduct" can do.

- Everyone is guided by an implicit code of conduct. It will take you where *it* leads, not where you want to go.
- The one you do not design for your destiny is one that will be designed by someone or something else.
- The "code" of mediocrity is one of the most powerful forces on earth.
- If you and your people do not consciously and aggressively struggle against it, you will inexorably be drawn into it.
- You can't achieve your own chosen destiny by going where everyone else is going.

That's why the most ideal code of conduct you can devise and implement is not just a good thing to do. It is a necessary thing to do.

CHAPTER 18

Values & Beliefs—The Tacit Mediators

EVERY CODE OF conduct implies a set of values and beliefs. And every set of values and beliefs implies a code of conduct. You may like the idea of using either the one or the other. Or both. What's provided in this short chapter is a possible set of values and beliefs that are most needed if you intend to pursue real achievement, like making a high-performance organization. But first, consider this:

When people speak to you, everything they say is cooked in and filtered through their personal values and beliefs. When *you* listen or observe, every observation and every interpretation you make is constructed out of and woven through with *your* values and beliefs.

Most of the "dragons" that affect our lives and everything we do with others abide in the values and beliefs that we can't help having and imputing to the world. Perhaps it is time to explore these matters more explicitly. What matters? The two most basic for our purposes are these:

One, there are those values and beliefs that abound in the world around us that will function as serious or even defeating impediments to any endeavor we may engage in.

Two, without the *needed* values and beliefs—without "the right stuff"—no one is going to lead themselves or their organizations to any significant level of real achievement.

This is not a detour. Nor is it an "academic" or a philosophical digression. It is practical, pragmatic, fundamental. There is a tremendous potential advantage in being able to figure out how this tacit dimension of values and beliefs—that mediates all human perception, thought, and behavior—will be either furthering your cause, or impeding it.

Quickies—

- Leaders have to know what propels their cause or what constrains it—whether in themselves or others.
- Values and beliefs either serve you or resist you. There are no neutral values or beliefs.
- You will "win" or "lose" in this tacit dimension. It's to your advantage to understand it as well as you can.

Values And Beliefs Are . . .

Values and beliefs are not something people "have." They are what *have us.*

Whether on the input side (listening, reading, observing) or the output side (speaking, writing, thinking, or doing), the values and beliefs that have people in their clutches—in their *thrall*—are what mediate everything. We do not deal with the world directly. The world does not affect us directly. All of our "minding" of the world or ourselves is mediated, filtered through our values and beliefs. They are what every thought, every perception, every choice or decision, and every bit of behavior must pass through. *We* are . . . what *they* are.

People are not born with any values or beliefs. They infiltrate the most basic part of our being from those around us. They are like contagious diseases, spread by those who are had by them to newcomers to the group. Those newcomers are admitted to full-fledged membership in that group (family, culture, tribe, whatever) only if and when they are properly infected and taken over by the values and beliefs that distinguish and characterize that particular group (religious, occupational, familial, community, whatever).

Values and beliefs are both "imported" and "exported." We are "infected" by other people who are *had by* certain values and beliefs. And, properly indoctrinated, we become carriers who, intentionally or not, try to "infect" others. We cannot live in *any* human group without exhibiting reasonably acceptable evidence that we are had by the same core values and beliefs as the others in that group. Some groups are less permissive than others. It's unlikely you will ever be acknowledged as a *bona fide* software engineer unless you *think* like those other "engineers" around you do—which is to say, unless you exhibit certain values and beliefs that are reasonably consistent with theirs. There is little possibility of being "reasonably consistent" with the values and beliefs of the Mafia or of radical feminism. You are either one of them or not. If you are one of them, you will think and do and say and have as "they" do. Or you will, simply, not be admitted. If you want to be seen and accepted as an executive, you may have to act like one, dress like one (up *or* down), and talk like one. You must exhibit the values and beliefs of this group, or never be quite accepted.

More thought-prodders—

- Whatever the human group, tribe, subculture, etc., if you want to be one of "us," you have to exhibit the same values and beliefs as "we" do.
- The most compelling evidence you can exhibit is that you are an effective "carrier"—that is, that you have effectively "infected" others.
- If you are merely pretending, you will be found out. It is only when your values and beliefs are *tacit*—only when they are driving you without your conscious awareness that you can be considered one of "us."
- Your values and beliefs mediate the world for you, and mediate you for all the rest of the world.

The "Software" Of Thought And Behavior

It may seem strange to present such ideas in a book like this. Or to present them in such an unconventional way. But, as we have seen, it is conventional understandings that ensure your mediocrity or "average-ness." You can't achieve something that is beyond "average" with an average or conventional way of thinking. Real achievement is not commonplace. And getting there requires thinking about the factors critical to that endeavor in a very unconventional way.

None predict to the outcome more than your values and beliefs and the values and beliefs of those people who have to make it happen. If you aren't had by the right set of values and beliefs for undertaking and carrying through the struggles and difficulties you will encounter on the path to real achievement, you won't get very far. If you don't in fact know what values and beliefs you are had by, you will likely attribute any impediments on your journey to the wrong source.

Desire is not an achievement. You will remember where we started: many try, few succeed. If you truly value your aim or your cause, you have to value all of the efforts—mental, physical, and spiritual—required to get there. If you believe in your cause, you have to believe in whatever it takes to get there.

There is no necessary correlation, as we have seen, between what people say and what people do. There *is* a close correlation between what people value and believe and what they accomplish.

Values and beliefs are the "software" that energizes, guides, channels, filters, and screens all of our attention and all of our actions. What we value and what we believe not only defines who we are, but our destiny—how we turn out.

Some provocations along those lines—

- If you don't value accomplishment over activity, your life will be more or less a random sequence of activities.
- If you don't get the "software" right, the hardware isn't going to make much difference one way or the other.
- What you don't understand of your own values and beliefs will make you a mere victim of them. The ones you haven't consciously chosen will choose you.
- What you don't understand of the values and beliefs of others—whether enemies, competitors, friends, or partners— leaves you naked and vulnerable on the playing field.

- Values and beliefs are not what make the world go 'round. They *are* the world around which everything else revolves.

The "Right Stuff"

The right values and beliefs are the "right stuff."

If *you* don't have "the right stuff," then you are not going to accomplish anything extraordinary, either individually or as a leader of others. And if those key others are not right-minded, right-hearted, and right-spirited (if they don't have "the right stuff"), then your mission will likely fail. You can always "hope," of course, that you get lucky, or that your competitors are less well equipped and prepared than you are. In that case, you may have some ordinary "success." But it will not be *your* accomplishment. It will just be what happened to happen.

The right values and beliefs are critical because values and beliefs do not take us where *we* want to go. They take us in the direction *they* go. Their direction and their ends are inherent in them. They are blind to everything but their own ends. Get them right, and they will carry you along to where you want to go. Get them wrong, and they will carry you along to wherever *they* are headed.

The Field Of Play

We thrive, or we fail, not because of our values and beliefs. But as a consequence of how those values *play us out* in all the rest of the world—the "real" world. Think of the world as a game in which we are players. It is a "game" the outcomes of which are beyond any person's control. We adapt, or we cease to be players. It is this world in which we have to accomplish. We either make things happen for our own purposes in this world, or we will simply be a byproduct of it. It is in that "real" world that leaders succeed, or not.

We got Machiavelli wrong because we looked at what we presumed he said through the lenses of our "modern" view of the world. What he advised his "prince" was to perform superbly those values and beliefs that would perpetuate the state, and to eliminate within himself those that would put the security of the state in jeopardy. That's all. Seems like good advice even today. The Roman Empire had a good long run. But it was eclipsed by a world outside of it that had passed it by. The values and beliefs that had made it "great" in times past led to its fall. In the more recent years before the "consumer revolution" in our own country, there was a sort of acquiescence to shoddy products and services that made it possible for many large organizations to grow and flourish for reasons other than "quality," "customer service," and the like. We still don't "get" it. Organizations fail today because they cannot rid themselves of the values and beliefs that made them "successful" but which no longer have that consequence on the changed playing field. What was good for General Motors may have been what was good for the country at some point in history, as that much-repeated quotation had it. But not today. When people had to be grateful for whatever they could get, good intentions may have sufficed. But these days you would be prudent to have product liability insurance, and to value a good lawyer over good intentions.

So here are some thoughts to ponder—

- It isn't values and beliefs as such that make the difference.
- It is how they play us out in the complex, dynamic world of sometimes conflicting values that makes the difference.
- To achieve greatly, and sustain it, requires "the right stuff."

The Contrary Values And Beliefs You Are Up Against

Here's what you are up against. And thus what you have to change if you need certain values and beliefs working for you rather than against you.

1. In general, work is not very highly valued these days. But the values that are not put into one's work cannot appear in

the products or the services you provide. What people don't value devalues the products of their work.

2. Training people to say, "Have a nice day" is not the same thing as equipping them to produce a "nice day" for customers and others. Saying, "Have a miserable day" isn't going to make it happen, unless it has already been made so, as for example by the perfunctory treatment you get from most flight and retail attendants.

3. An old Hungarian proverb has it that people should be rewarded for how well they do what they do, not for their position in an organization. We value our celebrities more than our plumbers. When everyone becomes a talk-show host (or devotee), who will fix the plumbing?

4. We are greatly concerned with our "rights" and our "entitlements." But "duty" is rarely mentioned.

5. We espouse certain values, but live by very different values. People will be as hypocritical with customers and fellow-workers as they are in their private lives.

6. Great performance is wholly incompatible with easy hypocrisy. Check it out.

7. The level of character you and your people do not routinely exhibit (basic values are consistent) can be no part of the assessment that customers, suppliers, or investors make of you.

8. You cannot perform at a level of character you do not have.

9. People who can't give to the organization more than they expect from it are deadbeats, and need to be dealt with accordingly.

10. What you don't value won't value you.

What They Might Have To Be

Well, you get the point. What follows is an example of the kinds of values and beliefs that can underwrite real achievement. They work only if they are a part of who you and your people are. These are unlikely to be your present values and beliefs. They are the kinds of values and beliefs to aspire to if you intend to pursue

great achievement. Here is a possible list of values and beliefs that can make a difference (because they have made a difference):
Some Guiding Values and Beliefs

We believe that good work, superbly done, is the richest source of human dignity and quality of life.

- *Can you imagine . . . what the performance of an organization would be like if most of the people in it were actually driven by that belief?*

We believe that the world passes by those who do not change with it.

- *Isn't it the case that people who stop learning, and thus changing, actually lose ground simply because the world is changing around them? Can you imagine . . . that world trying to keep pace with people who are learning every day?*

We believe we should never belittle ourselves by setting mediocre goals.

- *Aren't mediocre goals the way mediocre people achieved their mediocrity in the first place? Think small—be small?*

We believe in being forever dissatisfied with our performance.

- *Isn't it always the case that people who are satisfied with their performance go stale? Can you imagine . . . a whole organization of strivers?*

We believe that, to fulfill our *moral* obligation to ourselves and to others, DUTY must come first.

- *Obligation? Duty? Can you imagine . . . a whole organization of people who put their duty to others and to the organization first? Their customers would be astonished, wouldn't they?*

We believe that people should be the masters of their own destiny.

- *Can you imagine . . . a person who says to the world, "Make of me what you will"? Can such a person actually be "empowered"?*

We believe that the future belongs to those who ask the right questions.

- *What is the right question here? Or can a person escape the problem by pretending to have no future in mind and play the game of "victim"?*

We believe that trust and respect must be mutually *earned.*

- *Can trust and respect simply be traded? Or does it seem to you things work better if you and the other person actually have to earn the trust you then deservedly offer or receive?*

We believe that the primary measure of our success lies in the quality of life we provide to each of our stakeholders, internally and externally.

- *If your customers are not better people as a result of their interactions with you, are you?*

Well, it must be obvious how powerful it can be to have the right values and beliefs as widely and deeply distributed, and acted upon, as possible. These may not be just the right ones for you. But if you depend upon the hodge-podge collection of values and beliefs that people bring to your place from their friends and the media, you will be struggling with the problems these can create for the rest of your life. It may be to your advantage (even to try) to get people "on the same page" with respect to the beliefs and values needed to pursue your cause.

Leadership Lessons: Some Reminders

Before launching into the next chapter on the "core stratagems," it might be useful to briefly reprise some of the basics explored thus far.

- The way your mind works determines who you *are*. Who you are determines what you *do* and *how* you do it. Fix the source, not the symptom.
- People who haven't assumed responsibility for their own destiny will have difficulty understanding people (like you) who have. The solution: hold them responsible for their own destiny.
- You don't—no one can—control the outcomes. What you can control is everyone's preparedness for achieving your goals come what may.
- Instrument yourself and the people of your organization in such a way that you don't merely "have" a cause, but so that cause "has" you. Let the cause be the boss.
- There are only two basic reasons why people do what they do. One is that they *can* (competence and wherewithal). The other is that it is *necessary* (conscience, cultural systems, or even to avoid unwanted consequences).
- If you want to know what people mean by what they say, look at what they do.
- The meaning of communication is exclusively in the consequences.
- The only measure of performance is performance.
- The primary "motive" for better performance lies in the level of dissatisfaction with previous performance. People have a comfort zone only with your permission.
- People's habits (including your own) will take you where *they* go, not where *you* intend to go.
- A person's "experience" (or credentials) is not the same thing as that person's performance in the role they have for making your great achievement a reality.

- Most of what you have to learn about extraordinary achievement you have to learn by doing it.
- You must unrelentingly value the future you envision over the realities of the present, which you acknowledge.

So, when you're ready, let's move on.

CHAPTER 19

The Core Stratagems

IN THIS CHAPTER, we will confront head-on the "core" stratagems for the pursuit of real achievement. They have been implicit in much of what we have encountered in the preceding pages. But it is time to call them forth and deal with them directly, now that you have a way of understanding them as they have to be understood.

The *Strategic Distribution* Of The *Ownership* Of Problems

The first of these core stratagems is all about the *strategic distribution* of the *ownership* of problems. That's a lot of words packed together. A brief overview and then we will unpack them.

Most broadly, what this means is that the actual organization is not what's on the organization chart. The actual organization is structured around *who* owns *what* problems, and the processes that connect them. More informally, what this means is that what makes the organization "work" is determined by what person or group "owns" what problems, because this is what determines the flow of information to those nodes, and where decisions and initiatives originate that affect what others do.

In the past, we strove to locate this ownership in the offices of the "managers" of the organization. This was the "Who reports to whom?" kind of organization structure. But it never worked perfectly because there was always someone fouling up the works by taking ownership of a problem and dealing with it more or less unilaterally. The idea was that because they were at the "head" of the pyramid structure of the conventional organization, managers were the "brains." It was up to them to do the thinking, make the decisions, and see to it that others did what they were told to do.

The point is that the underlying organization structure will always depend upon who owns what problem. And the power of this logic predicts that if you get this right, you will have the blueprint for a high-performance organization. Let us then unpack our terms in reverse order. (It will simply work better for you that way.)

1. How "**problems**" get dealt with depends upon who owns them. A "problem" that no one owns is a problem that is unseen. To "see" a problem and talk about it is what makes any problem "real." How it is seen and made real in talk about it depends solely on who sees it, or who brings it into existence by how they talk about it. How it is dealt with depends entirely on who deals with it. We've considered all this before. What we want to bring to the fore here is that people's attention is always focused on *their* problems (as they understand them). And what "moves" people to action is the significance (to them) of where they are vs. where they are trying to get to by dealing with the problem. Problem: If an entrepreneur is the only person in her enterprise, she is the problem-seer, the problem-definer, and the problem-solver. What she does at work depends upon the problems she owns. Others may see different problems, and define them and go about solving them differently. Unless she persists in owning them. Which is more often than not the case.

2. To **own** a problem simply means to have the responsibility for it—in many ways: for anticipating it, for seeing it, for defining it, for doing something about it, and for being

accountable for the consequences of all of these, especially for what is done, or not done, about it.

What deserves your careful consideration here is that people treat the problems they "own" very differently from the problems others "own." You do.

Some people gladly own problems they ought not to own. You do. And there are many people who would be okay with having someone else own all of their problems.

In any system that involves people dealing with each other to some end, here's the crux: If the person who ought to own the problem is not the one who owns it, the system becomes dysfunctional. Here's an example with which we're all familiar: If the child owns the problem of the happiness and pleasure of the parents (and the rest of the community), the whole thing works far better than if the parents "own" the problem of the child's happiness and gratification. The latter, as we observe every day, creates dysfunctional families. And, in the extreme, dysfunctional children. Another universal example: In a schoolroom, if the teacher "owns" the problem of the students' learning, and the students do not "own" the problems of their own learning, very little learning beyond rote recall takes place.

In the same way, if the "boss" owns the problem of the subordinate's performance, so that the subordinate doesn't or can't own that problem, the system is dysfunctional. All kinds of problems will arise that are attributed to causes other than the key cause. If the "problem" of the performance of the company is owned solely by the chief executive, the whole organization is dysfunctional. That's a problem that ought to be owned by everyone in the organization—like the "problem" of quality.

If the system is dysfunctional, it cannot be fixed by fixing the people in it, or by applying a recipe on top of it. It can only be fixed by fixing the system, and that means making sure that the person or persons who ought to own the problem do in fact own it. As soon as your spouse's happiness becomes your problem, the system is dysfunctional. In the same way, if you own the problem of the employees' satisfaction, you will find that there is no way for you to succeed and you will forever be engaged in dealing with problems that are unrelated to your cause.

"Ownership" means that the person who ought to own the problem owns it.

Here are two generic caveats:

- One, if a person who works at your place does not own the problem of his or her personal destiny, that person will never be able to understand why you would choose a cause or a destiny for your organization. Or why that should be of any concern to that person.
- Very important to remember: You should never require a person to own (to be accountable for) anything that is not reasonably within that person's control. Preparedness and competence are. Outcomes aren't.

People who have no obligation for the health and welfare of the larger system to which they belong will be a dead-level drag on the spirit and the economy of that system, including your own organization.

The paradox here is that

- It is only by owning the problems of their own personal destinies that people can come to a realization of their inescapable *interdependence* with others in any larger endeavor.
- People who do not own the problem of their own performance and their own destinies in life cannot "see" that they have to put into the larger whole what they want to get out of it.
- You have to fix that disability first.

3. The **strategic distribution** of the ownership of problems simply refers to the need to get the ownership of every "problem" rightly situated. To repeat, if *you* own the problem

of the performance of the people in your organization, you will struggle and struggle with a problem you cannot solve. That's because, ultimately, they are the only ones who can solve the problem of their own performance, and therefore they should own that problem.

There's always a logic involved. If a person or a department owns the problem of quality, then none of the rest of the people have to own that problem. If "customer service" is owned by a small group of people, then the other people in the organization don't have to own that problem. If conformity to government regulations is a problem that is owned by a person or a department, then no one else has to own that problem in their workplace. If recruiting is a problem owned by the HR department, others don't have to get involved. The problem of recruiting people ought to be owned by everyone in the organization. The logic is this: *who* ought to own *what* problems in order for the performance of the whole to be raised . . . daily?

If you let it be assumed that people get paid at your place for performing *their* petty problems and concerns at work, that's what will happen. People get paid (if "Mother" has it to pay) for performing their *roles*. If they don't own their performance in their roles, someone else (you?) will have to. How much of your performance in your role gets siphoned off in this direction? All because the ownership of problems has not been strategically distributed. Because the people who ought to own the problem can't (competence) or won't (their feelings of the moment) means that others get drawn into owning problems they shouldn't own.

Rise to the challenge of the strategic distribution of the ownership of problems within your organization and your organization can then rise more fully to the challenges it faces in the larger world.

- The leader cannot get the level of competence and performance needed by decree or exhortation.
- What should he (or she) do with this problem?

Some thought-prodders:

- The problems that people don't own will serve them as an excuse in advance for any shortfalls in their performance, as they see it.
- The problems that people don't *own* will be problems they will feel no responsibility for.
- If you believe that you exhibit your superiority by being the go-to problem-solver for your people, then you will be an unseen and therefore insoluble cause of those problems.
- And . . . thus you would function as the chief inhibitor of the growth of your people's competencies and accountabilities.
- Your first duty? To not be a part of the problem, so that you might be a part of the solution.
- Your second? Selecting and casting people so that they own the problems of the performance of every part of the organization, so that you can concentrate on the performance of the whole.
- The more sense people have of owning the vital problems of the organization, those that they encounter, the more tied they will be to the life and the destiny of the organization.

Making Possible What's Necessary And Making Necessary What's Possible

That is not intended to be a cute play on words. It is intended to engage you in trying to figure out what all that means. In what way do those words constitute a core stratagem?

The first part of it—**making possible what's necessary**—means that one's goals and purposes, if those are necessary, require certain preconditions, like stamina or commitment or competence. What you are not equipped to do you will not do because you cannot. So this refers to equipping yourself (or others) with whatever is required to carry through those goals and purposes.

People have to own the problem of capacitating themselves to carry out the accomplishments called for in their roles. But some impediments to their performance may have to be removed by you. If the organization is not structured (remember problem ownership?) so that they can effectively perform their roles, you may be the one who has to fix that problem because they can't. If they do not have the resources they need, or the information infrastructure required, you may have to enable them by providing those. This is part of what is meant by making the necessary accomplishments **possible**.

You may have the wrong people. You may not have exactly the right roles for your "story" to unfold as intended. You may not have the right business strategy. You may not have the kinds of "smart" systems that would enable performance even if you have all the rest of it right. These are all enablers. If they're not right, it isn't going to happen. You make it **possible** by getting all of the preconditions right, so that your people have no excuse for not owning the problem of their own performance in their roles.

The other half of it is **making necessary** what's **possible**. You don't know what's possible. No one does. What is commonplace today was at one time considered "impossible." Heavier than air vehicles really can fly. The Pony Express, which never really made money, was the fastest way of getting information around in its day. The internal combustion engine was not "possible" until someone figured out how to make one. History is replete with examples of how what was considered "impossible" came to be a part of our everyday lives.

When someone says, "That's not possible," all they could mean is that they themselves, constrained as they are by their own thinking, beliefs, and attitudes, can't figure out how to do it. What's "possible" depends upon doing it. Nay-saying is not a *test* of what's possible.

The art of all great leaders has been their uncanny creativity in making **necessary** what no one has yet seen or experienced, and therefore probably believe to be "impossible"—that is, the art of making **necessary** whatever might be *possible*.

The lesson is this:

- What "can't" be done reflects no more than a failure of imagination.
- It is the leader's task to make it **possible** for people to first imagine that something could be accomplished, and then to make it **necessary** for them to accomplish that.
- Making necessary what's possible is the process of making reality out of imagination.

That's what Columbus did. That's what Gandhi did. That's what the world's first heart transplant surgeon did. That's what leaders have always done.

- That's what you could do.
- If you can figure out how to make necessary what you want to achieve.
- Doing it, accomplishing it, is what makes it "possible." Reality always trumps prophecy.
- Declaring something to be "impossible" is prophecy based on no more than one's own disbelief in oneself.

Accomplishments, Not Activities

Because it is also true of the larger culture, the cultures of most organizations permit, channel, even encourage people to think and do in terms of **activities**. "I have to study" is an activity that students use to identify their burdens in life. "I have to go shopping" is the second most time-consuming activity in America. "I have to go to work" is an activity. And what we do, most of the day at work, consists of *activities*. The typical "job description" is more often than not a list of *activities*. When the time for evaluation comes, and the cowardly "manager" meets the aggressive employee in the arena, the argument is, frequently, "But I'm doing my job, aren't I?!" Since that consists mainly of some activities, what recourse does the cowardly manager have?

What you want and need are **accomplishments**. But those are rarely in the "job description." They are left implicit, mainly in the daydreams of the manager. As we have seen, a "job description" is a good example of doing **A** while hoping for **B**. We list the activities but hope for the accomplishments.

Real meaning in life lies mainly in the pursuit of a worthy goal or a purpose, not in the mindless repetition of activities. People (including you) do not get *engaged* in activities. A person can only get fully engaged in an accomplishment.

[There is a real "catch" in this whole endeavor we are exploring in this book. It is this: If you don't understand how to accomplish your goals, you won't. But it is only when you do accomplish your goals that you will fully understand how to do it. Nice paradox. But that's the way it is.]

To get right into the differences between "activities" and "accomplishments," let's go to some specifics:

- For people who have no particular aim in life, an *activity* will seem to them like an *accomplishment.*
- In organizations, an accomplishment is a measurable contribution to the aims or the cause of the organization.
- Making it necessary for people to distinguish between activities and accomplishments is an ongoing task of leadership.
- People must make themselves capable of accomplishing what is required of them in their role.
- An accomplishment that is not understood at the outset, or which cannot be objectively measured, creates problems.
- The more closely related an accomplishment is to the goals of the organization, the more meaningful it is to the person.
- The accomplishment is *accomplishment-mindedness.* If people are not accomplishment-minded, they will not be accomplishers.
- What you want to achieve is that ordinary people will thrive on doing common things uncommonly well.
- Sheer activity requires just as much effort with a fraction of the return on accomplishments.

Relationship

This core stratagem operates so unnoticeably it is often given no thought at all. It is simple but powerful. Here it is in its briefest form—

- If two or more people intend to collaborate to some mutual end (collaborate, negotiate, make love, whatever), their *relationship* determines what can be done, and how.
- Just as it is your relationship with your customers that determine what's possible, or how much collaboration can be expected, it is your relationship with your people that determines what you can do with them, and how you have to do it.
- What can and can't be done is a function of the relationship.

Choice

To provide good and effective leadership, you must perceive and treat every person's circumstances and "problems" as a matter of choice. *Their* choice. This has to begin with you. You have to be the exemplar of seeing yourself as the owner of all of your circumstances.

You have to assume that people are the way they are *by choice*. A person is always the result of a whole series of choices (or failures to choose) over a long period of time. Choices in the past bear upon outcomes far into the future.

And we know that outcomes are always uncertain and uncontrollable. But people do have a choice about having a purpose in life or not. And people do own the problem of how well their ongoing choices contribute to their purpose in life. Indeed everything is going to turn out the way it turns out. But equipping oneself and preparing oneself to pursue worthy and chosen ends are conditions over which every person has control. That is what you (or I, or they) *choose*. We choose to be prepared and equipped to accomplish something on purpose. Or we choose not to be equipped and prepared.

A person who doesn't "get" that is not going to be very useful to you in furthering the choices you make about what kind of organization to have in order to pursue a cause that is yours by choice.

- The alternative to choosing your own or your organization's destiny is being a *victim* of whatever forces happen to push you this way or pull you that way.
- What isn't accomplished by choice you cannot take credit for.
- The choices you do not make determine the destiny you or your organization cannot have.
- People cannot choose who they are at the moment. But they always choose the competencies that enable them to *perform* to their advantage in a given situation. Preparedness.

Get Everyone In The "Learning Mode"

It seems likely that for every ten dollars spent on "change" in the past 20 years or so, we've realized a "return" of fifty cents or less. We're looking back on billions spent in the name of "change."

There is only one form of *sustainable* change. And that's when people change—in relevant and significant ways—their ways of knowing, of being, and of doing. And that kind of change occurs only when people learn something that makes it necessary for them to reshuffle what they know, to alter who they are, or to re-tool their ways of doing things.

Real learning is the source of real change. And real learning is possible only for those people who are in the "learning mode." People don't get more competent day after day because they are told to do so. People don't equip and prepare themselves for outstanding performance because they are told to do so. Or even if they agree that they should. People don't get smarter and more capable if they are fed larger amounts of "information" or even of "knowledge." They have to have goals that they have to achieve. And, if they *have to* change in order to carry out those goals, they will do so. That's why everyone in the organization needs to have a "learning plan," as we have seen. This is a plan for systematically eliminating shortfalls in their ability to accomplish what's given in their role, and with respect to the performance goals they have signed onto. Couple that learning plan with objectively measured performance and inescapable necessity for performing, and you will have an organization that will outperform all others.

- The premise here is simple. Performance in any role whatsoever can be improved upon every day . . . forever.
- Learning opens minds. Knowing closes them down.
- Learning requires a question. You have to think about that. Knowing leads to making statements. You don't have to think about that.
- If you want people to think about what they're doing, they have to be in "the learning mode."

There are two ways to "grow" an organization: outside-in and inside-out. Outside-in simply means that the organization grows to meet the demands of its customers or clients. Inside-out means that people grow in their competencies and capabilities, and this opens up more of the world to the organization.

Which way would you choose? To be victim or cause?

When people are in the "learning mode," their insatiable curiosity about their work—and about everything that affects their performance one way or the other—is a powerful source of real and lasting change.

It is performance that needs changing. And the people who can best figure out how to change performance for the better are the ones who *own* their performance in their role—today, tomorrow, and beyond.

Some ponderables:

- Most "resistance" to change is at the top of the organization.

- That's because the more elevated one's position, the more in the "knowing mode" that person is likely to be.
- People at the top may want "change." But they themselves often do not want to—or *can't*—change.
- Unfettered learning coupled with competence is a far better source of the right "change" than is managerial decree.
- The lesson for leaders: Demonstrate what being in the "learning mode" looks like and feels like. Then expect no less from others.
- People are going to take you where they're going anyway. Make their competence and their growth necessary. Then they'll take you where it would otherwise be impossible to go.

Bring Life Back Into Work

- If you apply the leadership lessons provided in this book, you **will** bring life back into work.
- If you cannot select—or develop—people who have the level of competence in their roles that enable them to give their hearts and minds to their work, you cannot have an organization that performs greatly.
- To the extent your people cannot give life to their work, your organization's performance will be life-less.

Real life and real growth are two aspects of the same thing. The life you or your people cannot have at your place is a life you cannot have. Learning is the source of real growth, which is growth in competence. And real growth is the source of life. To talk about bringing life to work accomplishes nothing. But you can do so by making necessary the kind of learning that enhances needed competence and thus performance.

Some thought-prodders:

- The more of a purpose in life one has, the more life one has.
- The sense of being fully alive you have in the present comes from the future cause you are serving.

- Every person is the steward of his or her own future. And every person is responsible for the future of the organization in which they are interdependent with others.
- Whether for an infant or a CEO, life comes from where you have to get to.
- And growth comes from growth in the capabilities required to get there.
- The leader is thus a life-maker.

PART VI

Envoi

SO THESE ARE the kinds of provisions you need to undertake your leadership journey. The rest is up to you.

It's good to know as much as you can at the outset of your journey. But, as the ancient wisdom has it, when it comes to matters like leadership, what you have to learn . . . you have to learn by doing it.

You have to practice thinking the way you would have to think. You have to practice being who you would have to be. You have to practice seeing and saying the world you are trying to get to. Your progress will always come in small advances. It's all about who you *are*, and thus about how you think and do in this world in order to lead yourself and others to the world you envision.

All that has preceded in these pages could hardly be "summarized." Nothing of all that you have to do can be reduced to a scheme, a formula, or a set of "secrets or "rules." You're the person who has to **author** the story of your leadership. You do this—always remember—with what **you** have to do it with.

The purpose of this book is to provision you with much of what you need to do it with. But what's here, explicitly and implicitly, will of itself do nothing for you. You have to do what has to be done. How it all turns out will be a measure of you, not of all these rich and powerful ideas, got from the world's wisdom and from years and years of hands-on experience and reflection. If all of the preceding enables you in some small way to achieve great success on your journey, then our journey together to this point has been, well, rather indispensable.

"Envoi" is the greeting I give you as we part ways here, and we stand together to envision the real journey, which now lies ahead of you.

The following chapter is not the last chapter in this book. It is for the purpose of tidying up and providing you with a thinking pad for launching your journey.

There is always time to have some fun with what we think we know, just in case there are better ways of knowing it. Let these next two pages provoke one or more of those.

CHAPTER 20

A Short Course On Real Achievement

[*In all the world, there is no human experience that can compare to the exercise of the deeply-developed competencies required for the pursuit of a great and worthy achievement.*]

FEW PEOPLE HAVE had such an experience. That's because few people have been a part of pursuing, alone or with others, a great and worthy achievement. This is in spite of the fact that it is the most humanizing experience that any person can have.

If you have a vision, and if you have the kind of tenaciousness and can develop within yourself the kinds of competencies required for seeing that vision through to reality, you will have called yourself to leadership. As a leader, you are in a position to provide that unique human experience for yourself and for all of those who contribute to the pursuit of a great and worthy achievement.

This is your privilege, because of your position. This is your moral obligation, because of your position.

You can do this only if you are fully competent to do so.

As you *think*, so will you *be*. And as you *are*, so will you *do*. To fulfill any task in this world, think your way through to accomplishing it. You have to be the person who makes it necessary. You have to do what needs to be done.

If you are "had by" the cause of making a great, high-performance organization, you will need to understand what competencies you need in order to carry out that task. That's what you have in your hands. You will need to provide the kind of leadership required to make it possible, and necessary, for people to develop those deep competencies required for seeing it through. The more competent people are in their role, the more pleasure they have in their work and thus the quality of their lives rises. It's win-win. In fact, the more competent people are at what they do, the more they can *play* at what they do. Useful creativity is a function of extreme competence.

If you succeed, be humble. Others conspired with you to make it happen. You were blessed.

If you do not succeed, go back and fix the only things over which you have control: how you think, who you are, and how you do what you do. And make all of the tools required an integral part of who you are.

This guidebook can provide you with much of what you need for the thinking part of it. How you make that a part of who you are, and how you make that color what you do and how you do it . . . will be a product of putting it into practice. It will be your utter determination that puts it all together, fitting you to the tools you need, and fitting the tools you need to you. Sometimes the right tools make even that passionate determination possible.

ACKNOWLEDGEMENTS

My thanks to those dozens and dozens of chief executives and top managers who have challenged my ideas over the years, and as a result made them work better in their many and various organizations.

My thanks also to the many thinkers and practitioners who, over the past eight millennia, have provided a rich legacy for our own present day thinking about this infinitely challenging subject.

And to my friends and colleagues who have read and critiqued one or more of this book's several incarnations, and have gently nudged me until I just had to do it in a way that might vindicate their belief in what I had to say.

They will know who they are. In any event, this is what they all made possible.

About The Author

Lee Thayer's career as a pioneer and influential innovator in the design and development of high-performance organizations extends from the 60s to the present day. Asked many times why he didn't "write a book" about his many successful (and sometimes unsuccessful) engagements with top executives in every kind of organization around the world over all those years, his reply used to be, "I'm too busy doing it to merely talk about it." But he finally acquiesced to the constant pressure to "talk about" his extensive experience in the trenches and the leadership lessons that can only be learned there. This book is the result.

Combining his early experience as an executive himself with his degrees in engineering and psychology, Dr. Thayer has developed a unique and functional framework for understanding *what it takes* to lead the way to great achievement, and *how to do it*.

He has served as a consultant for such firms as Pratt-Whitney, IBM, AT&T, Westinghouse, Boeing, InterNorth, McDonnell Douglas, Phillips, Shell, Rexnord, General Motors, Sealtest Foods, Hallmark, and the U.S. Air Force. More recently, he has been devoting his full time to scores of small to medium-sized organizations, where the impact is more readily apparent. He was the consultant behind the now well-known success story at Johnsonville Foods. He has been an invited speaker in most of the major leadership programs here and abroad—from Finland to Australia, and from China to Spain and Greece.

He is now deeply involved in his writing and speaking engagements, and his ongoing work as mentor and coach to CEOs and company presidents. His clients have commented on the fact that his experiences as a Naval officer orchestrating the movements of a squadron of ships at sea, and his experiences as a performer and arranger for jazz ensembles as a youth, have provided him with powerful insights into the challenges of orchestrating the performance of organizations. That, and his experiences as a successful entrepreneur and executive, have made him one of the most sought-after consultants in America.

His passion, he has reported in interviews, is "to help committed CEOs and other top executives to transform themselves into leaders, and their organizations into more vigorous, more adaptive, healthier, even more humanizing, high-performance organizations."

He can be reached via his company, The Leader's Compass, on the web at www.theleaderscompass.com or email at info@theleaderscompass.com.